"Occasionally, a where-to, how-to guidebook rises above mere functionality and becomes a piece of literature in its own right. The first two (the only two published so far) of Betty Pratt-Johnson's five-part series of paddling guides . . . are such books. They're fine examples of how guidebooks *should* be put together."　　　　　　　　　　　　　—James Raffan, KANAWA

"Whether you canoe, kayak, raft or just picnic . . . this guide is user friendly."　　　　　　　　　　　　　　　　　　　　　　　　　EXPLORE

"This is another fine guidebook from Pratt-Johnson for those people seeking to explore the fabulous waterways of British Columbia. . . well-researched, simply written . . . colorful and enthusiastic personal accounts."
　　　　　　　　　　　　　　　　　　　　　　　　　RIVER RUNNER

". . . a must for the paddler looking for new challenges."
　　　　　　　　　　　　　　　　　　　AMERICAN WHITEWATER

". . . well illustrated and carefully researched . . . color and enthusiasm. The information is so thorough, and it's so obvious that Pratt-Johnson has hugely enjoyed her five years of learning, that the book will be appreciated by whitewater veterans and may inspire many beginners."
　　　　　　　　　　　　　　　　　　　　VANCOUVER PROVINCE

"At a glance, the reader can tell who the run is good for. Choosing a trip . . . becomes easy . . . "　　　National Organization for River Sports, CURRENTS

"The author, Betty Pratt-Johnson, is a professional Outdoor Sports writer with an impressive track record of publications.
　". . . an interesting glossary . . . a thoughtfully planned index makes using the guide easy . . . this is a must for any paddler that may have been [there] and for those who are aspiring to explore the white paradise of British Columbia, Canada."　　　　　　　British Canoe Union, CANOE FOCUS

"Wer also von Flüssen träumt, deren Wasser noch trinkbar ist, oder schon plant, in den Westen Kanadas zu reisen, um Urlaub auf unverbauten und wenig befahrenen Wildbächen und herrlichen Flüssen zu machen, der neue Fluβführer von Betty Pratt-Johnson gehört zum Gepäck."　　KANU SPORT

"If running rivers is in your blood, both books are sure bets."
　　　　　　　　　　　　　　　　　　　　　　OUTDOOR CANADA

Come run a river

WHAT REVIEWERS ARE SAYING ABOUT BETTY PRATT-JOHNSON AND THE FIRST TWO GUIDEBOOKS IN HER WHERE-TO-GO WHITEWATER SERIES:

"A popular local canoeist and kayaker, Pratt-Johnson is also an award-winning magazine writer who previously authored a guidebook for divers in B.C. and Washington.

". . . this guide [covering greater Vancouver region] will lure you to white-water rivers . . Indian paintings on rocks, the biggest surfing wave in British Columbia, and the best lunch spots and whereabouts of hot showers."

EXPLORE

"Her writing style is to experience all the river runs herself, then give the reader detailed information on what to expect and how to get there."

SEATTLE TIMES

". . . this lady has a good sense of what a paddler needs to know to have fun and to get in and out of these routes safely. . . her adult entry to the sport of whitewater paddling may be what gives the text of these books its unusual clarity, freshness and vitality." —James Raffan, KANAWA

". . . local history, scenery, wildlife . . . easy-to-read, very professionally drawn maps, as well as lively photos. This author has outdone herself."

CANOE

"Betty has done a tremendous job of putting all the information a person could possibly want into an easy to understand format."

COMOX TOTEM TIMES

". . . not only fun to read but . . . also helpful in choosing from the many rivers and facilities available. Even if you don't paddle your own canoe, kayak or raft — and don't ever want to — you will find rivers described in this book where you can join organized rafting trips." WESTWORLD

"Fishermen will find the book useful too, as will less adventurous folk who are looking for scenic picnic sites rather than churning water."

KAMLOOPS NEWS

"For whosoever is dreaming of still clear brooks with drinkable water, or planning on touring the Canadian West for a pleasant vacation on relatively undisturbed and off-beat runs, Betty Pratt-Johnson's new river guide is a must!" —Translated from German, KANU SPORT

". . . among the best I've seen in the past year."

THE MIDWEST BOOK REVIEW

Books by Betty Pratt-Johnson

141 Dives in the Protected Waters of Washington and British Columbia

Whitewater Trips for Kayakers, Canoeists and Rafters on Vancouver Island

Whitewater Trips for Kayakers, Canoeists and Rafters in British Columbia: Greater Vancouver through Whistler, Okanagan and Thompson River Regions

Whitewater Trips and Hot Springs in the Kootenays of British Columbia: For Kayakers, Canoeists and Rafters

Everybody Loves an Octopus, her popular natural-history article which was published first in the United States, was translated into French and German and reprinted in a scuba diving magazine in Switzerland. It was then made available to readers around the world in 12 additional languages as well as in big print and it was selected as an example of good writing for the college anthology *Read to Write.* It is also included in the *1979 Science Annual* of the Americana Encyclopedia.

Betty Pratt-Johnson
WHITEWATER TRIPS

and Hot Springs in the Kootenays of British Columbia: For Kayakers, Canoeists and Rafters

The Third in a Series of Five Guidebooks
Covering 157 Whitewater Trips in
British Columbia and Washington

Adventure Publishing Ltd., Vancouver/Seattle

Canadian Cataloguing in Publication Data

Pratt-Johnson, Betty.
  Whitewater trips and hot springs in the
Kootenays of British Columbia
  "The third in a series of five guidebooks
covering 157 whitewater trips in British Columbia
and Washington."
  Includes index.
  ISBN 0-921009-18-6

  1. White-water canoeing - British Columbia -
Kootenay Region - Guide-books. 2. Rafting
(Sports) - British Columbia - Kootenay Region -
Guide-books. 3. Rivers - British Columbia -
Kootenay Region - Guide-books. 4. Hot springs -
British Columbia - Kootenay Region - Guide-books.
5. Kootenay Region (B.C.) - Description and
travel - Guide-books. I. Title.
GV776.15.B7P733 1989   917.11'45   C89-091296-3

Library of Congress Catalog Card Number: 89-085596

Published in Canada and the United States:
Canadian Address: **United States Address:**
Adventure Publishing Ltd.   Adventure Publishing Ltd.
P.O. Box 46545, Station G   1916 Pike Place, Suite 73
Vancouver, B.C.   Seattle, Washington 98101
Canada V6R 4G8   U.S.A.

Typeset in Canada by The Typeworks
Printed and bound in Canada by Hignell Printers

Photographic and Topographic Map Credits
Photographs throughout this book were taken by the author except those credited below:

Front cover photo by Dave Read; canoeist Joe Selby of Cranbrook on Kootenay River, with Pedley Falls behind
Page 6 (top photo), Colin Coe
Page 6, (bottom photo), Jean Macdonald
Pages 125, 134, and 157, aerial photography provided by the Ministry of Crown Lands, Government of British Columbia
Page 23, Brian Neilson
Pages 31 and 103, Madeline Waring
Pages 53 (top photo), 149 and 155 (bottom photos), back cover, John Pratt-Johnson
Page 63, Rick Earles
Page 77, Taoya White
Page 86 (bottom photos), Doug Leighton
Pages 87 and 113, Susan Murray
Pages 95, 109 and 115, David M. Lawson
Page 121, Cheri LePage
  The maps on pages 29, 33, 57, 71, 128, 132-133, 135, and 147 are based on information taken from the National Topographic Series map sheets 82F/6 © 1981, 82F/5 © 1981, 82N © 1985, MCR 220 © 1985, MCR 220 © 1985, 82K/15 © 1979, MCR 220 © 1985, and 82K/5 © 1978 Her Majesty the Queen in Right of Canada with permission of Energy Mines and Resources Canada.
  The maps on pages 37, 51 and 168-169 are based on information taken from the National Topographic Series map sheets 82F/NW © 1973, 82K/NW © 1980, and 82J/SW © 1977 with permission of the Surveys and Resource Mapping Branch, Ministry of Crown Lands, Government of British Columbia.

*Once you've been here, you'll
  never leave this place,*

It will never leave you.

ACKNOWLEDGMENTS

When I was very young, maybe five years old, I decided to be an explorer. My inspiration came from the *National Geographic* magazines lying around our house. When twelve years old I was told to write a school essay on any subject. Later I heard the teachers laughing — I wrote that I wanted life to be a "technicolor experience". They laughed, but it's happening. Paddling the known and unknown rivers and exploring the primitive and developed hot springs of the Kootenays, I've realized those childhood ambitions. The Kootenays experience is one of the most precious chunks of my life that I have to share. And, as I share it with readers of this guidebook, I want you to know who the many people are that I've enjoyed river running with. This guidebook is based on the fun we had. Thanks to . . .

• Ben Lemke who first took me paddling in the Kootenays. I am grateful not only for the happy times we shared during numerous paddling tours but also for the insights passed on to me about the lighthearted backwoods-mixed-with-modern spirit of Kootenays people. It *could* be catching. After our third Kootenays paddling trip, Ben didn't return to the lower mainland region. He's living now in Greenwood.

• The late Dane Wray who made me aware of the unusual geography of the Kootenays country — of the strange land formation of the Rocky Mountain Trench which allows the Kootenay and Columbia rivers to pass close to one another, but with one flowing north, one south. After my introduction to boating Kootenays rivers, I met Dane and asked if he'd like to join us on a paddling trip there. He wrote me telling of the Kootenays rivers and creeks he wanted to run listing their names like names from the Old Testament. It was sheer poetry. I had to keep going until I'd paddled or looked at every one.

• Klaus Streckmann for sharing his knowledge of how to explore but most importantly for sharing his love of it.

• The very special people with whom I experienced the intense thrill of making difficult river explorations that were probably first descents: Mike Bohn, Elie Bowles, Colin Coe, Ben Lemke, John Pratt-Johnson, Klaus Streckmann and the late Dane Wray.

• "Regulars" with whom I shared a great deal of paddling in the Kootenays, Dave Home, Charlie Marxer, Marian Porter, Don Ross, Mike Rott, as well as boaters I paddled one or two Kootenays rivers with; Dick Bird, Bob and Margaret Bear, Greg Fee, Brian Palmer, and Steve Schleicher.

• Local paddlers who joined us on a couple of occasions; Al Brown, Guy Crisfield, Roger Crisfield, Carol Jarvis, Ken Pepperdine, and Bert Peters.

Thanks also to the following Kootenays people who have shared their enthusiasm and expertise:

Peter Velisek of Slocan Park whom I've not yet met but who was always ready to tell me about his home rivers; Rob Gordon, kayaker from Invermere who provided facts about the Toby Creek races and who read the other write-ups covering the east side of the Rocky Mountain Trench; Joe Selby of Cranbrook who shared detailed written notes with me with which I checked many river facts; Fred Thiessen of the Ministry of Forests in Nelson who tirelessly helped me with land status facts as well as information regarding how to drive Kootenays logging roads safely; kayaker Paul Leeson of the Ministry of Forests in Cranbrook; Bob Lindsay, Fish and Wildlife Branch, Nelson; rafters Daryl Besplug, Rick Earles, and Jeff Freer; Peter Mackie, Ministry of Parks; Terry Halleran of Meadow Creek; Janey LaPointe at Mica Creek; Jack Fisher, West Kootenay Power; Netta Gansner of the East Kootenay Historical Society, Ken Zurosky and Daryl White at Fort Steele Heritage Town Archives who ferreted out the curious history of the canal at Canal Flats; Patsy Kachanoski at Fairmont Hot Springs; Lyle Wilson of Invermere who spontaneously stopped on the road when he saw our kayaks and offered our cold, wet group a roof for the night at Nipika; Van Redecopp of Kimberley who graciously dropped everything to share information with our scruffy group — we were covered with two-weeks-of-camping-out dirt when we arrived wanting to paddle.

My thanks to Oliver Nagy at the Water Survey of Canada who, once again, helped me most generously with information regarding riverflows. Thanks to Nora Williams and Betty Lum at the Map Library, University Library, University of British Columbia who were particularly energetic in helping me locate useful maps and facts and who telephoned me, on several occasions, volunteering newly found information — they never stopped thinking on my project. Thanks to Rosemary Hadley at the Geographic Information Centre, University of British Columbia; Bruce McBride, B.C. Archives and Records Service; Ron Hooper, Environment Canada; Kathleen O'Neill-White, Tourism British Columbia; the specialists at the Geological Survey of Canada who checked my write-ups with information regarding rocks and added to it; Marianne Lemke for translating the book review that was written in German into English; Doug Forrest, who is with Powerex and who is Manager of the Canadian Entity for the Columbia River Treaty as well as Irene Javor and Rory Tennant at the B.C. Hydro Information Centre, and Neill Lyons at Environment Canada, who is a member of the engineering committee for the Columbia River Treaty Permanent Engineering Board, for helping me track down facts regarding the Columbia-Kootenay River System.

Putting it on paper is the next step. It has been a pleasure, again, to work with Dr. Tirthankar Bose who has edited this book; graphics artist Kerry Jackson who drew the maps; Andy Cassidy who gave me photographic help; Vic Marks, Marian Bantjes and Marlene Solberg at the Typeworks who taught me to set the type and do the layout on the computer. Only the photographs and maps were left to be stripped in, and the hydrographs produced and pasted up — I am grateful to David Lim who completed these artistic jobs, and to Karen Petersen and Diana Pratt-Johnson who carefully checked the index.

But once again my greatest thanks go to my husband John who managed to live with me throughout the lengthy procedure of my producing yet another guidebook. I have enjoyed the process enormously but it isn't easy for concerned onlookers to take. The paddling is fun we shared; the book production is tedious and rewarding only to the one who discovers a delightful or extraordinary new fact or who ticks off yet another detail on the way to completion. I enjoy that part too; it brings the rivers alive a second time around but in a new manner. And an additional pleasure is still to come.

The final step in guidebook production is for people to use them. I love to get feedback as well; that's special. Without readers, there would be no point. So, to all who pick up this guidebook — I hope it's useful — thanks!

CONTENTS

What's Special About the Kootenays?   Page 7
How to Use This Guidebook   10

West Kootenay River Runs and Play Spot

1 GRANBY RIVER, Howe Creek through Eight Mile Flats   12
2 GRANBY RIVER, Canyon   14
3 COLUMBIA RIVER, Rock Island Play Spot   16
4 SALMO RIVER, To Seven Mile Reservoir   22
5 SALMO RIVER, Porto Rico through Ymir   26
6 SLOCAN RIVER, Crescent Valley to Kootenay River   30
7 LITTLE SLOCAN-SLOCAN RIVERS, To Passmore   34
8 WILSON CREEK, To Rosebery   38
9 LARDEAU RIVER, Rapid Creek through Devil's Elbow   40
10 DUNCAN RIVER, Westfall River to Giegerich Creek   44
11 DUNCAN RIVER, Hume Creek to Westfall River   48

East Kootenay River Runs

12 BUSH RIVER, To Kinbasket Lake   52
13 BLAEBERRY RIVER, To Columbia River   58
14 KICKING HORSE RIVER, Beaverfoot Bridge to Glenogle   62
15 VERMILION RIVER, Hector Gorge to Kootenay River   68
16 CROSS RIVER, Above Natural Bridge   72
17 KOOTENAY RIVER, Palliser Reach   76
18 WHITE RIVER, Lower Section   84
19 WHITE RIVER, Upper Section   90
20 BULL RIVER, 40 Mile to Sulphur Creek   94
21 BULL RIVER, Mini-Canyon   98
22 BULL RIVER, Canyon   102
23 ELK RIVER, Canyon   108
24 ST. MARY RIVER, To Marysville   112
25 FINDLAY CREEK, Mini-Canyon to Skookumchuck Road   116
26 TOBY CREEK, Through Slipping Rock Rapid   120
27 HORSETHIEF CREEK, 14 Mile Bridge to Westside Road   124
28 BOBBIE BURNS CREEK-SPILLIMACHEEN RIVER,   130
   Below Poet Creek

West and East Kootenays Hot Springs Map   137
1 AINSWORTH HOT SPRINGS, Commercially Operated   138
2 NAKUSP HOT SPRINGS, Commercially Operated   140
3 NAKUSP HOT SPRINGS, Primitive   142
4 ST. LEON HOT SPRINGS, Primitive   144

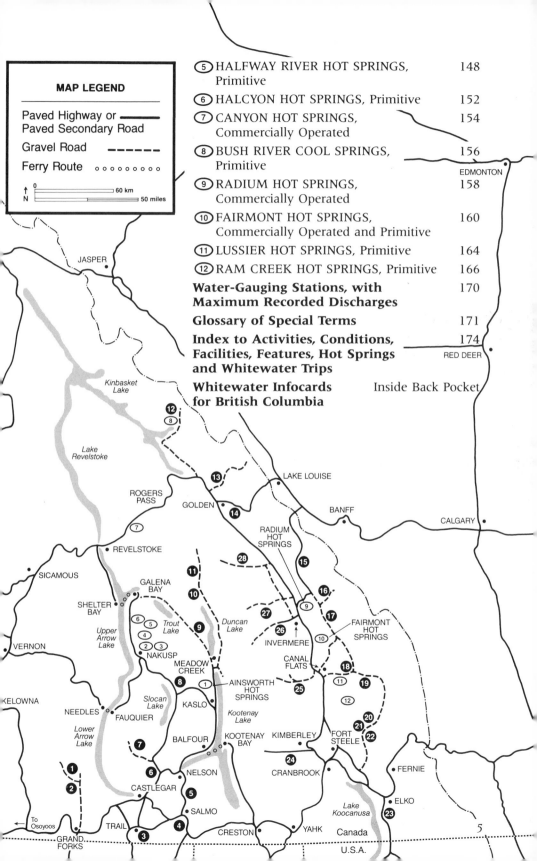

5 HALFWAY RIVER HOT SPRINGS, Primitive 148

6 HALCYON HOT SPRINGS, Primitive 152

7 CANYON HOT SPRINGS, Commercially Operated 154

8 BUSH RIVER COOL SPRINGS, Primitive 156

9 RADIUM HOT SPRINGS, Commercially Operated 158

10 FAIRMONT HOT SPRINGS, Commercially Operated and Primitive 160

11 LUSSIER HOT SPRINGS, Primitive 164

12 RAM CREEK HOT SPRINGS, Primitive 166

Water-Gauging Stations, with Maximum Recorded Discharges 170

Glossary of Special Terms 171

Index to Activities, Conditions, Facilities, Features, Hot Springs and Whitewater Trips 174

Whitewater Infocards for British Columbia   Inside Back Pocket

MAP LEGEND

Paved Highway or Paved Secondary Road ———

Gravel Road – – – – – –

Ferry Route ∘∘∘∘∘∘∘∘∘

0   60 km
N   50 miles

Frowning Hole on Findlay Creek

Nearing canyon on Bull River

WHAT'S SPECIAL ABOUT
THE WEST AND EAST KOOTENAYS?

Kootenay country — chock-full of places to go on roads that loop through delightfully confusing mountains and valleys. You'll find white-water paddling to suit all tastes. Incredible hot springs too. But the Kootenays region is special for a number of reasons — it's a rare place because of the people who live there; many locals put equal value on their TV satellite dish and their wood cookstove — it's the ultimate playground for visitors who delight in a quiet blend of history and the wilds.

Thrill-seeking rafters, hot-shot kayakers, laid-back open-canoeists, people who love to wander in unfenced natural places — all will find appealing rivers, creeks, hot springs, and camping in this richly varied region. First descents, well-worn water trails, primitive and commercially operated hot springs are all highlights in this book. Roaring rivers and quiet ones too. You'll find waterfalls to plummet over, some to walk around.

Spray in your face as you buck through the deep canyon on the Kicking Horse, the smell of sage beside the Horsethief, wild roses decorating the campsite on the road to Paradise near Toby Creek, gooseberries beside Findlay Creek, strawberries and orange tiger lilies growing wild beside the upper White, bighorn sheep roaming on the rocky hillside above the Vermilion, tired bodies curled up in hammocks slung between two trees beside the Kootenay; a natural bridge of rock over the Cross; steam rising to hide a sky full of stars as you soak in the hot springs at Lussier. Peach and white colored stalactites dripping gentle, hot rain on your shoulders in the hot springs caves at Ainsworth. You might find old mining artifacts in prospectors' caves beside Findlay Creek and the Elk Canyon, see bald eagles or hear a hawk shrieking like a cat high above the river.

For paddlers, the Kootenays is a summer place to go. If you like your water wild, go in early summer. If you like it gentle, go in the heat of August when the grass is yellow and the glacial milk is flowing. Timing is important.

In the West Kootenays, the runoff starts sooner on rivers like the Granby and Salmo — they usually peak in May, and riverflow is not maintained throughout summer because there's no lake above them to moderate flow and no glacial-melt. During June you can also dash down the lively Little Slocan River, Wilson Creek, and the upper Salmo — catch them before they're gone. Then, in June and July, head for the heart-stopping big boisterous waves and boulder gardens beside snow banks on the Duncan, the warm, super-smooth waves on the Slocan, fall into a hole and be "Maytagged" then move on to the brilliant blue lower Salmo to dart between giant boulders in remote Shenango Canyon — it's pushy enough that you might prefer to avoid it when it's peaking in May or June, and big enough to maintain flow that can be paddled in August. In June and July, the Lardeau is big: be careful. But in August, you can coast down it while peering through crystal clear water to the coarse gravel beds where the Gerrard rainbows pair off, then play at Devil's Elbow and lunch beside it on a sunbaked sandy beach. And throughout the summer, you can surf an excellent set of four waves on the gargantuan Columbia at Trail, then paddle into the boiling eddy and ride it upstream to surf again.

In the East Kootenays the watersheds are at a higher altitude — the ice melts in May, and most rivers peak in June or July. This is true except for the Elk and Bull rivers: they usually peak in May or June, then keep going for a

Lussier Hot Springs

long season, so you can still paddle them after their peak. And note that at high water the Bull can be ugly, the Elk awesome — when they're peaking, you might want to give them a miss.

Early July — that's what I think of as prime time for paddling in the East Kootenays, that's when you can descend the stairstep rapids of Toby Creek, leap a small waterfall on Findlay, explore the Horsethief, play at Keer's Rock on the St. Mary, meet a knobbly-kneed moose at one of the lovely rounded bends with swishy-smooth surfing waves and see hoodoos like sand castles in the sky on the hillside above the river — all this on the lower White.

Glacial-melt extends the season on some rivers, keeps the Bull, Blaeberry, Horsethief, Vermilion, Bobbie Burns and more, flowing. In August, you can float down the glacial-fed Bush to Surprise Canyon — be part of one of the most beautiful Rocky Mountain backdrops in the world. During August and September, you can drift down the placid part of the Kootenay, then brave the big waves, stop for a riverside sauna, savour the spectacular scenery which includes a 30-meter (100-foot) waterfall cascading into it like a "larger-than-life" movie set depicting the Canadian scene.

Aprés-paddling in the Kootenays is *very* special too: pamper yourself with a hot plunge after every run — you'll find seven primitive hot springs and five commercially operated ones to choose from. They are all described in this guidebook. Hot springs are part of the rich long-standing tradition of hospitality in the Kootenays; some resorts offered facilities to guests as early as the late 1800s. You'll find pubs to go to. Places to camp. Hikes to go on — there's lots to do. But to me, hot springing is the greatest after-paddling pleasure to be found: thus, every river description in this guidebook includes the time it takes to reach the nearest hot springs after your day on the river — travel time from take-out to hot springs ranging from 15 minutes to 2½ hours, most taking 1 hour.

The Kootenays country is a delectably lush region for history, hot springs, primitive camping, scenery, and wildlife as well as for rivers and creeks. It's been alive with people since the late 1800s and early 1900s — people who were mining, logging, farming, trapping or on holiday.

Wandering through the Kootenays today is still a lively, voluptuous experience; and paddling in the Kootenays — whether exploring Class 2, 3 or 4 water, you'll find some of the most exciting and most scenic yet least known waterways in the world. Each time I visit I feel like a privileged guest in a magically settled yet untamed place.

HOW TO USE THIS GUIDEBOOK

Locator maps show the river and the hot springs sites, each identified by its number — in white within a black circle. Symbols on the river locator maps show whom the sites are suitable for: kayakers, open-canoeists, rafters.

For kayakers: For open-canoeists: For rafters:

Site descriptions for rivers give you all the relevant information for each of the 28 one-day trips, including access, facilities, the season to paddle, detailed features of the runs, character of the water and the fun you can have at particular points. Riverflow is natural on all but two of the rivers in this guidebook; so hydrographs are useful to help you plan when to go — timing is particularly important to enable you paddle the kind of water you want.

Heard of Bert's Drop and want to go for it? Wishing for easy water to paddle? Want the novelty of sitting in your canoe and being lifted 15 meters (50 feet) in a navigational lock? Want to paddle alongside the first road through the Rockies? — look in the index under *historic sites*. Delve into the quick-reference index and find whatever you want. If you come across an unfamiliar "river" word, check out the glossary of special terms. For additional data about regional conditions, when to go, topographic maps, air photos, travel and accommodations guidance, paddling clubs and more, see the *Whitewater Infocards for British Columbia* in the pocket on the inside back cover of this guidebook.

Site descriptions for primitive and commercially operated hot springs give you all the relevant details for the seven primitive and five commercially operated hot springs including access, and where to obtain more information regarding the springs as well as what's special about each one.

Primitive hot springs are pools formed from hot water bubbling naturally from the ground and are minimally developed, if at all, and are available to everyone without charge. Frequently people who enjoy them have built a wooden tub or a rock and pebble dam and have sometimes used plastic to contain the hot water. Primitive springs are usually situated in the wilds.

Commercially operated hot springs are also pools formed from hot water bubbling naturally from the ground but they are developed, and a fee is charged for using them. Commercially operated pools are normally tiled with adjacent changerooms, hot showers, and other facilities.

When planning your tour, refer to the following maps and remember the time zone changes in the middle of the Kootenays region; East Kootenays clocks are set on Mountain or "Alberta" Time, and West Kootenays clocks are on Pacific Time. The West and East Kootenays map is part of the Contents on page 5. This map shows where the described river runs, the whitewater play spot, and the hot springs are. It also shows key towns and roadways — it's for boaters going for "all of it".

People planning a hot-springs-only tour will want to use the hot springs map on page 137. Use these maps along with a road map of the region: you can obtain one free from any Tourism Infocentre or from Tourism British Columbia. You might also want to obtain a free map of the *Provincial Parks of the Kootenays* from the Ministry of Parks or from Tourism British Columbia. And remember to consider the time-zone changes.

Every river and every hot springs location was reached in an ordinary van or car; a four-wheel-drive vehicle is not required.

The Columbia-Kootenay River System map which you'll find on pages 19 and 80 provides a bird's-eye view of the waterways and mountain ranges in the Kootenays region — every river and creek described in this guidebook eventually flows into the Columbia on its way to the sea and they're all shown on it. For me, this map not only sorts out which way the Columbia and Kootenay rivers are flowing, it also helps me figure out which hidden Kootenay valley I'm in.

Topographic maps and air photos are especially useful when exploring a region with radical topography like you find in the Kootenays and a greater number of topos have been included in this volume than in previous whitewater guidebooks in the series; thirteen portions of nine topographic maps, and portions of three air photos are reproduced in this guidebook. Use them. However, as always, be aware that air photos and topos are not the final answer to what you will find on the river; information on them is often incomplete, and, rivers change — sometimes daily. Yet air photos and topos *are* useful tools to familiarize yourself with *part* of what you can expect to find when adventuring into the rugged, little known Kootenay countryside.

After checking out all information, remember that you must paddle every river each time as if it were a new river — it is. Go with care and enjoy.

Come on, let's go . . .

GRANBY RIVER
Howe Creek through Eight Mile Flats

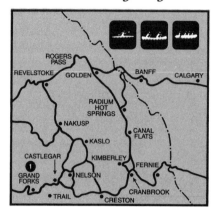

Who: Intermediate, advanced and expert kayakers, and guided novices; expert open-canoeists and guided intermediates; and all rafters, at high levels. At low levels, also novice kayakers and intermediate open-canoeists, but no rafters

Water to expect: Class 2, with a couple of Class 2+ to 3 drops (portagable); medium volume. Small rock river

Length of run: 7.2 kilometers (4.5 miles); 2 hours

Shuttle one way: 7.5 kilometers (4.7 miles); 15 minutes. Wide gravel

Why go: For a mellow paddle on a green stream through dry, rocky open-range country with ponderosa pines, birches, whitetailed deer, marmots, black bears. For the fun of wending your way through braided river. And, for the fun of trying a drop that might get you. It's near the end of the run, you reach it when you're warmed up. It's right beside the road, so you can check it out before paddling.

Topographic map: 1:50,000 Almond Mountain 82E/7.

Facilities: Camping is free, and there's a lot of room to pitch tents in the spacious Howe Creek Campground beside the river at the top put-in; you'll find picnic tables, pit toilets, fire rings, cattle, cow pies, and wild mushrooms. A smaller riverside campground, also provided free by the forest service, is at the midway put-in or take-out at Eight Mile Flats.

For an after-paddling warm-up, go via Grand Forks, Castlegar and Nelson to Ainsworth Hot Springs in the heart of the West Kootenays; it's 2½ hours from Grand Forks — and it's worth it. Once at Ainsworth, you could go on to paddle the Salmo, Duncan or Lardeau.

If you're heading north via Nakusp to Revelstoke then the Bush, the Blaeberry and Kicking Horse rivers in the East Kootenays, be sure to stop on the way at Nakusp, St. Leon, Halfway River or Halcyon hot springs. From Grand Forks, 4 hours. Or, 25 minutes past Revelstoke, you could stop at Canyon Hot Springs. See details about the springs and complete access directions for them in the hot springs section.

Guidelines: When the river's up, it's cold — so prepare for it. Width on this medium-volume stream ranges from 6 to 15 meters (20 to 50 feet) and there are narrow, braided sections with some sweepers. Also watch for the wreckage of a bridge that's halfway across the river; it's 2 kilometers (1¼ miles) downstream from the put-in at the campground at Eight Mile Flats. The river is not very pushy: gradient, in this top section, averages 12 meters/kilometer

logging roads with radio-controlled traffic

Season: April through July, during runoff; peaks in May. Mostly snow-melt but also rain-fed; natural riverflow. I paddled it in early June with riverflow of 111 m³/s (3920 cfs)

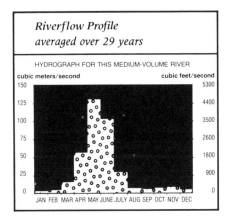

Riverflow Profile averaged over 29 years

HYDROGRAPH FOR THIS MEDIUM-VOLUME RIVER

(65 feet/mile) so you should be able to avoid all of the hazards if you watch for them.

Access to take-outs and put-ins: Located 1 hour from Grand Forks, head upriver on Granby River Forest Road on the east side of the river. To find it, cross the bridge in town, and turn left upstream. The road is paved for the first 43 kilometers (27 miles), but watch for logging trucks as you drive. At the "43 km" signpost there's a bridge across Burrell Creek and you'll see a wooden flume. Cross the bridge and continue upstream on gravel roads for 4.8 kilometers (3.0 miles) more to where you'll pass a left-hand turn toward Gable Creek; from there, continue straight upstream on Granby River Forest Road. Go 3.6 kilometers (2.2 miles) to a cattle guard near the "52 km" signpost, and leave a shuttle vehicle.

To put in, continue upstream for 6.0 kilometers (3.7 miles) to a bridge across the river. Cross it and go straight for 0.5 kilometer (0.3 mile) on Granby River Forest Road; turn right into another good gravel road and go 0.5 kilometer (0.3 mile); then right into a dirt track, and curve right down it for 0.5 kilometer (0.3 mile) to the camp.

A midway put-in or take-out point can be reached if you cross the top bridge over the Granby, as described above; then go 0.5 kilometer (0.3 mile) and, instead of turning right, turn left into a dirt track; continue 2.0 kilometers (1.2 miles) downstream on it to the campground at Eight Mile Flats.

Travel on these forest roads is open to the public; however, from Monday through Friday radio-controlled logging traffic could be on them, too, so drive with your headlights on. These roads are wide with lots of room, but it's still best to use them on weekends, holidays, and weekdays before 7 a.m. and after 6 p.m. To learn about logging traffic and possible fire-hazard closures, contact the Ministry of Forests, Boundary District, P.O. Box 2650, Grand Forks, B.C. V0H 1H0, telephone (604)442-5411.

GRANBY RIVER
Canyon

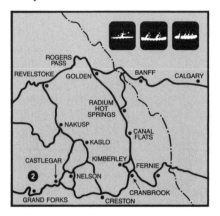

Who: At high levels, advanced and expert kayakers, and expert paddle rafters with guides; at medium levels, guided intermediate kayakers, and expert open-canoeists. At low levels, advanced and expert kayakers, but no open-canoeists or rafters

Water to expect: Class 3 to 4+. At low levels, boulder gardens; at high levels, continuous holes and rapids through a remote canyon. Possibly unrunnable when peaking; technical

Length of run: 5.5 kilometers (3.4 miles); 2 to 3 hours

Why go: For a demanding, technical run through the wilderness — lively holes and drops or boulder gardens all the way.

When I paddled the Granby Canyon, it was August and the riverbed was almost dry. We did some rock climbing to get through a couple of constricted drops. But the paddling was mellow, the water was warm, and it was a beautiful place to be. We could see the potential for a fabulous, continuous hole-filled run at high water, and I've talked with kayakers who've run it in spring when it's wild. Take your pick.

After boating, you could try fishing for rainbow or brook trout. The fishing is best in fall and spring. If you plan to angle, obtain a non-tidal sport fishing license. You can buy one in Grand Forks.

Topographic maps: 1:50,000 Almond Mountain 82E/7 and Deer Park 82E/8.

Facilities: A picnic table, pit toilet and fire ring are provided free by the forest service at an intimate campground close beside the Granby at Gable Creek put-in; there is a larger, more open forest service campground at the Burrell Creek take-out with a picnic table, pit toilet and fire rings.

Heading into the Kootenays country, the closest hot springs are at Ainsworth Hot Springs. It's a 2½-hour drive from Grand Forks via Nelson to Ainsworth Hot Springs where you can swim in hot pools through a cave with peach and white colored stalactites dripping hot rain.

Guidelines: You might be able to check water levels on an informal water-gauging scale, if it hasn't washed away. Look 10 meters (30 feet) upstream from the put-in bridge at Gable Creek for a weathered stick with red numbers painted on it that is strapped to some pilings. When this informal scale reads 1¼ meters (4 feet), it's high water; when the scale reads less than ⅓ meter (1 foot) it's bony, but plastic-boaters can still kayak it.

This run is difficult at all water levels, as the river descends quickly: gradient averages 17 meters/kilometer (90 feet/mile). At high levels it's one

Shuttle one way: 6.1 kilometers (3.8 miles); takes 15 minutes. Wide gravel logging road most of way

Season: April through July; peaks in May — exciting during runoff in June. Mostly snow-melt, also rain-fed. We paddled it in early August with extremely low, natural riverflow of 12 m³/s (424 cfs)

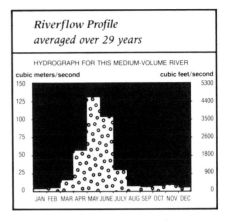

Riverflow Profile averaged over 29 years

HYDROGRAPH FOR THIS MEDIUM-VOLUME RIVER

long, continuous, pushy rapid filled with holes — and you'd better have a good roll. At lower levels, it becomes an extremely technical drop-and-pool river with some passages narrowed to a boat width — or less! River width ranges from 6 to 15 meters (20 to 50 feet) and trees grow close to the banks; there could be sweepers or fallen trees. This entire canyon requires paddling with care and it increases in seriousness as you go. It starts with Class 3 to 3+, and shortly below Gable Creek it becomes Class 4 to 4+.

Access to take-outs and put-ins: Located 45 minutes from Grand Forks, head upriver on Granby River Forest Road on the east side of the river; find it by crossing the bridge in town, and turning left upstream. The road is paved for the first 43 kilometers (27 miles), but watch for logging trucks as you drive. When the pavement ends and Burrell Creek Road goes off to the right-hand side, you continue straight. You'll see the "43 km" signpost, a bridge across Burrell Creek and a wooden flume in it. Cross the bridge over Burrell Creek and immediately turn left into the Granby-Burrell Campground, park, and walk ½ kilometer (¼ mile) along a dirt track and trail to the right; follow Burrell Creek to where it flows into the Granby and mark your take-out. Check out the trail as you walk: at the end of your paddle, you might be able to drive part of the way down it to pick up boats.

For the put-in, continue upstream from Granby-Burrell Campground. From the take-out, head up Granby River Forest Road for 4.8 kilometers (3.0 miles), turn left toward Gable Creek and go a short way down this narrower winding road to the put-in bridge.

Travel on Granby River Forest Road is open to the public; however, from Monday through Friday, logging traffic could be on it too, so always drive with your headlights on. Usually this road is free of logging traffic on weekends, holidays, and weekdays before 7 a.m. and after 6 p.m. To learn about logging traffic and possible fire-hazard closures, contact the Ministry of Forests, Boundary District, P.O. Box 2650, Grand Forks, B.C. V0H 1H0, telephone (604)442-5411.

COLUMBIA RIVER
Rock Island Play Spot

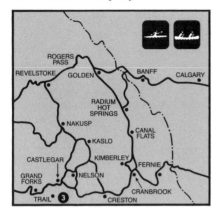

Who: Intermediate, advanced and expert kayakers and guided novices; expert open-canoeing groups; but no rafters

Water to expect: Class 2, some Class 3. Big water — enormous volume, waves usually about 1 meter (3 feet) high with big water boils and hydraulics

Length of run: Play spot that is 300 meters (1000 feet) long; surf for 5 minutes or all day

Shuttle one way: If you've got a support team to pick up anyone who swims, none required for the surfing

Why go: To play with power; to surf. The Columbia is a colossus — and at this easily accessible site there is a series of broad, oily-smooth surfing waves followed by an excellent eddy to ride upstream. You can surf, break through the boil at the side, cruise up the eddy, ferry out, then do it again. You can recirculate for hours. And a group of five or six boaters could ride the wave at one time.

The volume is incredible: paddling onto the continental giant at Trail makes me feel very small. This immense, polished mass of water seems like it isn't going anywhere. But it is! Almost before starting to ferry across, I was below Rock Island in the middle of this huge river that is 300 meters (1000 feet) wide — about to slip past what we had come for: the series of four surfing waves. They were almost 1 meter (3 feet) high that day. We played for a long time on them, recirculating up the slow, powerful eddy, ferrying out and surfing back through the big boils and whirlpools to the eddy again. Once you get started, these Rock Island play waves are a wonderfully unthreatening, safe place to practice surfing on big water — it is an excellent training ground for big-water hydraulics as there are no hazards downstream. Except for the play spot, the water is so unrippled you can hardly tell which way it is flowing.

Between surfing, you might enjoy sunning on the sandy beach or baking yourself on the hot rocks, and fishing for rainbow trout, brown trout or sturgeon. A 315-kilogram (690-pound) sturgeon was caught here in 1986 as well as one weighing only 186 kilograms (410 pounds)! In winter, watch for sturgeon leaping from the water to cleanse themselves of parasites.

The course of the Columbia River is strange: it flows both north and south soaking up every drop of water as it goes. All the rivers and creeks in this West and East Kootenays guidebook eventually feed into it. Seven of them flow into the Kootenay then the Columbia, and eleven of them flow directly into the Columbia *before* Trail — only the Salmo and Granby flow into the Columbia shortly *past* Trail. Near the source of the Columbia in the Rocky Mountain Trench of the East Kootenays, it was "touch and go" as to which of the larger

Season: Best on a hot summer day; available year-round, except during big releases from the Hugh Keenleyside (Arrow) Dam. We surfed it in early June with riverflow of 1830 m³/s (64,600 cfs)

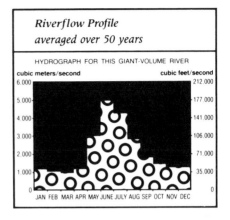

Riverflow Profile
averaged over 50 years

HYDROGRAPH FOR THIS GIANT-VOLUME RIVER

cubic meters/second   cubic feet/second

bodies of water Findlay Creek would flow into. Near the source of the Columbia at Columbia Lake, Kootenay River levels fluctuate with the spring freshet, but the river is usually about 2 meters (6 feet) higher than Columbia Lake is. Also, the lake and river are separated by a flat strip of land only 3 kilometers (1¾ miles) wide. These features were noticed by adventurer Baillie-Grohman who came to British Columbia in 1882. He signed agreements with the provincial government in 1884 and 1885 allowing him to build a canal to divert the Kootenay into Columbia Lake in order to reclaim fertile lands far downstream near Creston. The Canadian Pacific Railway and settlers at Golden feared flooding, objected, and the federal ratification required was denied. In 1886, a new federal agreement permitted Grohman's syndicate to build a canal, but not a diversion canal. Half of Grohman's dream was fulfilled: a connecting navigational canal was completed on July 29, 1889. It was the first canal in British Columbia and probably the least used canal ever dug anywhere in the world. Only two ships went through it. The *Gwendoline* was the first steamship to navigate it in May 1894 — it was heading south. A second steamer started north through the canal in the summer of 1902. But

Launching above Rock Island

17

the *North Star* got stuck. It was 3 centimeters (9 inches) too wide and 9 meters (30 feet) too long for the lock. To free the ship, the lock gates were burned, and the forward dam blown up. The lock was never rebuilt, but traces of the canal can still be seen. Today the canal also lives on in the name of the community first known as McGillivray's Portage, then Grohman: In 1909 the Geographic Board of Canada list established the new name as Canal Flats.

The Columbia River rises in the glassy, marshy waters of Columbia Lake near Canal Flats. It flows northward, quickly gathering volume from every river and creek draining into the Trench that hasn't found the Kootenay River first. It moves through Kinbasket Lake which has become enormous since the Mica Dam was completed in 1972. Then it takes a big bend and heads south through Lake Revelstoke newly created by the Revelstoke Dam completed in 1984. Finally the Columbia flows into the West Kootenays through the Upper and Lower Arrow lakes which are greatly enlarged since the Hugh Keenleyside (Arrow) Dam, which is at their outflow, was completed in 1968. And, 8 kilometers (5 miles) downstream past the Keenleyside Dam, the Kootenay River and Canal feed into the Columbia at Castlegar; another 27 kilometers (17 miles) downstream at Trail, just before the mass of water that is the Columbia crosses the border into the U.S.A., you can surf all but two of the rivers in this guidebook rolled into one at the Rock Island Play Spot — only the Granby and Salmo rivers merge with the Columbia past Rock Island.

Anyone wanting to boat the full length of the Columbia in Canada, which is 748 kilometers (465 miles), can do so. There are dams on the way, but you can get around them. Having encountered the Columbia so many times in both the East and West Kootenays while kayaking the rivers for this guidebook, I became fascinated with it. Now I fantasize paddling its entire length from Canal Flats to the international border; this would tie together the whole incredible Kootenays experience for me.

You could put in on Columbia Lake. Then, as you paddle out of the lake and the river trip starts, you pass beneath a highway bridge and reach a golf course; that's the signal to haul out for a soak in Fairmont Hot Springs. They're less than a kilometer (less than a mile) from the river. Past Fairmont, you go onto Windermere Lake where you might see windsurfers, then into the Columbia River again where you could enjoy bird watching while drifting lazily through flatwater marshes of the Rocky Mountain Trench and northwest through Golden to Kinbasket Lake. This is where the long spell of flatwater wilderness paddling begins. But no hurry. You'll find beautiful campsites beside the lake, and be sure to plan for time to stop for provisions, time to enjoy the wilderness, time to stop in the event that the wind blows up. The lake can become extremely rough. Do not go to the end of the lake; when the lake broadens, you keep left and go around the big bend of the Columbia at Mica Creek. You could get provisions and enjoy a free tour of the Mica Dam at Mica Creek. And you'll have to walk 2.0 kilometers (1.2 miles) on a road to get around the 600-meter (2,000-foot) thick dam. Put in again and paddle another great distance through more wilderness; travel the length of Lake Revelstoke to the Revelstoke Dam. Another free tour is offered here. At Revelstoke, you'll find a locked gate across the road on "river right", but it is

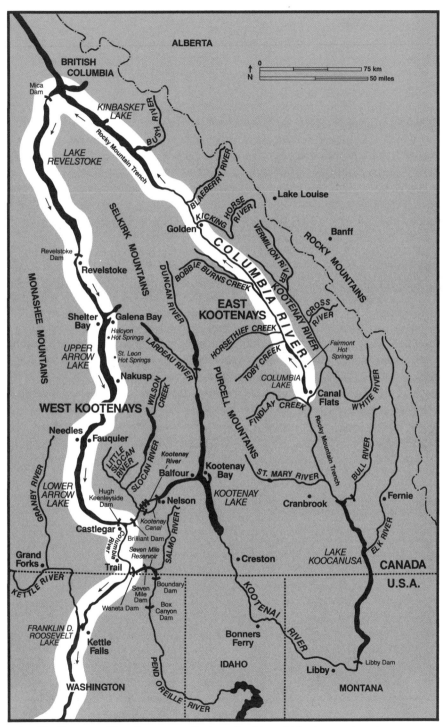

Columbia-Kootenay River System — all rivers in this guidebook pour into it; see arrows pointing in direction of riverflow on the Columbia

possible to take out on "river left"; then walk 5 kilometers (3 miles) along the east shore of the river around the dam. Past it, paddle beneath Trans-Canada Highway 1, and head south onto the Arrow lakes where the trip becomes a totally different experience. People have lived beside the Upper and Lower Arrow lakes for many years; a sense of history permeates the region even though it's sparsely settled today. Paddle down Upper Arrow Lake and arrive by water to savour Halcyon and St. Leon hot springs — in the late 1800s, that was the way visitors reached the elegant lakeside resort hotels here when they came to enjoy the springs. Halcyon is an easy walk from the lakeshore, less than a kilometer (less than a mile) while St. Leon will take a couple of hours to hike to. See descriptions and access directions for these primitive springs on pages 144-147 and 152-153 of this guidebook. And, before starting your trip, mark the lake take-outs so you can find them. After St. Leon, it's a long paddle down the long and skinny Arrow lakes. Near the end of Upper Arrow Lake, you could stop at Nakusp for provisions and to soak in another hot springs. From Highway 23 which runs close alongside the lake, it is 12 kilometers (7½ miles) up a paved road to the commercially operated springs; from there it's a 15-minute walk to the primitive springs. You might want to arrange in advance for transport — it's a possibility — or you could hitchhike. See directions to Nakusp Hot Springs (commercially operated and primitive) on pages 140-143. Then off for the final stretch of the Lower Arrow Lake to the Keenleyside Dam and an unusual treat.

Recreational boaters can piggy-back on the agreement that was made to protect logging, fishing and mining interests but which includes us. All boaters have the right, on the strength of the Boundary Waters Treaty (1909) and reconfirmed in the Columbia River Treaty (1964), to continue the free navigation that was available at the time the treaty was made:

The Boundary Waters Treaty states: ". . . navigation of all navigable boundary waters shall forever continue free and open for the purposes of commerce to the inhabitants and to the ships, vessels, and boats of both countries . . ."

At the Keenleyside Dam, this "free navigation" is achieved by use of a navigational lock which raises and lowers boats between Lower Arrow Lake and the Columbia River. The lock operates from 8 a.m. until 4 p.m. every day of the year except possibly Christmas and New Year. This service is provided without charge — it's free. Recreational boaters might be asked to give precedence to commercial traffic for whom the agreement was actually made, so it could take as much as ½ to 1 hour to get through the lock, or it could take as little as 15 minutes. There's a bit of water action when the lock fills and empties, but canoeists and kayakers should be able to handle it. Could be fun. I haven't done this one yet, but I want to.

And, If you don't want to paddle the whole Columbia, but you want the experience of the lock, you could launch upstream from Castlegar and go for a day-paddle through the Keenleyside Dam. The normal maximum vertical lift possible is 23 meters (75 feet). To arrange a ride down, or up, in the lock, contact Kootenay Canal Generating Station, P.O. Box 100, South Slocan, B.C. V0G 2G0, (604)359-7287.

Topographic map: 1:50,000 Rossland-Trail 82F/4.

Facilities: Camping is available, for a fee during peak season, at Beaver Creek Provincial Park. To reach it, head east and shortly past Waneta Plaza turn right onto Highway 22A. You'll find picnic tables, pit toilets and fire rings at the campground. The nearest hot springs are 1¾ hours away at Ainsworth Hot Springs where you'll find a beautifully developed commercially operated hot pool in a cave. There's a warm pool for swimming too. You go via Castlegar and Nelson to Ainsworth Hot Springs.

For information on camping facilities alongside Kinbasket Lake, Lake Revelstoke, and the Upper Arrow lakes as well as for details about using the navigational lock at the Keenleyside Dam, contact B.C. Hydro Information Centre, 970 Burrard Street, Vancouver, B.C. V6Z 1Y3, (604)663-2114.

Guidelines: The Columbia is vast: it's width at Trail is 300 meters (1000 feet). It helps to have a roll or a close buddy for Eskimo rescue. And use common sense. Avoid even the smallest wave on this "Big-Daddy-of-Them-All" if it's runoff time and there is a release from the Keenleyside Dam. To find out current discharge at Birchbank, telephone the office of the Water Survey of Canada on weekdays after 1 p.m. at (604)666-3977.

Collecting from an 88,400-square-kilometer (34,100-square-mile) drainage area, the Columbia River at Trail can be stupendous. Maximum daily discharge — an all-time high of 8835 m^3/s (312,000 cfs) — was reported on June 14, 1913, at Trail. Riverflow is no longer measured at this station, so I refer to measurements taken 13 kilometers (8 miles) upstream at Birchbank: the greatest flow ever reported there during the period of record was 8466 m^3/s (299,000 cfs) on June 26, 1959. When we paddled, it was relatively low: 1826 m^3/s (64,500 cfs). What the Columbia is like when there is a big release from the Keenleyside Dam I would not like to guess!

A pointer for novices: to remain upright on boils, keep your paddle moving all the time.

Access to put-in and take-out: Located in the city of Trail with many roads leading to it: you can approach from Castlegar, Fruitvale, Rossland or Salmo via Highway 3B, Highway 22 or 22A. The take-out is the same as the put-in. The play spot is beside Highway 3B just west of Waneta Plaza.

From Castlegar or Rossland, go into Trail, cross the bridge in the center of town and continue east on the Salmo-Creston Highway 3B toward Fruitvale. From the bridge, go 5.2 kilometers (3.2 miles) and park beside the highway on the right-hand side at the top of a gravel road to the riverbank.

From Salmo, head west to Trail via Fruitvale on Highway 3B. It takes half an hour. You'll know you're nearing Trail when you see signposts to "Beaver Creek Provincial Park" but do not turn left to it. Continue straight at the junction, stay on Highway 3B; then, heading down the hill into Trail, you'll see Waneta Plaza on your right-hand side. The play spot is a short way past it. It's difficult to see road-side parking for it when moving fast; so slow down, and measure the distance. The parking spot is 0.6 kilometer (0.4 mile) past the "Waneta Plaza" signpost. It's on the left-hand side of the highway. From there, a short walk down a gravel road to the sandy beach where you put in.

SALMO RIVER
To Seven Mile Reservoir

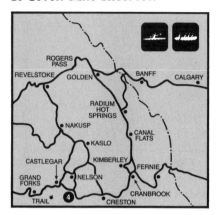

Who: Advanced and expert kayakers, no open-canoeists, and expert rafters with guides. At low levels, also guided intermediate kayakers

Water to expect: Class 4 boulder drops, Class 3 rapids, one Class 5 boulder drop (portagable) at high levels; unrunnable when peaking. At low levels, steep Class 3+ to 4 drops and pools, with one Class 5 drop (portagable). Continuous, pushy, technical through a remote canyon

Length of run: 11.6 kilometers (7.2 miles); 5 to 7 hours, depending on play time

Why go: Sparkling warm blue water, and it builds — through rock gardens, boulder gardens and boulder drops, culminating at Bert's Drop.

A gorgeous run all the way; an exciting run all the way! There's continuous Class 3 and 4 past the Black Bluffs through Shenango Canyon. From rock gardens to boulder gardens to boulder drops, and the boulders are so big you can't see the paddlers eddied out behind them. It's like becoming a Knight, Rook or Queen in a giant watery game of chess, except that none of the moves are in straight lines. Why is the Salmo so special? It is remote, it is challenging. It is a classic example of a progression in difficulty.

Topographic map: 1:50,000 Salmo 82F/3.

Facilities: Vacant Crown land all around near the put-in where you could pitch your tent, but no developed campgrounds. The swimming's good at the reservoir, so you might find a place to camp beside it. However, I've been told that since the water level fluctuates there's no camping near the take-out. For a hot shower, return to Wildwood Campground, which is open from the May holiday weekend until freeze-up or go to the campground at Hidden Creek. Both are near Salmo. Or you could head to one of the hot springs: the closest one is 1½ hours from the take-out at Ainsworth Hot Springs.

Guidelines: The river is wide at the put-in — about 60 meters (200 feet) but farther downstream it narrows in some passages to 5 meters (16 feet) wide; average width is from 10 to 45 meters (30 to 150 feet). The gradient is 12 meters/kilometer (65 feet/mile). The lower Salmo is a long run; its start is deceptively easy but the water soon develops and it keeps you awake throughout. It builds from Class 2 to 3, to 4, to 5.

When you've paddled about an hour you'll soon be at Shenango Canyon. Watch for a cabin hidden in the woods on the left-hand side. If you've been at all nervous so far, this is where you take out — don't go into Shenango Canyon. Walk up the hill. It's the last chance to get out of the canyon. The cabin is privately owned and there is a locked gate across the road, so you will

Shuttle one way: 17.0 kilometers (10.6 miles); 20 minutes. Pavement for 10.2 kilometers (6.3 miles), the rest is gravel

Season: May through August — best in June and July, but do not paddle when peaking. Snow-melt and rain-fed; natural riverflow bounces up after a couple of days of rain. We kayaked it in late June with riverflow of 82 m³/s (2900 cfs)

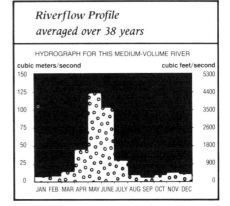

Riverflow Profile averaged over 38 years

HYDROGRAPH FOR THIS MEDIUM-VOLUME RIVER

have to walk up the hill and carry your boat. It's 1.6 kilometers (1.0 mile) to Highway 6. If you do use this road, be careful to respect the private property and be especially careful not to start a fire in this dry country.

If you don't climb out, be ready; around the next corner to the right is where the fun begins. From the cabin on you need to read the water carefully, and you need a roll. The entire canyon is demanding — but the main thing you *must* look for ahead is Bert's Drop and it's extremely difficult to see.

You don't want to run this one without scouting it. You might not want to run it at all. It's Class 5. In the past, local paddlers have flagged it, but do not count on their markers. If you want to be certain to spot the drop, hike in

Bert's Drop

from the take-out to mark it. If you don't mark it, paddle *very* carefully. In addition to reading the water and watching as the canyon narrows and paddling under control all the way, watch for a low cable across the river. It's about 6 meters (20 feet) upstream from Bert's Drop. After the cable, there's a power transmission line which is 24 meters (80 feet) high across the river and a white ball hanging from it into the canyon. Bert's Drop is soon after that.

When the boulders become choked, the passages narrower, and the drops steeper, expect Bert's Drop, the steepest of them all. When you guess you're almost there, pull out on "river left" well in advance, walk downstream and take a look. One friend's life jacket shredded — while he wore it! — when he purposefully went over this drop that plunges 2½ to 3½ meters (9 to 11 feet) with a rock in the middle at the bottom; he took it on "river right" and went into the hole at the base of the falls. The drop is named after Bert Peters who used to live beside the Salmo.

Bert "saw god" and was sobered for years by inadvertently dropping into the hole on "river left" the first time he kayaked this section; he was the first one over it. He has returned to paddle it a couple of times — it was a matter of principle, like getting back onto the horse that threw you, he says. He paddled with our group, but none of us ran the drop that day. I don't run Bert's Drop, and a lot of splendid boaters I know don't either. Whether you can run it at all and *where* you can run it depends partly on water level. Stop and scout.

After Bert's Drop it's a 20- to 25-minute flatwater paddle to the take-out. There used to be a couple more exciting rapids and chutes before the Salmo flowed into the tumultous Pend-d'Oreille River — they were the best ones. But the entire Salmo from Bert's Drop onwards is now flooded and flattened by the Seven Mile Dam which was completed in 1980. The Seven Mile Dam, along with the Waneta Dam completed in 1954, has transformed the once-grandiose Pend-d'Oreille River into a lake. This quiet body of water that is now backed up across the international border to the Boundary Dam is usually referred to as the Seven Mile or Pend-d'Oreille reservoir, but I like the commonly used name of Pete's Pond — Pete is production supervisor at the Seven Mile Dam. The mellow body of water between the Seven Mile and Waneta dams, which stretches to within a few steps of the Columbia River, is referred to as the Waneta Reservoir. None of these names are official, but the Pend-d'Oreille River has been drowned. It no longer exists. The name of "Pend-d'Oreille River" should be struck from the *Gazetteer of Canada.*

It's a lake take-out — great for swimming — but some whitewater thrills have already disappeared because of the dams, and more will go: Seven Mile Reservoir is due to be raised 5 meters (16 feet) in the next few years. So take note; you might want to kayak it before Bert's Drop is flooded and gone.

The first descent of the lower Salmo was was probably on June 18, 1979, when a group explored it with riverflow of 39 m³/s (1380 cfs). No written notes were made, but as far as can be recalled, Ralf Kuntzemann, Dan O'Brien, Bert Peters, and Peter Velisek were on that trip. Since then, many runs have been made on this gorgeous river.

Paddle power

Access to take-out and put-in: Located 30 minutes south of Salmo between Creston and Castlegar near the U.S.A. border.

From Salmo, head south on Highway 3/6, then Highway 6, to Nelway at the Canada/U.S.A. border. From here it's 8.2 kilometers (5.1 miles) to the take-out. Turn right into Pend-d'Oreille Road, which used to be Highway 22A. After 1.6 kilometers (1.0 mile) the road becomes gravel; there are many new roads in this developing region, but stay on the main one. When I was last there, we passed a couple of forks in the road on the way to the take-out, the first one veering off uphill on the right-hand side; we stayed left along the lower road. At the next junction, a road curled down to the left; here, you continue straight for 1.3 kilometers (0.8 mile) to the Bailey bridge at the take-out. Don't park too close to the water as sometimes the level of the reservoir fluctuates during the day; the last time a friend of mine paddled there, he arrived to find his new car with water up to its axles.

Before heading to the put-in, you might want to hike a fisherman's trail upstream along the east bank of the Salmo to scout the Class 5 Bert's Drop; it is 1.0 kilometer (0.6 mile) upstream from the take-out.

To reach the put-in, return to Nelway, turn left and go on Highway 6 for 8.0 kilometers (5.0 miles) to an almost-indistinguishable dirt track. If you reach Highway 3, you have gone too far and should return south on Highway 6: the turnoff into the dirt road is 2.3 kilometers (1.4 miles) south of the Highway 3/6 junction.

At the dirt track, turn west and go 0.6 kilometer (0.4 mile) into a field where flax is growing beside the put-in.

SALMO RIVER
Porto Rico through Ymir

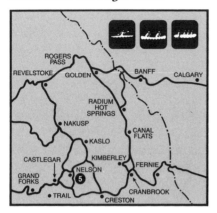

Who: At high levels, intermediate, advanced and expert kayakers; expert open-canoeists; and guided paddle rafters. At low levels, also guided novice kayakers and guided intermediate open-canoeists, but no rafters

Water to expect: Class 2 and a couple of Class 3 drops; small volume, small rock river

Length of run: 8.9 kilometers (5.5 miles); 3 hours

Shuttle one way: 8.9 to 10.3 kilometers (5.5 to 6.4 miles); takes 15 minutes. Paved but rough road and

Why go: "Cloud 9" play waves, a mini-canyon, a pub stop are scattered along this pretty little stream. I saw an otter — or was it a mink — dive in front of my boat in one of the quiet parts; and there might be slalom gates hung over a stretch near the take-out. After paddling you can fish for small rainbow trout. The Salmo is a river with many moods and contrasts.

When to go? Catch the upper Salmo with plenty of water in it if you can. The latest date when there's usually enough water to canoe it is mid-July. You might want to be there for the Salmo Raft Race which is an annual event on the Canada Day July 1st holiday weekend: the race takes off from Porcupine Creek, where this run ends, and goes into town. For information, contact the Salmo Travel Infocentre, Salmo and District Chamber of Commerce, P.O. Box 400, Salmo, B.C. V0G 1Z0, telephone (604)357-9332.

Topographic map: 1:50,000 Nelson 82F/6.

Facilities: Hot showers, flush toilets and camping — or just pay for a hot shower — at Wildwood Campground which is convenient to reach and is beside the Salmo; and, if you haven't done any swimming yet, there's an old-fashioned swimming hole there. Wildwood is 2.0 kilometers (1.2 miles) west of Salmo just off Highway 3 and it has a spacious woodsy feeling.

You'll find hot showers, flush and pit toilets, sauna and steam bath, firewood and many other services at the big open area at Hidden Creek Ranch Events Centre where there is no charge for camping, but you might give a donation for it. Hidden Creek is between Salmo and the take-out.

Also, as at most places in the Kootenays, there is a great deal of vacant Crown land where camping is permitted — much of it beside the river; scout from Porto Rico-Ymir Road shortly past the put-in bridge. You can look around, pick a place, and pitch your tent.

At hot springs time, it takes 1 hour and 20 minutes from the take-out to reach Ainsworth Hot Springs.

Guidelines: This run through the village of Ymir (pronounced Wy-mur) is

highway — the alternate route is all smooth, paved highway

Season: April through July. Best in runoff, early to late June; it is fleeting. Snow-melt and rain-fed; natural riverflow. We paddled it in mid-June with riverflow of 26 m³/s (920 cfs)

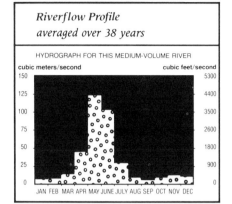

Riverflow Profile
averaged over 38 years

HYDROGRAPH FOR THIS MEDIUM-VOLUME RIVER

cubic meters/second   cubic feet/second

150	5300
125	4400
100	3500
75	2600
50	1800
25	900
0	0

JAN FEB MAR APR MAY JUNE JULY AUG SEP OCT NOV DEC

pleasantly playful. The river descends gently over mostly a small rock and gravel bottom at a steady rate of 9 meters/kilometer (45 feet/per mile). It starts with a bubbly, small surfing wave at the put-in bridge, and more follow. However, this river, as all narrow rivers in tree-clad British Columbia, must be paddled with care: logjams litter the top part and could be found anywhere along the route. We climbed over one fallen tree that was blocking the entire channel, and its branches were hanging into the river forming a strainer. With pushier water during runoff, that could be dangerous.

Paddling through Ymir, you can see the one hotel in town from your boat. The first time we passed it, a giant daisy was painted on the purple siding; the next year the daisy was gone — but the spirit was still there. It's a good

Playing near put-in

Climbing around logjam

pub stop. Past Ymir, the Salmo widens from 10 to 30 meters (30 to 100 feet) and it becomes deeper too. Red volcanic conglomerate riverbanks rise steeply. You paddle through a mini-canyon. The river twists around and there are a couple of Class 3 drops before the walls open out. Starting at the last huge rock wall on the right-hand side, you might see slalom gates. Then you're at the take-out.

Access to take-out and put-in: Between Nelson and Salmo off Highway 6. The take-out is 35 minutes from Nelson and 10 minutes from Salmo.
• From Nelson, when 15 or 20 minutes south of town on Highway 6, you'll pass Porto Rico Road on the right-hand side, then Porto Rico-Ymir Road on the left-hand side. You could turn down it and go 0.8 kilometer (0.5 mile) to the put-in bridge. From the put-in, you might continue south alongside the Salmo on a winding paved road filled with pot-holes, scouting the river as you go. You'll cross a bridge. Shortly past it, there is a "T" in the road. Turn left and go through Ymir, then turn left onto Highway 6 and go 2.1 kilometers (1.3 miles) to a side-road. Turn left into it, cross the railway tracks and a bridge over the Salmo River; almost immediately, turn left again over Porcupine Creek and it's a few steps to the take-out.

Or, after looking at the put-in, you could return to Highway 6, turn left out of Porto Rico-Ymir Road and head south on the highway for 9.1 kilometers (5.7 miles) then turn left into the side-road to the take-out.
• From Salmo to the take-out, head north on Highway 6. Measure the distance from the center of town: go 9.2 kilometers (5.7 miles). Past a sawmill, turn right; cross the railway tracks and the Salmo River, and almost immediately turn left over Porcupine Creek; park and walk a few steps to the river.

For the put-in: return to Highway 6, turn right and go for 1.9 kilometers (1.2 miles) to the Ymir turnoff. From here, you could either keep left to bypass town and continue along the highway for 6.3 kilometers (3.9 miles) then turn right into Porto Rico-Ymir Road and go to the put-in bridge.

Or veer into the right-hand road and go through Ymir. When just past town, turn right at the "T" crossroad, go over a bridge and follow the winding rough pavement filled with potholes alongside the river to the second bridge, which is the put-in. It's a really easy take-out and put-in on this one.

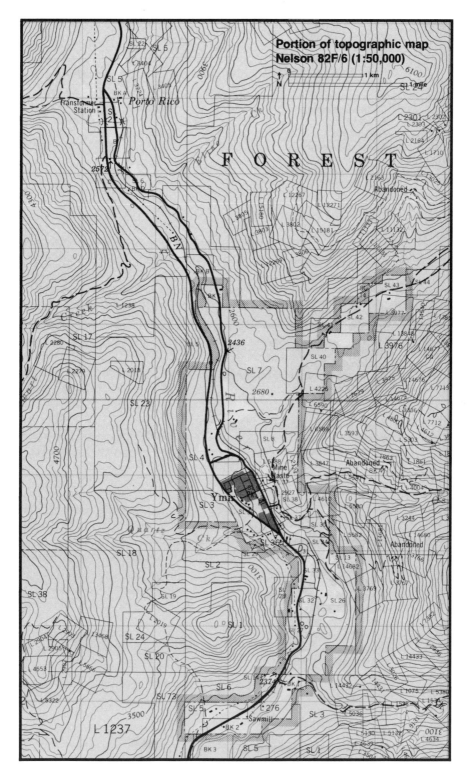

Portion of topographic map
Nelson 82F/6 (1:50,000)

FOREST

SLOCAN RIVER
Crescent Valley to Kootenay River

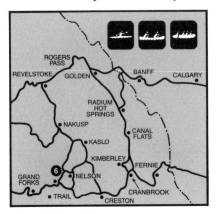

Who: Intermediate to expert kayakers, and guided novices; expert open-canoeists; all rafters

Water to expect: Class 2, with two Class 3 to 3+ rapids; medium- to large-volume and warm

Length of run: 4.8 kilometers (3.0 miles); 1 to 3 hours, depending on play time

Shuttle one way: 4.3 kilometers (2.7 miles); 10 minutes. Paved highway; easy to hitchhike or bicycle

Season: April to October. Best from

Why go: Surfing waves are so smoothly-scooped-out on the Slocan that they almost do it for you. It's where I first successfully river-surfed — and that's why I love the Slocan. But Facchina's Rapid, the continuous rapid that goes on for ½ kilometer (⅓ mile) with big waves — and big holes! — is the true highlight. After it, there's one more short rapid and *that's* the white water. When the rocks begin to show in August, it turns into more technical paddling. But water — and lots of it — is the special message of the Slocan that lures most boaters. It's a brief non-threatening fun run, you can do it again and again; and the water is warm.

Green trees line the broad banks in this broad valley; it's lovely to laze along through the floaty parts, the sun drenching you. People live alongside, yet while running the river you see only an occasional house on the hill. And once we saw a girl leading a horse to the river to drink. Beneath the take-out bridge, it's like a holiday resort: swimmers swing Tarzan-like over the water on a long rope, then drop and drift to the swimming raft; others dive from a springboard. On shore, people picnic. Sandy beaches are at both take-out and put-in and between runs you can lounge on either of them in the shade or in the sun.

Frequently, after paddling, when we've reached the hot-springs-time-of-day, we like to play our "cfs-guess" game. Each one makes a guess about riverflow. It's an excellent way to improve your awareness — and it's fun.

So, one sunny day in July while soaking in Halcyon Hot Springs, we came up with these cfs figures for the Slocan run we'd just done: Betty Pratt-Johnson 85 m³/s (3000 cfs); Klaus Streckmann 227 m³/s (8000 cfs;) Mike Rott 255 m³/s (9000 cfs); Mike Bohn 283 m³/s (10,000 cfs); Ben Lemke 496 m³/s (17,500 cfs). I wrote the numbers down — but never checked on it and never awarded a prize. On writing this book I decided to follow up on at least one "cfs-guess" and go public with the results; when I checked this one I found that the riverflow was 369 m³/s (13,000 cfs); several years later, the winner of this "cfs-guess" is Mike Bohn, and Mike, I'm sending a book to you.

June runoff to August. Snow-melt and rain-fed; natural riverflow usually peaking in June, with a lake to moderate flow. I've paddled it from late June through early July with riverflows ranging from 183 to 369 m³/s (6450 to 13,000 cfs)

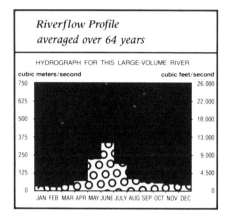

Riverflow Profile
averaged over 64 years

HYDROGRAPH FOR THIS LARGE-VOLUME RIVER

cubic meters/second		cubic feet/second
750		26,000
625		22,000
500		18,000
375		13,000
250		9,000
125		4,500
0		0

JAN FEB MAR APR MAY JUNE JULY AUG SEP OCT NOV DEC

Topographic map: 1:50,000 Castlegar 82F/5.

Facilities: Informal campsites are not available beside this run. The land is all privately owned. However, a free forest service campsite is 45 minutes away from the Slocan at Grizzly Creek. To reach it, go north of the put-in to Passmore, cross the Slocan and head up the gravel logging road. After crossing Koch Creek, which is the first bridge you come to, turn left and head upstream for about 10 or 15 minutes, turn left across Koch Creek and immediately over the bridge you'll find the campground beside Grizzly Creek with picnic tables, pit toilets and fire rings.

You'll find primitive camping with no facilities but closer and also free, by going up the same logging road at Passmore. However, after crossing Koch Creek, do not turn left. Instead, turn right into the first narrow dirt track you

August on the Slocan

Sunshine at take-out beach

come to. Drive in and pick a spot on this undeveloped Crown land where you'll find lots of space to pitch tents. From Passmore, it's 20 minutes.

For after-paddling hot springs: you could reach Ainsworth Hot Springs via Nelson in about 1 hour. Or, if you're heading north on Highways 6 and 23 by way of the free Galena Bay-Shelter Bay car ferry to Highway 1, you'll pass turnoffs to four springs along this "hot springs route". From the take-out, it will take 2 hours to reach Nakusp; then, it's a 15-minute drive off Highway 23 to the commercially operated Nakusp Hot Springs where you will find beautifully tiled hot pools and hot showers as well as a commercially operated campground; walk 15 minutes beyond the resort to the primitive hot springs. Or, heading north on Highway 23 again, you'll pass turnoffs to three more primitive springs: from the highway it takes 25 minutes to reach the springs at St. Leon, 35 minutes to the Halfway River springs, 2 minutes to Halcyon.

Guidelines: Plan to run the Slocan at least twice: a short run to sum up where you want to spend your time, then a play run. Almost immediately after you put in, the broad river bends left; stay on the right-hand side and look for the small hole to play in on "river right"; there are no hazards below it. Soon after, on "river left", you'll find an excellent series of six or eight regularly-spaced surfing waves; again, no hazards downstream.

Facchina's Rapid, the highlight, is next: it's a continuous rapid that goes on for ½ kilometer (⅓ mile). Past the surfing waves, around a broad bend to the right and left and you're into it: big holes, big waves everywhere. It's busy water with the simplest passage on the right-hand side. Maneuvering is required — playing too! Then there's a calm stretch followed by a short rapid; at low water, it becomes a chute with a short technical drop. Then you're at the take-out bridge, ready to do it again.

This is a broad river with width ranging from 45 to 60 meters (150 to 200 feet). In June, waves might be as great as 2 meters (6 feet) high, but you can find out. Riverflow information is available year-round from Water Survey of Canada; phone weekdays, 1-4 p.m. (604)666-3850. The gradient is a steady 6 meters/kilometer (30 feet/mile), and the water is pleasantly warm all summer.

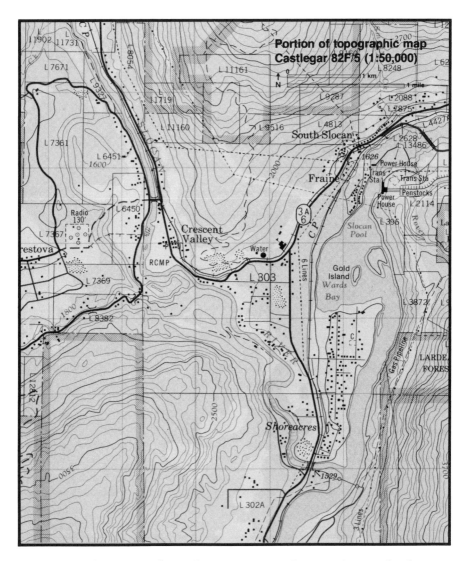

**Portion of topographic map
Castlegar 82F/5 (1:50,000)**

Access to take-out and put-in: Between Castlegar, Nelson and Nakusp. It is 20 minutes northeast out of Castlegar on Highway 3A; 15 minutes south west of Nelson on Highway 3A/6; and 2 hours south of Nakusp on Highway 6, then 3A.

To reach the take-out which is at the Highway 3A bridge over the Slocan just before it flows into the Kootenay: from the junction of Highways 3A and 6, go 2.4 kilometers (1.5 miles) south to the take-out bridge over the Slocan. You'll find room to park on the downstream side of the bridge on "river left".

To reach the put-in, return north up Highway 3A toward Nelson and Nakusp; at Highway 6, turn left and go 1.9 kilometers (1.2 miles) to the building that used to be the RCMP (Royal Canadian Mounted Police) post at Crescent Valley. See it on the topographic map above. Put in at a beach just south of it.

LITTLE SLOCAN-SLOCAN RIVERS
To Passmore

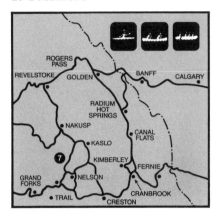

Who: Intermediate to expert kayakers, expert open-canoeists and all rafters; at lower levels, guided novice kayakers and intermediate open-canoeists but no rafters

Water to expect: Class 2 to 3+. A small-volume stream with riffles and braided stretches, plus a continuous Class 3+ rapid

Length of run: 15.6 kilometers (9.7 miles); 3½ hours

Shuttle one way: 19.6 kilometers (12.2 miles); 30 minutes. Gravel logging road with radio-controlled traffic

Why go: The Little Slocan is intimate — yet wild. Another mood. A contrast to the domesticated "Big Sister" Slocan it flows into.

A boisterous rapid with continuous waves and holes runs for 180 meters (600 feet) and is the highlight on this run. What else? A couple of small surfing waves, gentle riffles, a braided section. Beside the stream, we saw three black bears, a teepee, daisies. But the best thing about the Little Slocan to me is that the continuous rapids are an excellent confidence-builder for boaters graduating from Class 2+ to something more. Fun for all. Enjoy!

If you have time to fish, you might catch a rainbow trout — use a fly.

Topographic map: 1:50,000 Passmore 82F/12.

Facilities: A large space of primitive Crown land that's good for informal camping is at the end of a narrow dirt track which cuts off the logging road just 0.6 kilometer (0.4 mile) past the bridge over Koch Creek as you head upstream. Turn right into it. Also, it's worthwhile climbing down from the campground to see the cascades and waterfall on Koch Creek; there's an eddy before the cascade where you can collect drinking water for camping.

Hot springs for after paddling: if you're headed north through New Denver, you could continue to Nakusp, St. Leon, Halfway River or Halcyon hot springs which are about 2 hours away. If you're heading toward the Lardeau or Duncan rivers, stop at Ainsworth which is 1¼ hours away.

Guidelines: Gentle Class 2 riffles warm you up for the bouncy, continuous 180-meter (600-foot) long Class 3 rapid; expect it about ½ hour after putting in. All waves and holes when we were there, and it required maneuvering. At lower water this would be a technical rock garden. Below it, there are no permanent hazards but there could be sweepers or fallen trees; we saw sweepers at other points on this narrow stream that is 15 to 20 meters (50 to 70 feet) wide.

Beyond the bouncy rapid, there's action again where Koch Creek flows in, then a long braided section to the confluence of the Little Slocan and Slocan

May and June, spring runoff. Best in late June. Snow-melt and rain-fed; natural riverflow. It flashes up and then it's gone. We paddled it in early July during runoff. Precise riverflow unavailable; my guess is 25 m^3/s (880 cfs)

Through daisies to put in

where we played on a couple of small but nice surfing waves. From there, it's a leisurely 1.0 kilometer (0.6 mile) paddle to the take-out on the Slocan.

The Little Slocan descends at a rate of 9 meters/kilometer (45 feet/mile) and most of it is in one cascade — that's shortly after putting in where it drops at the rate of 12 meters/kilometer (65 feet/mile).

Surfing

Informal campsite beside Koch Creek

When looking for the put-in, follow access directions carefully and *do not put in on Koch Creek*. While exploring — we did! — and we came uncomfortably close to the Class 6 waterfall before realizing it and aborting the run.

Access to take-out and put-in: Located up a logging road off Highway 6 between Castlegar and Nelson and New Denver. It's near Winlaw, Vallican, Passmore, Slocan Park and Crescent Valley.

From New Denver, head south on Highway 6 through Silverton and Winlaw to Vallican and Passmore and turn right into Passmore Lower Road. It takes about 1 hour to get there.

From Castlegar or Nelson, head toward Crescent Valley on Highway 3A and turn north into Highway 6; go 16.4 kilometers (10.2 miles) north on Highway 6 and turn left into Passmore Lower Road; it will take you about 25 minutes from either place. Once on Passmore Lower Road, you'll cross the broad Slocan; immediately over the bridge, turn right into a narrow road beside the river and park at the roadside, wherever it looks easiest to take out.

To reach the put-in, return to Passmore Lower Road, turn right and go up Little Slocan Forest Road. New logging roads veer off all along — it's like a honeycomb; but you stay on the main one for 12.4 kilometers (7.7 miles) until you cross Koch Creek. From there, pass Koch Road which goes off on your left-hand side, but you continue straight on the main road. Go for 5.5 kilometers (3.4 miles) more, then follow the right-hand fork into Tedesco Road. Go along it for 1.8 kilometers (1.1 miles) to Tedesco Bridge, but do not cross the bridge as the property on the other side of it is privately owned. Just before it, park in a large opening on the left-hand side, and get well off the

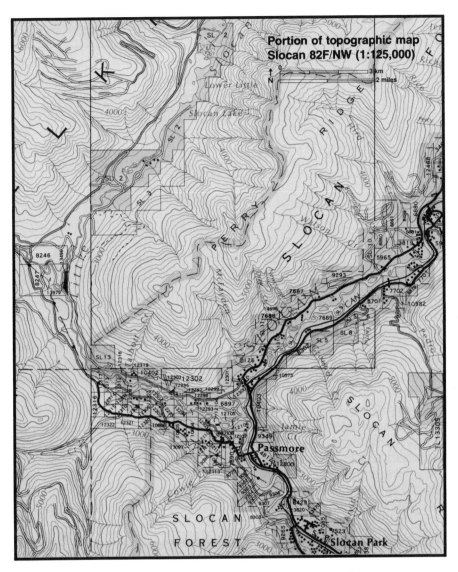

Portion of topographic map
Slocan 82F/NW (1:125,000)

road to avoid being hit by logs projecting from logging trucks — we saw one truck careen around the sharp corner before we climbed down the bank through the daisies and put in.

Travel on Little Slocan Forest Road is open to the public; however, from Monday through Friday, radio-controlled logging traffic could be on it, too. If travelling on a working day, follow a radio-controlled vehicle when possible or else proceed very cautiously. The driver of the first truck you meet will notify other vehicles of your location on the road. Always drive with your headlights on and it's a good idea to travel in convoy. The best times to use this road are weekends, holidays, and weekdays before 7 a.m. and after 6 p.m. To learn about logging traffic and possible fire-hazard closures, contact Slocan Forest Products Ltd., Slocan, B.C. V0G 2C0, telephone (604)355-2216; or contact the Ministry of Forests, Arrow District, 845 Columbia Avenue, Castlegar, B.C. V1N 1H3, telephone (604)365-2131.

WILSON CREEK
To Rosebery

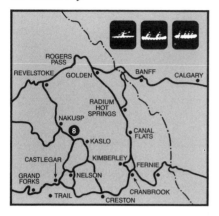

Who: At high levels, advanced and expert kayakers and guided intermediates; expert open-canoeists; and intermediate to expert rafters. At low levels, intermediate to expert kayakers; expert open-canoeists and intermediate open-canoeists with guides but no rafters

Water to expect: Class 3 to easy Class 4, depending on level. Small volume, continuous flow or holes, then small rock river

Length of run: 2.1 kilometers (1.3 miles); 20 minutes

Why go: "A lot of mile!" is the way one kayaker summed up Wilson Creek. During runoff it is continuous holes and waves; there is one eddy; and it eases up only when it reaches the bridge. A great paddle when you don't have much time but want to get your boat wet. Fast and fun. It's excellent also for boaters graduating to something more who want a short stretch of lively water. If you end up swimming, you'll just wash out into Slocan Lake.

Topographic map: 1:50,000 Rosebery 82K/3.

Facilities: A lovely informal campsite with fire rings provided free by the Chamber of Commerce; it's at the take-out. And there is organized camping for a fee on the other side of the creek at Rosebery Provincial Park where you'll find picnic tables, pit toilets and fire rings.

If you're wet and cold — or even if you're warm! — no nicer place to go after paddling than to Nakusp Hot Springs where there are both commercially operated hot pools and primitive hot springs in natural rock basins beside Kuskanax Creek. You can slip from one of the primitive hot pools down a natural rock slide and plunge into a rock pool filled with freezing cold creek water. Then climb up for a hot soak again. Be warned: after kayaking Wilson Creek for 20 minutes in the morning, we spent a whole sunny afternoon playing in these gorgeous hot and cold pools! They're only 1 hour from Wilson Creek.

Guidelines: Straightforward and uncomplicated. However, do keep a sharp lookout for sweepers on this stream that is 20 to 30 meters (70 to 100 feet) wide; gradient is steady and averages 13 meters/kilometer (70 feet/mile).

Putting in is difficult as there is no eddy; you need someone who can hold boats as people climb in, then leap in and take off immediately. From the first second you're on the water, there are continuous rapids throughout the first half of this short run on Wilson Creek. The only eddy we found was a quarter of the way along on "river left"; past it, there's a dogleg to the right. You can see this section from the road. Holes are scattered everywhere. Not gobblers,

Shuttle one way: 2.1 kilometers (1.3 miles); 5 minutes. Gravel logging road with radio-controlled traffic

Season: Runoff time — a June and July creek. Dependent upon snow-melt, also rain-fed; natural riverflow. I have paddled it during runoff from early through late June. Precise riverflow unavailable; my guess is riverflow ranging from 25 to 60 m³/s (880 to 2100 cfs)

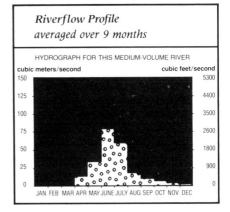

Riverflow Profile
averaged over 9 months

HYDROGRAPH FOR THIS MEDIUM-VOLUME RIVER

cubic meters/second   cubic feet/second

150	5300
125	4400
100	3500
75	2600
50	1800
25	900
0	0

JAN FEB MAR APR MAY JUNE JULY AUG SEP OCT NOV DEC

but they can upset you. And you must maneuver. Most of the way it is the kind of water where you don't stop. To slow down, turn and surf on a wave or play in a hole. Then you reach riffles around a small, gravelly island which has had a logjam on it whenever I've kayaked Wilson Creek. A short way past it, you're at the bridge. Then, the take-out.

Scout from the road when driving to the put-in. If you want to take a close look or if you want an excuse for an evening walk, you can hike the well-worn fisherman's trail along the west side of the creek: start in the provincial park at the bridge and head upstream — there's angling for rainbows and Dolly Vardens.

Access to take-out and put-in: From Highway 6 between New Denver and Nakusp, beside Slocan Lake at Rosebery. It is 10 minutes from New Denver, 25 minutes from Nakusp, 45 minutes from Kaslo, and 1¼ hours from the Slocan River put-in at Crescent Valley.

For the take-out, if heading south through Rosebery, cross the bridge and turn right into the Chamber of Commerce Campground beside the creek.

For the put-in, return to the highway, cross it and continue 1.8 kilometers (1.1 miles) on the logging road up the east side of the creek. View the creek as you go. Then, park as far off the road as you can; logging trucks were hauling when we were there. Make your own path through the trees and put in; it was an extremely difficult put-in because there was no eddy.

Travel is permitted on Wilson Creek Forest Road where logging traffic is radio-controlled. This road is open to the public 24 hours a day, however, usually the best times to use it are weekends, holidays, and weekdays before 7 a.m. and after 6 p.m. and always drive with your headlights on. To learn about road use and possible fire-hazard closures, contact Slocan Forest Products, Slocan, B.C. V0G 2C0, telephone (604)355-2216; or contact the Ministry of Forests, Arrow District, 845 Columbia Avenue, Castlegar, B.C. V1N 1H3, telephone (604)365-2131.

LARDEAU RIVER
Rapid Creek through Devil's Elbow

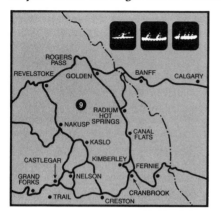

Who: At high water, intermediate and expert kayakers, expert open-canoeists and expert rafters. At lower levels, all kayakers; intermediate and expert open-canoeists; and all rafters willing to portage

Water to expect: Class 2; at high water, Class 3. At runoff, if could be unrunnable. Large volume; small rock river with braided sections and lots of logjams

Length of run: 21.9 kilometers (13.6 miles); 3½ to 4 hours

Shuttle one way: 12.9 kilometers

Why go: To ride the eddy fence at Devil's Elbow; to find a route through the maze of braided river before it; to bounce down some of the nicest continuous Class 2 rapids I've found; to look through clear clear water at round, even river rocks; to discover what's *beside* the river and *in* it; to see beaver, deer, Dolly Vardens pairing off; to see one of the most unspoilt, pristine spawning stretches in British Columbia.

And you can camp at the ghost town of Gerrard situated 10 minutes from the put-in where the Lardeau flows out of Trout Lake. In the early 1900s Gerrard was the home of 40 people; there was a railway through it from 1902 to 1928. Today it is a dot on some maps and little more, but you'll find a provincial park campground on the part of the former town site that was the old railway switching area; and, beside the bridge over the Lardeau at the outflow of Trout Lake, there's a plaque telling the story of the Gerrard rainbow trout. They are unique. The Gerrards don't die after spawning; perhaps that's why they become so large. The record Gerrard catch to date was 16 kilograms (35¾ pounds) in the 1980s. One of the first fisheries enhancement efforts in the world was to ship them around the U.S.A. That was in the 1940s. Transplants were attempted in many places, but the Gerrard rainbows have survived and flourished only in the Lardeau River in the Kootenays of British Columbia, their birthplace, where, every year they spawn over a period of about three weeks in May — they do it over Mother's Day.

In winter, the Gerrard rainbows provide excellent fishing in Kootenay Lake. It's considered a trophy lake. You might catch kokanee, too, from April until July or mid-August. Kokanee are landlocked sockeye salmon. They also return to the Lardeau to spawn and then mature in Kootenay Lake. In addition, there's a significant population of Dolly Varden char in Kootenay Lake. Fish for them from September through June. They migrate into the Lardeau in July and August and spawn in September. When we paddled the Lardeau in late July, we saw some of the first of the Dolly Vardens pairing off beneath the bridge at Gerrard. They were at the top of the 300-meter (1000-foot)

(8.0 miles); 15 minutes. Gravel highway which is frequently used by logging trucks

Season: May through September, peaks in June. Snow-melt, glacial-melt and rain-fed; lake above it moderates the natural riverflow and extends the season. We paddled it in late July with riverflow of 70 m³/s (2470 cfs)

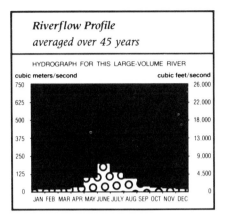

Riverflow Profile
averaged over 45 years

HYDROGRAPH FOR THIS LARGE-VOLUME RIVER

JAN FEB MAR APR MAY JUNE JULY AUG SEP OCT NOV DEC

stretch of coarse clean gravel that makes the Lardeau perfect for spawning. There is a permanent fishing closure on the Lardeau and its tributaries, so bring your rod for Kootenay Lake and bring your whitewater boat for the Lardeau.

If you're going to angle in the lake, check current fishing regulations for possible closures and buy a non-tidal sport fishing license.

Topographic maps: 1:50,000 Poplar Creek 82K/6 and Duncan Lake 82K/7.

Facilities: A pleasant 15-minute walk through huge trees signposted as the John Fenger Memorial Trail is 0.9 kilometer (0.6 mile) downstream from the put-in; there is a pit toilet there. The trail is named in memory of a well loved local resident — the Kootenays country is like that, people and places matter. South of the take-out, there's great food and ambience 15 minutes away at the café at Meadow Creek.

Ainsworth Hot Springs is another 60 minutes down the road. It's a commercially operated hot springs where you can wander through a horseshoe-shaped cave. There's a warm pool for swimming, and a hot circular "social" pool with a ledge around it where you can sit and talk. There are change-rooms, hot showers, hotel rooms and a restaurant.

You'll find a variety of campgrounds near this run — all free. Ten minutes upstream from the put-in, at the ghost town of Gerrard, there's a provincial park campground with picnic tables, pit toilets and fire rings. It's near the southwest tip of Trout Lake; there's a signpost to it on the south side of the bridge over the Lardeau. A few minutes downstream from the take-out, similar facilities are provided free by the forest service at a campsite perched on the edge of Duncan Lake. The lake is beautifully warm for swimming and for practicing rolling your boat. Space is limited at this site, but, if there are only one or two cars in your party, you might fit in. Go south for 7.9 kilometers (4.9 miles) toward Meadow Creek, turn left and follow the signs to Howser; continue to Duncan Lake and turn left to the campground beside it.

Camping is also free at Kootenay Lake Provincial Park-Davis Creek Campground on the outskirts of the village of Lardeau, 25 minutes south of the Lardeau River take-out. If you have a very large group, this is the place to stop. In addition to the usual picnic tables, pit toilets and fire rings, you'll find spacious wooded campsites where you can pitch your tents on moss beneath huge trees beside the cobbled beach of Kootenay Lake.

Guidelines: Scout Devil's Elbow when heading upstream to put in. It's a short distance past the bridge over the Lardeau which locals refer to as Gold Hill Bridge. Notice the squirrelly water. Look for the tongue — but I should warn you, if you stop to look and it's a sunny day, you might never make it to the put-in to run the river. At the level we found it, you could recycle up the eddy fence and run the drop again and again and again; and, with that late summer riverflow, there was a crescent of sandy beach at the river bend. It was a perfect place to eat lunch. You might want to spend all day there.

If you miss Devil's Elbow as you drive upstream, you'll reach a bridge over Cascade Creek: the Elbow is 0.8 kilometer (0.5 mile) back downstream from it.

The other thing to look for on this run is wood. The Lardeau is infamous for it: logjams and fallen trees litter every bend, and, if boaters are not watchful and aware, these trees can be killers — even on an easy stretch and even at low water. Most of the logjams on this run are in the warm-up section between Rapid and Poplar creeks, so be especially watchful at the start. But wood is not only in the obvious places like the braided sections: while paddling, we noticed that most things that looked like holes were caused by half-submerged stumps and sweepers. I can remember when I was a novice and couldn't tell the difference between a wave and a hole. You don't want to make that mistake here. It's not the place to learn to differentiate. Watch for wood all the way; and, when in doubt about any whitewater patch, avoid it.

Rivers change. It is not possible to map logjams and sweepers. New fallen trees and branches lodge in the river daily. You must find them for yourselves. So, the answer is to take a look, and if your group can paddle under control on the parts of the river you can see from the road on the day you're there, you can check out the rest of the river by running it. Run the river the first time to find the rapids, the standing waves, the holes to play in, the logjams and trouble spots.

Then run it again to play. River width ranges from 23 to 45 meters (75 to 150 feet), but logjams can narrow it to nil. Shortly after putting in, I climbed over and pulled my boat over one passage that was completely blocked by a pile of trees. Gradient averages 5 meters/kilometer (25 feet/mile); the rate of descent is gentle.

The order of water to expect is as follows: braided water with logjams and much natural brush and "trash" on gravel bars from Rapid Creek to Poplar Creek, followed by six or eight excellent Class 2 rapids from Poplar Creek to a short way past the Devil's Elbow — the most difficult one being the Elbow. This is followed by a couple more rapids, and then a quiet easing off to clear blue water by the time you reach the take-out. And, below the run, the water-gauging station for the Lardeau is at Marblehead between the Duncan Dam and Meadow Creek.

Photo stop on sunny gravel bar

Access to take-out and put-in: The Lardeau River runs alongside Highway 31 — this "highway" is a rough gravel logging road. The river and the road are way back of nowhere in the delightfully confusing mountains and valleys of the West Kootenays; the nearest town is Kaslo, and Nakusp is not much farther away. Revelstoke, too. You can reach the Lardeau take-out in 2½ or 3 hours from each of these places.

From Nakusp, you could approach Lardeau from the north *or* the south but let's start with north: go toward the Galena Bay-Shelter Bay ferry on Highway 23; before you reach it, turn right onto Highway 31 following signposts east toward Trout Lake, then south to Gerrard, Howser and Meadow Creek.

From Revelstoke, head west on Highway 1, then almost immediately turn south on Highway 23 and take the free car ferry from Shelter Bay to Galena Bay. Shortly after coming off the ferry, turn left onto Highway 31 and again, follow signposts toward Trout Lake, Gerrard, Howser and Meadow Creek.

From Nakusp (this time heading south), follow Highway 6 through Rosebery to New Denver, Highway 31A to Kaslo, then Highway 31 north through Lardeau to Meadow Creek.

To reach the take-out from Meadow Creek, head upstream. It's 15 minutes away; go north for 16.0 kilometers (9.9 miles) to a lay-by on the left-hand side of the road where there is a litter barrel and room for five or six cars to park. Leave a shuttle vehicle.

For the put-in, continue upstream — again toward Gerrard — and cross a bridge over the Lardeau which locals refer to as Gold Hill Bridge; when you're 0.8 kilometer (0.5 mile) past it you can view Devil's Elbow. Then continue for 7.0 kilometers (4.3 miles) crossing Cascade and Poplar creeks; just before Rapid Creek, park on the left-hand at the roadside.

Travel is permitted 24 hours a day on Highway 31 which is open to the public. However, logging traffic is usually on it too, so drive with your headlights on. The best times to use it are weekends, holidays or weekdays after 6 p.m. and before 6 a.m. To learn about logging traffic, contact the Ministry of Forests, Kootenay Lake District, Rural Route 1, Ridgewood Road, Nelson, B.C. V1L 5P4, telephone (604)825-4415.

DUNCAN RIVER
Westfall River to Giegerich Creek

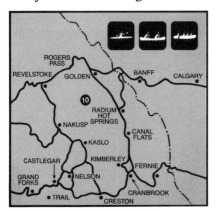

Who: All kayakers, expert open-canoeists and all rafters

Water to expect: Class 2+ and 2, Class 3- drops; swiftly flowing, small rock river

Length of run: 10.9 kilometers (6.8 miles); 2½ hours

Shuttle one way: 10.5 kilometers (6.5 miles); 15 minutes. Gravel logging road with radio-controlled traffic

Season: June through September; best in warm weather of July and August. Snow-melt, glacial-fed and rain-fed; natural flow, as the Duncan Dam is

Why go: Away from it all! And — action enough on this large-volume stream swishing through the woods to know you've paddled. We had novices tipping and swimming. It's continuous Class 2+ with a Class 3 drop thrown in at the start and finish. Average width is 50 meters (160 feet). The river has a steady gradient of 8 meters/kilometer (40 feet/mile), is mainly gravel bottomed but has some swirly squirrelly water in it. There are Dolly Vardens too.

Beside the river we saw two coyotes, three moose and many deer — one with antlers, in the rain forest; we saw devil's club and ferns. I've just learned that rainfall is extremely high in the West Kootenays region; rainfall in this remote valley is second only to that in the coastal region. The high rainfall and the glacial-melt give this river a long season — into October if you're hardy and don't mind the cold.

Topographic maps: 1:50,000 Westfall River 82K/14 and 1:50,000 Trout Lake 82K/11.

Facilities: This is a raw newly-opened-up valley: that's the feature to be reckoned with when planning your trip to the Duncan. There is a great deal of rough, vacant Crown land where you can camp. We found an excellent informal campsite on a beach beside the put-in where we pitched our tents for a couple of nights.

However, before heading into the Duncan region, you'll need to have supplies and also be ready to keep moving on the road. The short stretch of Duncan River Forest Road from Cooper Creek to the Argenta/Johnsons Landing turnoff is broad and easy to travel on. Past the Argenta turnoff, there's no stopping. The narrow track clings to the steeply rising mountainside high above the east shore of Duncan Lake. You might want to wait until logging traffic is off the road before heading up it, and, when you reach the river, there are no facilities.

Buy gas and groceries at Kaslo or Revelstoke. You might be able to get gas at Meadow Creek, but don't count on it on the weekend. If you want to pause

below the run. The river is freezing cold. We paddled it in late June with riverflow of 124 m³/s (4380 cfs)

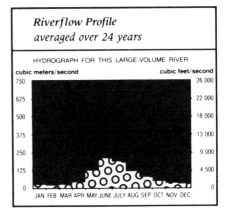

Riverflow Profile
averaged over 24 years

HYDROGRAPH FOR THIS LARGE-VOLUME RIVER

before driving up the narrow lakeside road, you could camp beside Glacier Creek at the southern end of Duncan Lake. It's immediately past the turnoff to Argenta; turn left, then right. Space to pitch tents in the woods beside the creek — or stop *before* you reach Meadow Creek. Camping is free at all sites. If heading south from Galena Bay on Highway 31, you could stop at Gerrard. If heading north, choose from a couple of spacious provincial parks: 15 minutes past Kaslo, look for the Lost Ledge site; beyond that, the Davis Creek site at Lardeau — both beside Kootenay Lake with picnic tables, pit toilets, fire rings and lots of room to pitch tents on the moss beneath a canopy of large trees.

If you're heading south on the way out, stop at Ainsworth Hot Springs; it's a medium-sized commercially operated hot-swimming-pool-type springs that is open year-round. The hot pools wind through a horseshoe-shaped cave with branches leading off. A natural steam bath is hidden at the top of

Boat-mending time beside campfire

one of them — climb a hot water cascade over smooth rock to find it. Look for it when you first go into the cave so you can still tolerate the heat; it's so intense, it takes your breath away. Ainsworth Hot Springs is 45 minutes south of Lardeau, 2¼ hours from the take-out. If heading north, stop at Halcyon.

Guidelines: Watch for sweepers and fallen trees: recent logging operations increase the possibility of them. When we paddled in June several trees were across the river, but were submerged; in October they were exposed and kayakers carried around them. Between times, these same fallen trees must must have been difficult-to-spot "killer logs" — paddle carefully every time.

This river was Dave Home's suggestion — his gift to our group this trip. The area was newly opened up by logging and our run on June 29, 1981, might have been a first descent. Mike Bohn, Colin Coe, Dave Home, Carol Jarvis, Ben Lemke, Marian Porter, Betty Pratt-Johnson, John Pratt-Johnson, Don Ross, Mike Rott and Klaus Streckmann were on this run.

Access to take-out and put-in: The Duncan is situated in the West Kootenays about as far into the "boonies" as you can get in the southeastern mainland region of British Columbia. It is 2 hours from Kaslo, 4½ to 5 hours from Revelstoke.

From Revelstoke, head south on Highway 23, then 31 through Meadow Creek to Cooper Creek. From Kaslo, head north on Highway 31 through Lardeau; 5 minutes past Lardeau at Cooper Creek, you'll see a weigh-scaler's shack. You could stop and ask where they're hauling. Then turn east following signposts toward Argenta and Johnsons Landing; cross a bridge over the Duncan River and when you reach the Argenta and Johnsons Landing junction, do not turn right. Continue straight on Duncan River Forest Road and head up the high, narrow twisting strip of road along the east shore of Duncan Lake. From the Argenta junction, it takes 1¼ hours to reach the head of the lake, and then you'll cross the Duncan River at East Creek. The water-gauging station is located 300 paces downstream from this bridge. From here, it's 10.5 kilometers (6.5 miles) and takes 10 minutes to the next bridge over the Duncan which is the take-out. At the end of the run, you'll have to climb 40 paces up a steep path.

Leave a shuttle vehicle, and go upriver 11.0 kilometers (6.8 miles) to put in beside the bridge over the Duncan which is just upstream from where the Westfall River flows in.

Travel on Duncan River Forest Road is open to the public; however, radio-controlled logging traffic usually is on it too; always drive with your headlights on. If travelling on a working day, follow a radio-controlled vehicle. The safest times to use this road are weekends and holidays or weekdays after 6 p.m. and before 6 a.m.

To learn about logging traffic and possible fire-hazard closures, stop at the weigh-scaler's shack at Cooper Creek junction, or contact the Ministry of Forests, Kootenay Lake District, Rural Route 1, Ridgewood Road, Nelson, B.C. V1L 5P4, telephone (604)825-4415.

Watching for wood through rain forest

DUNCAN RIVER
Hume Creek to Westfall River

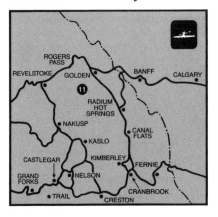

Who: Advanced and expert kayakers; no open-canoeists; and, because of the unknown quantity of the boulder garden, no rafters

Water to expect: Class 3, 4, and 5 (portagable). Technical big water, boulder gardens, continuously flowing and cold

Length of run: 9.7 kilometers (6.0 miles); 2½ hours

Shuttle one way: 8.4 kilometers (5.2 miles); 20 minutes. Gravel logging road with radio-controlled traffic

Season: A "summer river" — paddle it

Why go: Wilderness at the end of the road, waves — and not wimpy ones, waves that are 2½ meters (9 feet) high. A head wall. Snowfields at the roadside in summer that keep it flowing; look at the topo map and you'll see Deluge Mountain and Snowman Peak above the river. The Duncan flows through raw country, and it's different. Believe it or not, we saw a goose surfing at a play spot near the take-out.

Topographic map: 1:50,000 Westfall River 82K/14.

Facilities: On the way into the Duncan region, again, stock up on gas and groceries at Kaslo or Revelstoke — you might find gas at Meadow Creek, but don't count on it on the weekend. On the way into the region from either direction, you'll find a variety of camping that is free. Heading south from Galena Bay, you could stop at the provincial park at Gerrard. Heading north, when 15 minutes past Kaslo, you could go to the Kootenay Lake-Lost Ledge Provincial Park Campground, or, another 5 minutes up the road, stop at the spacious Davis Creek Campground at Lardeau with picnic tables, pit toilets, fire rings and lots of room to pitch tents. Great places to get sorted out. To camp just before driving up the narrow part of the forest road high above Duncan Lake, turn left immediately past the Argenta turnoff, then right and you'll find space to pitch a couple of tents in the trees beside Glacier Creek. It's the last place you can stop after entering the logging road — either stop here, or go to the top of the lake. Beyond the head of the lake, it is a newly-opened-up region where you'll find a great deal of Crown land — it's my favorite type of facility. Pick your place. We pitched tents beside the Westfall River.

On the way out of the Duncan, stop at Ainsworth Hot Springs, it's a commercially operated indoor/outdoor springs. The "indoor" pools follow two passages into a dimly lit cave. Deep in the cave you'll find secret places to hide. At the entrance to the cave there is a small sociable pool, with ledges for a dozen people to sit around and talk. And there's a large warm pool for swimming. Ainsworth Hot Springs is 2½ hours south of the take-out.

from June through September. Snow-melt, glacial-fed, and rain-fed; natural flow, as the Duncan Dam is below the run. We kayaked it in late June with riverflow of 162 m³/s (5720 cfs)

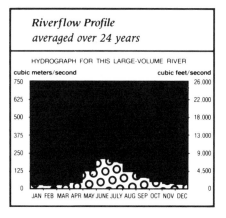

Riverflow Profile
averaged over 24 years

HYDROGRAPH FOR THIS LARGE-VOLUME RIVER

cubic meters/second		cubic feet/second
750		26.000
625		22.000
500		18.000
375		13.000
250		9.000
125		4.500
0		0

JAN FEB MAR APR MAY JUNE JULY AUG SEP OCT NOV DEC

Guidelines: Every run must be treated as an exploration. Watch for sweepers and logjams as well as new boulders and rubble in the riverbed. The riverbed is subject to constant change and is extremely unstable due to loose scree slopes above it, and due to active logging operations in the area. Also beware

Snow banks in July

of hypothermia: a solid roll is necessary. The river rises from snow and ice fields in the Purcell and Selkirk mountains, and it's freezing cold.

Gradient averages 10 meters/kilometer (55 feet/mile). Width averages from 15 to 30 meters (50 to 100 feet) but there are many narrower passages in the Boulder Garden. The biggest waves are near the start, and, in combination with the Head Wall, they make this section a Class 4; you can scout Head Wall from high above the road as you're heading upstream to put in.

One-third of the way on the run, you reach the Boulder Garden which tempted us, but which we decided to portage. It looked like Class 5; we carried around 1.8 kilometers (1.1 miles) of river before we found a reasonable put-in; again, you can scout it when heading upstream. Downstream from the Boulder Garden portage, you'll find easy Class 3 to the take-out.

Colin Coe, Betty Pratt-Johnson, John Pratt-Johnson, and Klaus Streckmann kayaked this section. The area was newly opened up by logging operations, and our exploration on June 30, 1981, was probably a first descent.

Access to take-out and put-in: The Duncan River is south of Revelstoke, and north of Kaslo. It is remote from any settlement and is reached by way of a narrow logging road that twists high above Duncan Lake. From Revelstoke, head south on Highway 23, then 31 via Trout Lake to Meadow Creek; from Kaslo, head north on Highway 31 through Lardeau. When 5 minutes south of Meadow Creek or 5 minutes north of Lardeau at Cooper Creek junction, look for the sawmill and the weigh-scaler's shack. You could stop and check where the logging trucks are hauling; then, turn east into Duncan River Forest Road following signposts toward Argenta and Johnsons Landing. Cross a bridge over the Duncan River and when you reach the Argenta/Johnsons Landing junction, do not turn right. Continue straight on Duncan River Forest Road and head up the high, narrow twisting road along the east shore of Duncan Lake. It takes 1¼ hours to the head of the lake, and then you'll cross the Duncan River again. From here, it's 15.9 kilometers (9.9 miles) to a bridge over the Duncan at its confluence with the Westfall River: this is the take-out.

When heading upstream to put in, you might take a second shuttle vehicle for it, in the event that you portage for a long way as we did. Scout as you go. When you've gone 2.8 kilometers (1.7 miles) you'll see a very rough four-wheel-drive road veering down on the left-hand side. It's about ½ kilometer (⅓ mile) to the river. This would be an easy place to put in after the portage, but you'd lose a lot of good river by using it. You might prefer to bushwhack, as we did, in order to gain a longer run.

• Boulder Garden: the Boulder Garden starts 5.7 kilometers (3.5 miles) upstream from the take-out bridge, and I am not sure how far it goes. We have not paddled 1.8 kilometers (1.1 miles) of river downstream from it, and we have not seen that section of river. The Boulder Garden was inviting but the weather was cold and rainy when we paddled it and we did not want to scout from shore any more that day. However, I have returned in winter when the

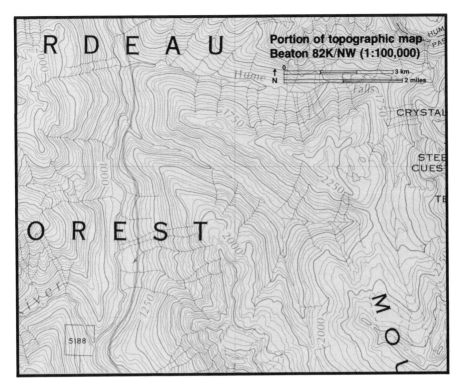

bush cover was not so great. It looks like almost the entire length of the river might be runnable except a short 100 meter (300 foot) section which is immediately downstream from where we began our portage. You can see the start of the Boulder Garden from the road. As you head upstream, you'll pass narrow waterfalls sparkling between scree. Look for the Boulder Garden deep in the canyon — the viewpoint is just past the "94" signpost.

• Head Wall: after scouting the Boulder Garden, proceed upstream past more waterfalls spilling in, and heaps of snow beside the river — go 1.3 kilometers (0.8 mile) farther, and, just before the bridge over Beatrice Creek, look down the steep bank to Head Wall.

Then continue upstream for 1.4 kilometers (0.9 mile) to the bridge over Hume Creek. It flows from alpine lakes and glaciers below Mount Hatteras, Tetragon Peak, Deluge and Crystalline mountains. The road dips down as you approach Hume Creek; there are a narrow lay-bys on both sides of the bridge. Find road-side parking, if you can! — scramble down the creekbed and put in.

Travel on Duncan River Forest Road is open to the public; however, the road is heavily used by radio-controlled logging traffic too; always drive with your headlights on. If travelling on a working day, follow a radio-controlled vehicle. The safest times to use this road are weekends and holidays or weekdays after 6 p.m. and before 6 a.m.

To learn about logging traffic and possible fire-hazard closures, stop at the weigh-scaler's shack at Cooper Creek junction, or contact the Ministry of Forests, Kootenay Lake District, Rural Route 1, Ridgewood Road, Nelson, B.C. V1L 5P4, telephone (604)825-4415.

BUSH RIVER
To Kinbasket Lake

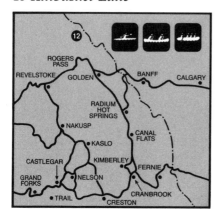

Who: Top run to Surprise Canyon: intermediate, advanced and expert kayakers, and guided novices; expert open-canoeists and guided intermediates; intermediate, advanced and expert rafters, and guided novices. Lower run: all kayakers, all open-canoeists, all rafters

Water to expect: Top Run: Class 2- to 2, depending on level, with a Class 2+ to 3 canyon. Lower run: Class 1 and 2- and medium volume. Steadily flowing, with few obstacles

Length of run: 12.9 kilometers (8.0 miles); 4 hours for full run. Top run is

Why go: For Surprise Canyon, a drift past staggering mountain scenery, bird-watching, hiking, primitive cool springs at the midway put-in or take-out.

This is the most beautiful setting for any river I've seen anywhere. It's a big, broad valley with craggy Rocky Mountains rising behind, and myriad small creeks cutting through narrow rocky gorges, feeding into the Bush. The Bush is riffled, slowly flowing, smooth and straightforward with a sudden twisting, turning and narrowing in Surprise Canyon providing brief excitement at the end of the top run. From there, it's a totally mellow, scenic paddle on the ever broadening river to Kinbasket Lake with bird watching on the way.

We were lured to explore this wilderness spot by the rumor of primitive warm springs beside the Bush. There was so much rain the week before we were there that the cool springs were chilled and drowned and we could not tell the cool and cold water apart to say that we'd found them. But the forest service recreation officer has confirmed to me that the cool springs *are* there beside the trapper's cabin we found, and they're part of the forest service recreation site; a hunting guide we met at the campground said the cool springs do not freeze up in winter. They're probably never warm enough for a hot soak after a cold river run, but they're another fun thing to look for beside the river. We also enjoyed hiking from the campsite up the beautiful Valenciennes River gorge. There's wildlife too. We saw a bald eagle and Canada geese from the river. While hiking and while scouting the river, we saw bear scats, mule deer droppings, rose hips, mushrooms, and blueberries.

The Bush River and Bush River Cool Springs are on my list for a return visit.

Topographic map: 1:50,000 Rostrum Peak 82N/14.

Facilities: Camping is free beside the Valenciennes River put-in and take-out where the forest service provides picnic tables, pit toilets and fire rings. The primitive cool springs are directly across the Bush from the campground. With extremely low water you might be able to wade the stream. But it's probably better to ferry across the river in a canoe or kayak, even though we found

6.9 kilometers (4.3 miles);
2 to 3 hours

Shuttle one way: Top run to Surprise Canyon: 3.8 kilometers
(2.4 miles). Lower run: 7.3 kilometers (4.5 miles); 10 to 20 minutes. Gravel logging roads

Season: June through September. Glacial-melt, snow-melt and rain-fed; natural riverflow that responds to sun by rising quickly. We paddled it in early August; precise riverflow data unavailable; my guess is with riverflows of 63 and 65 m³/s (2220 and 2300 cfs)

Kinbasket Lake, snowcapped peaks behind

it difficult to pull a boat up the bank through the tangle of scrubby brush into the trees. Climbing through the bushes is scratchy and rough too, and we en-

Putting in at the Valenciennes

Looking north — braided river above Surprise Canyon

countered mosquitoes — but I always love poking around to see what's there. We found a rough trapper's cabin beside a small pond which is formed by the cool springs. They bubble through the rocks a little north of the cabin.

For a hot plunge on the way out of the region, if heading west it will take 2½ hours from the take-out to Canyon Hot Springs; and you'll be moving from the Mountain or "Alberta" time zone into the Pacific time zone which will give you an extra hour to reach the springs. If heading east, it will take 3¾ hours to reach Banff. If heading east and then south down the Rocky Mountain Trench, allow 3½ hours to Radium.

Guidelines: Surprise Canyon is the one passage to be aware of and to check out, because it could be blocked by a fallen tree. It comes just before the mid-way put-in or take-out at the Valenciennes; there is a sudden narrowing, canyon walls rise on both sides, and the river turns sharply to the right. With high riverflow, the water is swirly before this blind corner: the canyon narrows to a width of about 8 meters (25 feet) — a radical twisted bottle-neck on the Bush which has been broad and braided with an average width of 20 meters (70 feet) up to this point, and, there are tall trees on the high cliffs above, which could fall into the canyon and block the narrows.

This steeply walled canyon goes for 100 meters (300 feet) and it is not noticeable from the road. Even though we tried to see all we could before putting in, we had no hint of the deep canyon until we were on the river and heading into it. We had studied the 1:50,000 topo map that covers the Bush, and you can see some narrowing where the canyon is, but the steep sides are not apparent. When home again, I found a larger scale map in the library. It is from the Columbia River Basin MS series which is no longer in print. Much on these maps is outdated. However, this old 1:31,680 topo MS 35, on which 1 inch equals ½ mile, *does* show the extreme narrowing in Surprise Canyon. (I am happy to have discovered this series, because a great many rivers in this book are covered in it.) In any event, probably the best way to check out the canyon is by paddling cautiously into it. Then, if the water is mellow, you might be able to ferry across and check that the final, narrow passage is unobstructed. If the water is high, you might have to climb the steep right-hand bank and look down into it. That's what we did.

Before Surprise Canyon, and after it all the way to Kinbasket Lake, the river is straightforward. It is swiftly flowing with riffles and some standing waves up to ⅔ meter (2 feet) but with few obstacles. When we paddled, it felt pleasantly full of water with no rocks showing. If new boaters did not look at the topo map, they might be tempted to push off on their own on this one, because the water is not difficult. But anyone looking at the topo would think again: the approach to Surprise Canyon is shown on it as dropping at the rate of 21 meters/kilometer (110 feet/mile); however, that *must* be a mistake. The river just does not feel that steep when you paddle it. The overall gradient on the topo shows an average of 5 meters/kilometer (25 feet/mile) drop — *that's* what it feels like. But I have to admit the river moves right along and you have to be cautious because it becomes so wide, and, if you have to swim it could take a long while to reach the side.

The Bush drains the Columbia Ice Fields, so glacial milk clouds the river and keeps it flowing for a long season, and glacial-melt coupled with rain affects it noticeably. Sunshine followed rain when we were there, and the water level rose ⅓ meter (1 foot) while we were on it. There are a great many glaciers feeding into the Bush from Ladylove, Cockscomb, Ego and Bush mountains. Glacial water is cold — prepare for it; go onto the river as a group, wear wet suits, paddle as a team.

Access to take-outs and put-ins: The Bush River run is located 1½ hours off the Trans-Canada Highway; the turnoff to it is between Golden and Rogers Pass. From the Trans-Canada, you head northwest on the Big Bend Highway which is a good gravel road. The old Big Bend was part of the Trans-Canada Highway before the Rogers Pass was built and was so-named because it followed the big bend in the Columbia River where it flows north through Kinbasket Lake then arcs southward past Mica Creek and finally past Revelstoke. The turnoff is near Donald which was an important town of the Kootenays in 1889 but now almost a ghost town. Today the turnoff into the Big Bend Highway is not easy to spot, so measure the time and distance:

Heading east on Trans-Canada Highway 1, look for the Big Bend cutting off to the northwest when 45 minutes east of Rogers Pass Summit. You'll go down a big hill, cross the Columbia River, and pass the Donald sawmill on your left-hand side. The Big Bend Highway turnoff is 2.9 kilometers (1.8 miles) east of the bridge over the Columbia, and 2.1 kilometers (1.3 miles) east of Donald. Turn left into it. Heading west, look for the Big Bend Highway cutting off on the right-hand side when 8.1 kilometers (5.0 miles) west of the bridge over the Blaeberry River. And turn right.

Travelling up the Big Bend, which becomes Bush River Forest Road after 4.2 kilometers (2.6 miles), you'll drive for 30 kilometers (19 miles) through countryside that's been scarred by logging. The region is honeycombed with confusing logging roads. Keep noticing where you are: you'll pass Blackwater, Comfort, Help and Aid lakes. From Help Lake onward, the country is pretty. To find your way to the take-out, keep to the east shore of Bush Arm of Kinbasket Lake until you cross Goodfellow Creek. Just past it, turn left into Chatter Creek Forest Road and go down it to the lake where you'll find the take-out bridge for the lower run.

For the midway take-out or put-in, return to Bush River Forest Road and head upstream for 6.6 kilometers (4.1 miles) to a bridge over the Valenciennes River; the campground is beside the Valenciennes, the cool springs are on the opposite side of the Bush.

For the top put-in to make the run through Surprise Canyon, continue 3.8 kilometers (2.4 miles) upstream to a bridge over the Bush.

Travel is permitted 24 hours a day on Bush River and Chatter Creek Forest Roads which are open to the public. However, logging traffic could be on them too, so drive with your headlights on. To learn about possible fire-hazard closures, contact the Ministry of Forests, Golden District, 600 Ninth Street North, P.O. Box 1380, Golden, B.C. V0A 1H0, telephone, (604)344-7500.

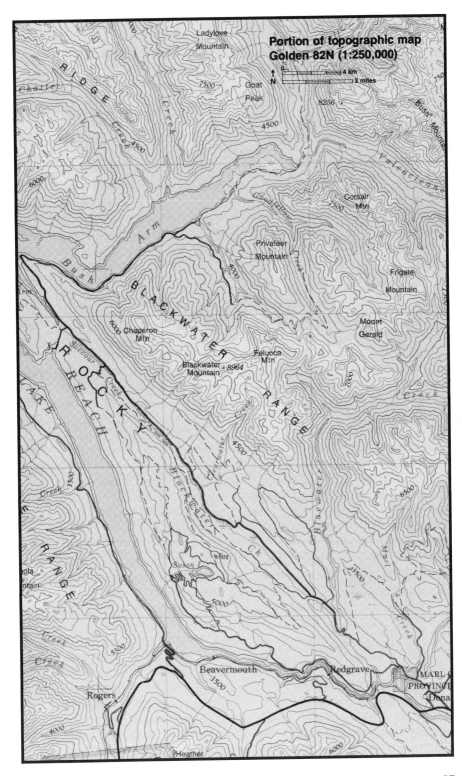

**Portion of topographic map
Golden 82N (1:250,000)**

Ladylove
Mountain

Goat
Peak

Corsair
Mtn

Privateer
Mountain

Frigate

Mountain

Mount
Gerald

Chaperon
Mtn

Felucca
Mtn

Blackwater
Mountain

Fire

Susan

Beavermouth

Redgrave

Rogers

Heather

BLAEBERRY RIVER
To Columbia River

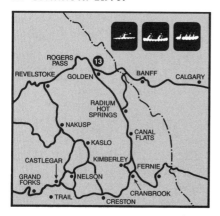

Who: Intermediate, advanced and expert kayakers; expert open-canoeists and guided intermediates; and all rafters, at high levels. At low levels, also guided novice kayakers and intermediate open-canoeists

Water to expect: Class 2- to 2, depending on level. Braided and some swirly water at high levels

Length of run: 12.6 kilometers (7.8 miles); 2 to 3 hours, leisurely run

Shuttle one way: 20.6 kilometers (12.8 miles); 20 to 30 minutes. Gravel logging roads

Why go: Glacial blue water flows through mountain meadowlands into a twisting canyon that looks like it's bulging with fossils — there *probably* are fossils here, but we didn't stop to look. You're away from it all on this lovely river. It's an excellent stretch for any boater who's passing by on Highway 1 to drop into for a couple of hours break from civilization.

At high levels, it's a good seasonal warm-up for veteran boaters. At low levels during August, a gentle initiation into whitewater fun for new boaters. It's a confidence-builder for guided intermediate open-canoeists and guided novice kayakers. At all levels, this run is a scenic place to go. It includes riffles, a braided section through the meadow, a couple of bubbling rapids, a couple of play spots, and swirly, boily water through a convoluting canyon with steep, scrap-paper-like shaley walls bulging over the river. The variety of experiences on this one piece of water and the degree of difficulty increasing as you go make it an excellent stretch for new paddlers under guidance, or even when they are on their own after the run has been checked out that day. The region has been settled for many years, but there is a delightful sense of wilderness as you paddle.

Non-paddlers can get onto the Blaeberry with a commercially operated rafting trip from late May through August. This one is not a quickie, and it is modeled for the group: a two-day trip might include river running, twilight horseback riding, and a short walk from the overnight lodge to see Thompson Falls.

Topographic maps: 1:50,000 Golden 82N/7 and Blaeberry 82N/6.

Facilities: Picnic tables, shelters with wood stoves, pit toilets, and fire rings provided free at the put-in; and there are good launching points at this campground. You'll also find a baseball diamond and a horseshoe pitch which are maintained by a community group, the International Order of Old Bastards (I.O.O.B.). We met members when we were there in early August. They were camping beside the Blaeberry, staying in many varieties of recreational

Season: May through September, peaks in June or July. Snow-melt, glacial-melt and rain-fed. Natural flow. I've paddled it from early July through early August with riverflows ranging from 17 to 65 m³/s (600 to 2300 cfs)

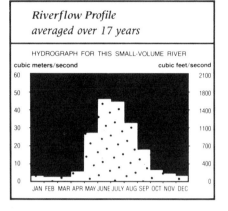

Riverflow Profile
averaged over 17 years

HYDROGRAPH FOR THIS SMALL-VOLUME RIVER

cubic meters/second   cubic feet/second

vehicles and they were congenial good fun. They claim to have a membership of 1500 in the Golden region where they've been active since 1976 — millions of members throughout the world. The organization originated in Australia after the Second World War. The Golden chapter members usually gather for their annual picnic on the early August holiday weekend — good to know if

Expert's flashy start — but check depth!

you want to either avoid the crowd or join with them on British Columbia Day. Paddlers are welcome to use these facilities maintained by the I.O.O.B. and they're free. It's a non-profit organization. But you might want to support them: at the time of writing, lifetime membership is $8 and all of the money goes back into the community. To become a member, contact the I.O.O.B., P.O. Box 2585, Golden, B.C. V0A 1H0. You'll also find Crown land where you can camp across the river.

Our group found that the privately owned Blaeberry Campground near the take-out was an excellent place to meet — with telephones and hot showers. We gathered there from various parts of the province at the start of a week-long trip.

For after paddling, Canyon Hot Springs is a 1-hour drive from the take-out heading west on Highway 1 and you'll be moving into the Pacific time zone from the "Alberta" time zone so you'll be there in *no* time. If heading south on Highway 95 into the Rocky Mountain Trench, it takes 1¾ hours to reach Radium Hot Springs; or, slightly south again, you could go to Fairmont, Lussier or Ram Creek: see access directions to them in the hot springs section.

Guidelines: For flashy fun, some kayakers start this run by jumping from the bridge wearing their boats. But check how much water there is.

For the rest of us, a gentle rapid starts the run, and you can put in before it or after it. The river width averages 22 meters (75 feet) where it is a single channel; gradient averages 3 meters/kilometer (15 feet/mile). After putting in, a few riffles are followed by a long braided section where the river broadens and meanders. Watch for sweepers and fallen trees snagged on the sides and on the gravel bars. Then, when you see a bridge ahead, look for a good drop to play in just before the bridge; next you're into the squirrelly swirlies in the short, twisting canyon which narrows to 15 meters (50 feet) wide — keep your paddle moving all the time, and you'll stay upright. And suddenly you're under the highway bridge and into the headwaters of the Columbia River. Paddle into the lagoon on "river right" to take out.

The glacial-melt from Mummery and Cairnes glaciers keeps the Blaeberry flowing for a long season, but it's not as cold as some glacial rivers are. Probably because it warms up in the sun when it meanders through the big open valley before the put-in.

From late May through August, you can obtain an eyeball report on river-flow from Hydra River Guides Ltd., P.O. Box 2708, Banff, Alberta T0L 0C0, telephone (403)762-4554.

Access to take-outs and put-ins: Located 10 minutes west of Golden beside Trans-Canada Highway 1.
• From the Highway 1/95 junction at Golden, head west for 15.6 kilometers (9.7 miles) and you'll cross a bridge over the Blaeberry. Just past it, turn left into Blaeberry River Road, cross the railway tracks and curve left down to a lagoon at the edge of the still headwaters of the Columbia River. This is the take-out.
• From the Rogers Pass Summit, it takes 45 minutes to reach this take-out. Heading east on Trans-Canada Highway 1, when you come down a big hill

In scenic canyon on Blaeberry River

and cross the Columbia River, measure the distance: the Blaeberry River Road turnoff is 10.1 kilometers (6.3 miles) farther along the highway. When you reach it, turn right and follow it to the take-out lagoon. If you miss Blaeberry River Road because of high-speed travel on the Trans-Canada, you'll cross the highway bridge over the Blaeberry.

To reach the put-in, return to Highway 1: turn left and go 0.2 kilometer (0.1 mile), then right off the highway into Blaeberry School Road which is a good gravel forest road. Go up it and turn right into Golden-Donald Upper Road; soon you'll cross the river and you might want to look at it. This is your only chance to see the river and it is a good midway put-in or take-out. There is an incredible maze of forest roads in this valley which has been inhabited for many years and many of the routes will work, but from the bridge the easiest route is to turn left off Golden-Donald into Oberg-Johnson Road. Continue on it for a short way and then turn left again into Moberly School Road. Follow it to where Blaeberry Road curves off to the right and then curves left. From the junction of Oberg-Johnson and Moberly School Roads, it's 7.7 kilometers (4.8 miles) to the put-in bridge at the campground near Redburn Creek.

But, if at any point you come across the I.O.O.B. signposts — the easiest way of all to find the put-in is to follow them.

Travel is permitted 24 hours a day on these forest roads which are open to the public. However, logging traffic could be on them too, so drive with your headlights on. To learn about possible fire-hazard closures, contact the Ministry of Forests, Golden District, 600 Ninth Street North, P.O. Box 1380, Golden, B.C. V0A 1H0, telephone (604)344-7500.

KICKING HORSE RIVER
Beaverfoot Bridge to Glenogle

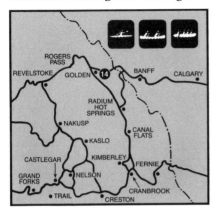

Who: Advanced and expert kayakers; no open-canoeists; advanced and expert rafters, at medium levels from Beaverfoot Bridge through Hunter Creek and Palliser to Glenogle. At low levels, also guided intermediate kayakers with a solid roll and intermediate rafters

Beaverfoot Bridge to Hunter Creek when levels are low, also intermediate kayakers and guided novices; expert open-canoeists with flotation; and all rafters

Water to expect: Class 3 to 4, with a Class 4+ rapid (portagable) and Class 2 at the start. At very high levels during runoff, possibly Class 4+ to 5 and possibly unrunnable. Swiftly flowing, continuous and cold. Straightforward,

Why go: Spray in your face as you buck through the Roller Coaster in the deep canyon, play in Hopi Hole, run Portage Rapid. It's a big, tough river with a super-easy shuttle — you get a whole lot of fun for little effort.

Portage Rapid is an excellent, demanding boulder garden. *It's pushy.* At the top of it, there's a rock named Black Bart, and, after Portage you blast through Shotgun, where the river funnels past a rock slab with a set of three or four standing waves at the bottom of it. Then play in the endo hole before heading on into Roller Coaster, the bucking bronco pure-joy-ride. It's a wonderful series of waves through the canyon. You can see part of it from the road. The waves are far below — 24 meters (80 feet) beneath Park Bridge and they still look big — all water!

What about the scenery? It's a mix. The Rocky Mountain backdrop is beautiful and you *might* see it, as you go, at the start of the run when the river's not too demanding; you might also hear train whistles and traffic then. The railway and the highway both run close beside the river, and, if you had time to look they would detract from the total scene. It's no wilderness. But you're soon too busy to notice. You paddle this one for the big-volume, exciting water — and you get it!

Non-paddlers can "go for it" too, on one of several commercially operated rafting trips. Rafts are on the river every day from June through August, except when the water's too high, and there's a variety of offerings, a trip for every taste. The usual run is a day-trip, either the one described here from Beaverfoot (Cozier) Bridge through Glenogle or some rafts put in slightly higher upstream. For people with limited time, there are half-day trips: you can drift down the top part and run through Hopi Hole for a gentle introduction to white water and brief excitement in the Hole — or go for a wild half-day run through Portage and the Roller Coaster. For people who have lots of time, with some operators you can go beyond that and run through the steeply walled rock-choked canyon — the wildest part of all — into Golden. The Kicking Horse is becoming more and more well known and non-paddlers

except 1 rapid — but pushy! Big water

Length of run: 17.2 kilometers (10.7 miles); allow 8 hours for full run from Beaverfoot Bridge to Glenogle.

Beaverfoot Bridge to Hunter Creek, 8.4 kilometers (5.2 miles); 3 to 4 hours

Shuttle one way: 15.2 kilometers (9.4 miles) for the full run; 15 minutes.

To Hunter Creek, 8.0 kilometers (5.0 miles); 10 minutes. Paved highway, and 1.2 kilometers (0.7 mile) on gravel logging road; easy to bike or hitchhike

Season: June to mid-September; peaks in July and early August — best when weather is warm. Glacial-melt, snow-melt and rain-fed; natural flow. Flashes

up with rain and sun. We paddled it with July riverflow of 78 m³/s (2750 cfs)

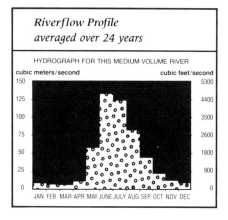

Riverflow Profile
averaged over 24 years

HYDROGRAPH FOR THIS MEDIUM-VOLUME RIVER

might want to experience it because of that. Also, the Kicking Horse was designated for recognition and thus for long-term management as a Canadian Heritage River in January 1989. The section designated is the first 67 kilometers (42 miles) of it, the headwaters which are in Yoho National Park. At the time of writing, the provincial government of British Columbia has not yet lent support to the Canadian Heritage Rivers System program; therefore, the run described here is not part of the heritage waterway. But it would be fitting if the designation could be enlarged to include this popular run too as well as the final stretch into Golden where the Kicking Horse flows into the Columbia. To date, nine rivers in Canada have been designated as Heritage rivers

Below Shotgun

and six more have been nominated for it, the Kicking Horse being the only one in British Columbia.

Topographic maps: 1:50,000 McMurdo 82N/2 and Golden 82N/7.

Facilities: You'll find a variety of campsites near the run. At the Beaverfoot Bridge put-in there's undeveloped Crown land beside the river on the north side of the bridge. There are no facilities here except a great deal of space to pitch tents, and there might be logging traffic going past. Between the Beaverfoot put-in and the final take-out at Glenogle, camping is free at two spacious sites that are beside the Kicking Horse and away from logging traffic: at the Palliser access where there is one picnic table but no pit toilet; and at the Hunter Creek recreation site, which is largely undeveloped but where the forest service provides one picnic table, one pit toilet and fire rings. You'll find lots of room to pitch tents at both sites, and you'll probably meet people on commercially operated rafting trips at all of these put-in and take-out points.

When 15 minutes from the put-in heading east towards Calgary, there's camping for a fee in Yoho National Park with picnic tables, pit toilets and fire rings; and there are a great many more campgrounds in the heart of the park.

Downstream from the take-out, 15 minutes away in Golden, there's camping for a fee in the city park beside the Kicking Horse. To reach it, turn off Highway 1 onto 95, and go into the center of Golden; turn left at 9th Street and continue to the end of it. You'll find the riverside campground with hot showers and a swimming pool too. It's open June to September.

Hot springs are available in every direction: heading west, Canyon Hot Springs is a 1½-hour drive away and it's just off Trans-Canada Highway 1. You go via Rogers Pass to this delightfully intimate, commercially operated swimming-pool-type development, an outdoor hot springs pool which is enhanced with extra heat and underwater music. You'll find changerooms with electric outlets and hot showers, and a spacious, privately operated campground — open from May to September. Canyon Hot Springs is in the Pacific time zone, so when checking the hours it's open, remember you have an extra hour to reach it after paddling the Kicking Horse which is on Mountain or "Alberta" Time. If you're heading south to paddle: Radium Hot Springs is a 1¾-hour drive from the take-out, only 5 minutes off Highway 95. It's another excellent commercially operated outdoor pool and it's open year-round. Heading east, you could stop at the hot springs at Banff.

Guidelines: Don't be fooled by the millpond look at the put-ins. There's a stretch of Class 2 water for warming up at each access, but action develops. Since the water is so swiftly and continuously flowing and so cold — rescue so difficult, this river can become awesome. Sum it up before you go.

River width from the Beaverfoot Bridge to Glenogle ranges from 20 meters to 50 meters (70 to 160 feet) narrowing to 15 meters (50 feet) at Shotgun with very low water. In the first part of the run from Beaverfoot to Palliser, watch for a cable across the river as warning of the Class 2 Cable Car Rapids; past Palliser, watch for the Class 3+ to 4 Hopi Hole, which you can ride or avoid. Beyond the Hunter Creek access, the Kicking Horse descends at the rate of 15 meters/kilometer (80 feet/mile). When you are 10 minutes past the

Hunter Creek "rec" site, you're definitely into something much much more:
• Portage Rapid, the big-bad-drop of the river which is a Class 4+ boulder rapid, goes on for 180 meters (600 feet). Portage starts at a point where the railway tracks run close alongside on "river left".

Be alert for it when you're ten minutes past the Rafters' Lunch Stop at Hunter Creek: you'll see a large pool with a beach on "river right" which is the Hunter Creek "rec" site. Past this pool and beach, the river swings away

At Shotgun, looking upstream into Portage Rapid

from the railway tracks around an unused gravel stockpile that is 20 meters (70 feet) high. On the other side of the pile you meet the tracks again and you should eddy out about 100 meters (300 feet) downstream. Definitely worth climbing from your boat to scout Black Bart, the Shark's Tooth, and Shotgun. It's easy to carry around all of it if you want to.

At the top of the rapid, a string of rocks projecting from "river right" going about one-fourth of the way into the river. Black Bart is in the middle of them, and might be beneath the surface. Not far downstream, look for the Shark's Tooth, a pointy rock about one-quarter of the way across the river nearest to "river left". At very high water *it* might be covered. At medium levels, Black Bart is covered with water. But at all except the highest levels, you can see the rock which is closest to "river right". This gives an indication of where Black Bart is, so that rafters especially can avoid getting caught on top of it, and it gives all boaters a clue about where to ferry across to pick a clean line to avoid the Shark's Tooth. And scout Shotgun. Again, rafters will want to find the deepest passage near the wall on "river right", while kayakers will want to look for — or look out for, if it's very high water — an endo hole 75 meters (250 feet) beyond Shotgun near "river left". Play time. And that's the end of the Portage Rapid section.

Just beyond Portage Rapid, when it's high water in June and July, look out for a house rock in the middle of the river and keep to the right-hand side of it to avoid a reversal — it can be a keeper.

• Roller Coaster Rapid follows: when you see Park Bridge where Highway 1 crosses the river, watch for the great waves in the canyon. They were 1 meter (3 feet) high when we paddled with medium riverflow; at very high levels, wave height can be 3 to 5 meters (10 to 15 feet).

The glacial-fed Kicking Horse rises and falls quickly with rain and sunshine. When we paddled it, it was bright blue and beautiful and fun. I've seen it when it was muddy brown and roaring and to be avoided — maximum recorded discharge was 402 m^3/s (14,197 cfs) on June 19, 1916. A whopper of a day! For an up-to-the-minute eyeball report on riverflow from June through August contact one of the rafting operations. Alpine Rafting Company, P.O. Box 1409, Golden, B.C. V0A 1H0, (604)344-5016: from 9 a.m. till 9 p.m. you'll reach a person with the rafting operation, after 9 p.m. it's a live answering service. Clearwater Rafting Adventures Ltd., P.O. Box 597, Midnapore, Alberta T0L 1J0, telephone (403)256-2484. Glacier Raft Company, P.O. Box 2319E, Banff, Alberta T0L 0C0, telephone at Banff (403)762-4347 and at Golden (604)344-6521. Hydra River Guides Ltd., P.O. Box 2708, Banff, Alberta T0L 0C0, telephone (403)762-4554. Or contact Kootenay River Runners, P.O. Box 81, Edgewater, B.C. V0A 1E0, telephone (604)347-9210. Many of these rafters are on the river daily.

Paddlers wanting to go onto the Kicking Horse but wanting an easier trip could paddle to Palliser or to the Rafters' Lunch Stop at Hunter Creek "rec" site, then go by raft into the wild part. But be warned that at high water this "easier" Hunter Creek section has solid Class 3+ water with big holes, the Hopi Hole being one. Intermediate kayakers and expert open-canoeists might tackle the section from the Beaverfoot (Cozier) Bridge to Palliser or to Hunter Creek at very low water, but never at high water, and from Palliser to Hunter Creek never even at medium levels. Do not underestimate the Kicking Horse.

All paddlers *must* catch the Rafters' Take-out at Glenogle as the section of river from Glenogle to Yoho (5 Mile) Bridge and into Golden is extremely dangerous and seldom paddled; there's a good eddy at Glenogle, and it's easy to make it if you've noted its location — just don't get carried away with the fun and forget where you are. Beyond the Glenogle take-out, there is a monster hole, then a constricted, steeply walled rock-choked inaccessible canyon from Yoho Bridge into Golden. You can see the beginning of it beneath Yoho Bridge. This section of river is sometimes kayaked by experts and it's raftable by experts who know it, but I recommend that recreational boaters planning to paddle it should see it first from a commercially operated raft.

Access to take-outs and put-ins: Between Golden and Calgary alongside Trans-Canada Highway 1. From Calgary, it's 2½ hours. From Golden, it's 15 minutes to the take-out which is upstream from Yoho Bridge referred to by many locals as 5 Mile Bridge. Locals have named the access points too, and, a couple of those names, Palliser and Glenogle, are difficult to relate to any physical feature. When you reach the spot there is no settlement, because these are names of railway points designating how far the tracks stretch from Field — Field is at Mile 0. There is a marker board near the tracks at Palliser to indicate it's the 22.4 Mile Point and one at Glenogle to indicate it's the 28.1 Mile Point beyond Field. These markers are small, they're for railway purposes only, and they're not even at the actual access point. Neither Glenogle nor Palliser is obvious when you're driving at high speed along the highway. So when watching for them, don't look for a town or a gas station or a grocery store. Instead, measure the distance.

Glenogle take-out is also frequently referred to as the Rafters' Take-out: heading upstream, the turnoff into it is 2.0 kilometers (1.2 miles) past Yoho (5 Mile) Bridge immediately past some concrete guardrail barriers along the highway. If you reach Yoho Rest Area, you've gone too far. The rest area is 1.5 kilometers (0.9 mile) upstream from the Glenogle take-out and is a good pit-toilet stop, but the bank is too steep there for taking out. There's plenty of room to park at Glenogle and a gentle slope to walk up from the river, but it's not easy to spot from the river either. When dropping your shuttle vehicle and before leaving Glenogle, look at the take-out eddy and note it carefully. This is a *must* take-out.

Hunter Creek put-in or take-out, often referred to as the Rafter's Lunch Stop, is located midway along the run at the Hunter Creek recreation site. The access road is very rough and filled with potholes but is only a kilometer (less than a mile) to the river. The turn-off into Hunter Creek "rec" site is 5.2 kilometers (3.2 miles) upstream from Park Bridge and is immediately west of the Trans-Canada bridge over Hunter Creek.

Palliser put-in or take-out: this is a popular put-in with kayakers who want to avoid the flatwater paddling at the start and is a good take-out for open-canoeists. Yet you still get Hopi Hole from this put-in. The narrow gravel road from the Trans-Canada Highway to the river at Palliser is difficult to spot as it is unmarked. It cuts off the highway and veers steeply down from it at an acute angle to the southwest. If approaching from the Yoho Park side, you'll find the Palliser turnoff 3.4 kilometers (2.1 miles) past Beaverfoot Road and 1.1 kilometers (0.7 mile) past a viewpoint with a large parking area; if approaching from the Hunter Creek side, it's 2.4 kilometers (1.5 miles) past the Hunter Creek Bridge and 1.3 kilometers (0.8 mile) past a lay-by where there's room for one car to stop. Once you're on the Palliser road, it descends to the river in an easy gradient, and, at the time of writing the gravel surface is smooth. Head down it for 1.2 kilometers (0.7 mile) to the water; there are a great many roads in the small area between Highway 1 and the river at this former sawmill site. When there are choices, follow the right-hand fork. Go to a picnic table where the road is closest to the river.

Beaverfoot (Cozier) Bridge put-in: from the Rafter's Take-out at Glenogle to the top put-in, go upstream 14.0 kilometers (8.7 miles) and turn right off the highway into Beaverfoot Forest Road, which is a gravel logging road. From the bridge at Hunter Creek, you'll go 5.8 kilometers (3.6 miles) to Beaverfoot. If you reach Yoho Park, you've gone too far. Beaverfoot cuts off the highway just 0.7 kilometer (0.4 mile) before you reach the park. Cross the railway tracks, curve down a hill and cross the Beaverfoot (Cozier) Bridge to the other side of the Kicking Horse — it's only 1.2 kilometers (0.7 mile) from the highway. The Cozier Mill used to be here; you can still see evidence of it. There's room to park, and an easy spot to put in.

VERMILION RIVER
Hector Gorge to Kootenay River

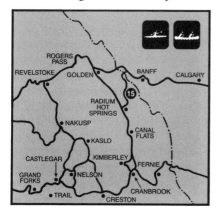

Who: Intermediate, advanced and expert kayakers, and guided novices; expert open-canoeists and guided intermediates; but no rafters at this take-out

Water to expect: Class 2 and 3, a short Class 3+ rapid; mandatory portage of 180 meters (600 feet) at the take-out. Small volume. Small rock river with steady gradient

Length of run: 14.8 kilometers (9.2 miles); 4 to 5 hours on the river plus a 15-minute bushwhack

Shuttle one way: 12.7 kilometers (7.9 miles); 10 minutes, and allow

Why go: Gentle rapids, superb game-watching, unthreatening play spots, sunny sandbars and glacial blue water — with a dramatic backdrop of Rocky Mountains.

But mostly the game is ever-so-special: while on the river, part of our group saw five bighorn sheep wandering wild on a steep hillside above the river. Natural mineral licks are in the limestone on the slopes luring mountain goats to the region and you might see them too. When completing the shuttle, we saw two elk.

These are the reasons I first loved the Vermilion — now I've gleaned more fascinating facts: this stretch is significant for "river people" because it is the beginning of the complex Kootenay system. Riverflow on the Vermilion averages 4⅓ times that of the upper Kootenay River where they meet at the take-out for this run through Kootenay National Park. Thus, technically the Kootenay is a tributary of the Vermilion. And, look at what the combined flow turns into!

The Vermilion River is significant, too, because of the road beside it; the Banff-Windermere wagon route, was the first "highway" through the Rocky Mountains — history buffs will enjoy interpretive displays at many stops in the park with stories of the early days.

Topographic maps: The federally produced 1:200,000 map of Banff, Kootenay and Yoho National Parks MCR 220 is the topo that's easiest to use for this run; a portion of it showing the run is reproduced on page 71. You can purchase this map from federal map sales offices, from park headquarters in Radium or seasonally from park information offices at Radium and at Marble Canyon. The 1:50,000 maps Spillimacheen 82K/16 and Mount Assiniboine 82J/13 are the largest scale topos available for the run, but are difficult to read as the Vermilion wanders back and forth across the map borders.

Facilities: You'll find picnic tables at the put-in and take-out; camping for a fee in Kootenay National Park at McLeod Meadows which is 5 minutes from

20 minutes more to place marker. Paved highway, easy to bike or hitchhike

Season: May through August; best June and July. Natural flow; snow-melt and rain-fed, then glacial-melt keeps it flowing. We paddled it in early July; precise riverflow unavailable; my guess is 50 m³/s (1770 cfs)

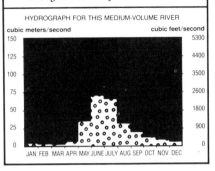

Riverflow Profile
averaged over 11 years

HYDROGRAPH FOR THIS MEDIUM-VOLUME RIVER

Rock jump in Hector Gorge

the take-out, and at Redstreak in Radium: both campgrounds have kitchen shelters and flush toilets, and there are hot showers at Redstreak.

Radium Hot Springs is 25 minutes from the take-out, and you'll find a commercially developed hot-swimming-pool-type outdoor springs with change-rooms and hot showers. It's got civilized amenities yet a wild feeling.

Guidelines: Hector Gorge comes soon after putting in: this is where the action is. The steeply walled gorge goes on for 5½ kilometers (3½ miles) — high, sparsely-treed shale banks compress the riverflow into small surfing waves at corners: the river narrows to 30 meters (100 feet). Hector Rapids is a Class 3 stretch; it's usually a rock garden with a few scattered boulders. At higher water but not peak levels, it becomes Class 3+ to 4 and it's difficult to portage. But for the most part, this run is a quiet scenic one. So, if you like playing the white water, do it in Hector Gorge at the start of the run and, later, stop for lunch on a sunny sandbar downstream.

Beyond the gorge the river is wide, the glacial valley broad, the road never too far away. The Vermilion spreads out, becoming mostly a small rock river with smoothly flowing water, then branches into a great many channels around sand and gravel bars. You'll find the overall gradient gentle averaging 4 meters/kilometer (20 feet/mile); width ranges up to 50 meters (160 feet). Shortly before the take-out, we paddled beneath a bridge. The bridge might be gone. But if you reach one, it's a sure sign you're nearing the end of the run; stay on "river right" so you'll spot your marker. Past the bridge, the river widens and sweeps in a broad curve to the right and you are at a "meeting of the waters": the confluence of the Vermilion and Kootenay rivers. This is the end of the Vermilion, which is the larger river at this point, and the start of the Kootenay, and it's the take-out. Ferry across and pull out on the left-hand bank of the Kootenay as you face upstream then portage 180 meters (600 feet) along brushy fisherman trails beside the river to the picnic site: end of run.

Access to take-out and put-in: Located alongside Banff-Windermere Highway 93 in Kootenay National Park between Vermilion Crossing and McLeod Meadows, the Vermilion take-out is 2½ hours from Calgary, and it's 25 minutes from Radium.

• To reach the take-out from Calgary and Banff: when you're past Kootenay Crossing, watch for Dolly Varden Picnic Site on the left-hand side — that's where the take-out is.

• From Radium, when you're past McLeod Meadows, watch for Dolly Varden Picnic Site on the right-hand side. Stop and find your way from the picnic site to the Kootenay River: walk on fishermen's trails for 180 meters (600 feet) downstream following the Kootenay to where it flows into the Vermilion. Hang a marker and look at the gravel bars and the general scene where you'll ferry across to take out. This take-out is difficult to spot from the river, so note it well.

For the put-in, return to the picnic site and drive upstream 10.8 kilometers (6.7 miles) to Hector Gorge Lookout for a bird's-eye view; from the lookout, it's 1.9 kilometers (1.2 miles) more to Hector Gorge Picnic Site. Turn left into it and you'll find plenty of room to park. Walk across the highway and then 14 paces down a short, grassy bank to put in.

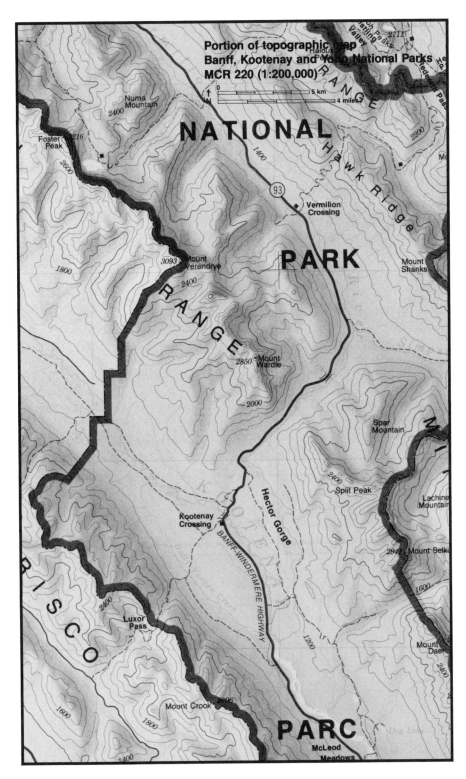

Portion of topographic map
Banff, Kootenay and Yoho National Parks
MCR 220 (1:200,000)

0   5 km
4 miles

NATIONAL

PARK

PARC

Numa
Mountain
2400

Foster
Peak
216
2600

1800

RANGE

2400

3093 Mount
Verendrye

2850 Mount
Wardle

2000

Hawk Ridge

93

Vermilion
Crossing

Mount
Shanks

2200

Spar
Mountain

2400

Split Peak

Hector Gorge

Lachine
Mountain

2941 Mount Selki

1600

Kootenay
Crossing

BANFF-WINDERMERE HIGHWAY

Mount
Daer

2400

BRISCO

2400

Luxor
Pass

1200

1600

1800

1800

Mount Crook   2606

1400

McLeod
Meadows

Dog Lake

CROSS RIVER
Above Natural Bridge

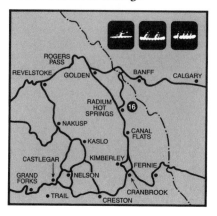

Who: At high levels, intermediate to expert kayakers and guided novices; intermediate and expert open-canoeists; all rafters. At low levels, also novice kayakers; and novice open-canoeists with guides; but no rafters

Water to expect: Depending on level, Class 2 to 3-. Small volume. Small rock river with braided sections

Length of run: 3.5 kilometers (2.2 miles); 2 hours — but you could play all day at the take-out

Shuttle one way: 4.6 kilometers

Why go: An excellent river for open-canoeists, and for new kayakers wanting to play. The run is short: so if you want a warm-up, you can run it once. If you want more, you can run it again and again. In fact, it's a special treat for all boaters to swish through the woods and play in the smoothly scooped-out surfing waves at the rounded swoopy bends in this mellow stream. Look at the take-out and you'll see what I mean.

The water is blue and crystal clear, not glacial, not too cold. The scenery is lovely, the primitive campsites spacious — even if you don't paddle, it's worth coming to the Cross to see the waterfall, the natural bridge of rock above it, the convoluted canyon leading up to it. And from the Cross, it takes only ½ hour to reach the commercially operated hot pools at Radium where you can swim in a cool pool or lounge in a hot one, see Rocky Mountain bighorn sheep from the hot pool, and take a shower. The springs are open year-round. It's a river for all seasons too: when the Cross is choked with ice, cross-country skiers follow groomed trails to the snow-covered natural bridge. You can walk to it the rest of the year. The river got its name because in 1845 a Jesuit priest erected a cross near its source at the summit of White Man Pass.

Topographic map: 1:50,000 Tangle Peak 82J/12.

Facilities: Beside the Cross, you'll find undeveloped Crown land where primitive camping is free; many riverside sites are spacious. If the weather is sunny you might head upstream from the put-in for 2.8 kilometers (1.7 miles) to a rough, dirt track on the left-hand side. It's filled with potholes but is passable when dry, and it leads to a couple of large gravel bars.

Beside the Kootenay, there's camping for a nominal fee at Nipika Riverbend which is 5 minutes from the take-out on the Cross. If you're planning to stay at Riverbend, please contact Lyle and Dianne Wilson, P.O. Box 903, Invermere, B.C. V0A 1K0, telephone (604)342-3130. You'll find a place to pitch your tent or hang your hammock, fire rings, pit toilets, daily raft trips on the Kootenay run by several commercial rafting operations, and lots of river people.

(2.9 miles); 10 minutes.
Gravel logging roads

Season: May through August. Snow-melt and rain-fed. Natural flow. We paddled it in early July; precise riverflow unavailable; my guess is 19 m³/s (670 cfs)

Low water at take-out bridge

Radium Hot Springs are not far away — it takes only 30 minutes to reach these commercially operated pools which have been part of Kootenay National Park since 1922. They're open year-round. At Radium, after a hot soak you can take a warm shower and blow-dry your hair.

Guidelines: The run starts quietly in a braided section and builds — to harmless, unthreatening surfing waves; you could play all day at the delightful corner before the take-out. You really could. Because the water is crystal clear and blue and not too cold.

The river descends at the rate of 8 meters/kilometer (40 feet/mile). Stream width varies with riverflow from 18 to 45 meters (60 to 150 feet) as the

Watching for fallen trees

73

channels split into braids and then merge into a single watercourse and split again. Sweepers and logs are scattered down the gravel bars in the braided sections, and could be dangerous — especially at high water. A fallen tree might easily block the stream at narrow corners like the take-out. Watch for them.

Access to take-out and put-in: Located off Settlers Road on the east side of the Columbia-Windermere Valley in the Rocky Mountain Trench. The take-out is ½ hour from Radium, 1¼ hours from Canal Flats, and 3 hours from Calgary.

• From Calgary, head west on Banff-Windermere Highway 93 through Kootenay National Park; past Kootenay Crossing, watch for McLeod Meadows. When you're 8.2 kilometers (5.1 miles) past the McLeod Meadows Campground, turn left into Settlers Road which is a gravel logging road. It is well signposted. You can easily see it if you're travelling during daylight hours, but it's difficult to spot at night. From Settlers Road and Highway 93, go south on Settlers for 12.1 kilometers (7.5 miles) and you'll see a signpost to "Nipika Riverbend Campground".

• From Radium, head east on Banff-Windermere Highway 93 for 16.4 kilometers (10.2 miles) and turn right into Settlers Road. Again, go south on Settlers for 12.1 kilometers (7.5 miles) to the Nipika signpost.

• From Canal Flats, head north on Kootenay River (Ravenshead) and Settlers Roads, the gravel logging roads that follows alongside the west bank of the Kootenay River; a couple of logging roads lead off to bridges across the Kootenay, but you continue straight, staying on "river right" to Settlers Road; from Canal Flats, go 64 kilometers (40 miles) to the Nipika signpost at Settlers. It takes 1¼ hours.

To reach the take-out from the "Nipika Riverbend Campground" signpost on Settlers Road, head down the hill, cross a bridge over the Kootenay. Pass Nipika Campground, and you'll reach a fork in the road signposted to a mine on the right-hand side; you stay left and continue upstream on Cross River Road for 3.1 kilometers (1.9 miles) to a lay-by with room for two cars to park; this parking spot is 0.7 kilometer (0.4 mile) past the "2 Mile" signpost and you can walk in from here to see the natural rock bridge.

• For the natural bridge: climb down the bank and make your way through the woods until you find a well-worn trail beside the river — there are many of them, and all lead to the picturesque canyon, waterfall and natural bridge. Veer left following one of the pine-needled paths downstream until you reach the falls; it takes 10 or 15 minutes to get there.

• For the take-out, continue from the lay-by: drive upstream for 3.0 kilometers (1.9 miles) and shortly past the "4 Mile" signpost you'll see a small but good gravel road leading off to the left; this is Cross River Small Business Enterprise Program (Cross River SBEP) Road; go down it to the take-out bridge.

To reach the put-in, return up the hill to Cross River Road. Turn left and head upstream: from this point, it is 3.5 kilometers (2.2 miles) to the put-in. The logging road climbs, then winds down the hill close to the bank and dips into a hollow where there's room to park at the roadside; and there's a rough track to the river that has been blocked to vehicles, but you can easily walk on it; it's about 60 paces to the water.

Natural rock bridge

Travel is permitted on Settlers, Cross River, Cross River Small Business Enterprise Program (Cross River SBEP) and Kootenay River (Ravenshead) Forest Roads, all of which are open to the public. However, logging traffic might be on them too 24 hours of the day except on Saturdays, Sundays and holidays — so drive with your headlights on. To learn about logging traffic and possible fire-hazard closures, contact the Ministry of Forests, Invermere District, P.O. Box 189, Invermere, B.C. V0A 1K0, telephone (604)342-4200.

KOOTENAY RIVER
Palliser Reach

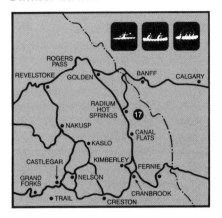

Who: Intermediate, advanced and expert kayakers, and guided novices with an Eskimo roll who are confident; expert open-canoeists and guided intermediates; and all rafters

Water to expect: Class 2+ and 3. Steady gradient. Straightforward big water; very long, committed run through a relatively inaccessible canyon

Length of run: 44.6 kilometers (27.7 miles); 6 to 8 hours, minimum

Shuttle one way: 34.5 kilometers (21.4 miles); 45 minutes. Gravel logging road

Why go: It's a must. If you run rivers, sometime you'll want to paddle the Kootenay; this large languorous river with scenery that includes a waterfall cascading into it like a picture-postcard-come-alive has exciting whitewater stretches too — watch for Horseshoe Rapids.

The entire run is like a "larger-than-life" movie set depicting the rugged Rocky Mountain Canadian scene inhabited by nothing but red-coated Royal Canadian Mounted Police and wild game. It's like what all the world imagines Canada to be. It's here. On the Kootenay. The beauty of the scene is marred only by patches of red in the green trees caused by the mountain pine beetle and recent logging activity. You'll bounce through big boisterous powerful waves past high, dry earth cliffs, sliced off rock walls, waterfalls, and, we didn't see any Mounties, but you'll see game: dusk is the magical time for it. We saw many small deer, a coyote, mountain sheep, two mule deer, and an elk after our long day on the river and on our way to luxuriate in the hot springs.

It's a river for all water people, and that includes non-paddlers too. Rafts are on the Kootenay every day from June through August giving tourists a bouncy ride; open-canoeists and kayakers wanting raft support for a large group can also organize that. You might be able to squeeze in at the last moment, but it's better to book in advance; see the "Guidelines" section for the name of the rafting operator who is active on the Kootenay.

This book covers one-day trips; note that the Kootenay is excellent for a long one-day trip as described here, but it's also the best canoeing river in the region for multiple-day-tripping. It is a major waterway. Every river in this book eventually flows into the Kootenay or into the Columbia.

The Kootenay and Columbia rivers start in the East Kootenays. While the Columbia heads *north*, the Kootenay follows the Rocky Mountain Trench *south*. The Kootenay crosses the international border into Montana as Lake Koocanusa, curls through Idaho as the Kootenai River, then loops north into the West Kootenays of Canada where it becomes the Kootenay River again. It flows through the south and west arms of Kootenay Lake, past Nelson, then

Season: May to mid-October. Best July and August. Natural flow, peaks in June. Rain-fed, snow-melt and glacial-melt. We paddled it in early July with riverflow of 192 m³/s (6780 cfs)

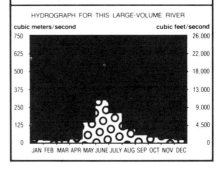

Riverflow Profile
averaged over 36 years

HYDROGRAPH FOR THIS LARGE-VOLUME RIVER

cubic meters/second   cubic feet/second

750	26,000
625	22,000
500	18,000
375	13,000
250	9,000
125	4,500
0	0

JAN FEB MAR APR MAY JUNE JULY AUG SEP OCT NOV DEC

September sunshine on Kootenay

Putting in at Riverbend

Bridge Rapids in August

78

into the Kootenay River and the Kootenay Canal. The river spills in waterfalls through the Corra Linn, Upper Bonnington, Lower Bonnington and South Slocan dams and power plants, while water in the canal flows through the Kootenay Canal Dam; then canal and river merge at Brilliant near Castlegar and pour through the last dam on the Kootenay producing the last large burst of power before the Kootenay River disappears into the Columbia.

The source of the Kootenay is a short way upstream from the take-out for the Vermilion run described on pages 68 through 71 of this guidebook. From there to the Columbia River is a long way: the Kootenay flows for a total of 655 kilometers (407 miles), of which 444 kilometers (276 miles) are in Canada. The four dams on the stretch of river that runs for 5 kilometers (3 miles) between Nelson and Slocan Pool supply 65% of the power needs for the homes of 200,000 southern interior British Columbians — the dam at Brilliant supplies power for local industry, and the dam in the Kootenay Canal can contribute up to 5% of the B.C. Hydro power grid which serves homes and businesses in other parts of the province. The Kootenay flows for miles, cuts a wide swath, creates a lot of power: it *is* a must paddle.

Topographic maps: 1:50,000 Tangle Peak 82J/12 and Fairmont Hot Springs 82J/5.

Facilities: Nipika Riverbend Campground is at the put-in, and it's an ideal place to camp. The Kootenay run and the shuttle for it are long ones, and you've got a better chance of having a leisurely day on the river if your tents are pitched at one location for a couple of nights. Nipika is pleasantly low key: it's a privately owned user-maintained site where you drop your fee in a box. If you're planning to go, please contact Lyle and Dianne Wilson, P.O. Box 903, Invermere, B.C. V0A 1K0, telephone (604)342-3130. Staying at Riverbend, you'll see all the action; this is where the rafts leave from. And, for after paddling, Radium Hot Springs is only 30 minutes away.

Guidelines: The Kootenay is big and broad: river width averages 45 meters (150 feet) — "two throw-bags worth" according to one rafter, and width at the take-out is 75 meters (250 feet). The Kootenay River descends at the rate of 4 meters/kilometer (20 feet/mile) — volume, not gradient, makes this one exciting. And the volume keeps up: the paddling season is long as glacial-melt keeps the river flowing. In June the water is bright blue, but can become white with glacial flour in August. Throughout the paddling season it's big volume, but much of the way you can cruise. It's big, but not in the usual whitewater sense of "big" water. There is much Class 2, there are some lovely Class 3 standing waves but nothing squirrelly. All is straightforward on this one — no strange hydraulics when we paddled it. But big waves? Yes!

When planning to paddle the Kootenay you might want to check on riverflow before you go. For an eyeball report on what the river is doing, contact Kootenay River Runners, P.O. Box 81, Edgewater, B.C. V0A 1E0, telephone (604)347-9210. They're on the river in rafts every day.

On the river, the easiest way to stay out of trouble is to scout the drops before the river bends, and on this river that seems to be especially when it's bending to the left. If you go with a good team, take time to scout, and go

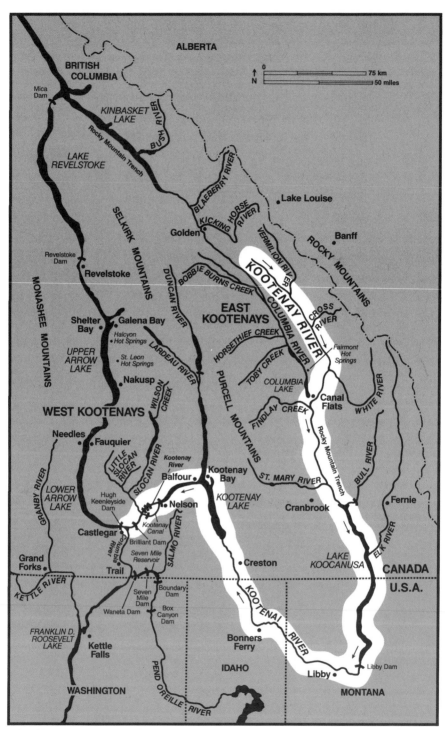

Columbia-Kootenay River System — all rivers in this guidebook pour into it; see arrows pointing in direction of riverflow on the Kootenay

carefully, almost everyone can paddle it — newer paddlers could organize raft support for this long trip. The order of drops and features to expect:

• Bridge Rapids beneath the put-in bridge warrants a quick look before going into it — it's Class 2 to 2+. From here, expect the next drop soon. It's only 2.4 kilometers (1.5 miles) past the put-in and could take as little as 15 or 20 minutes to reach.

• Surprise Rapids, also called Ledge Rapids, washes out at higher water; so much so I didn't even note this spot when I paddled it. At low water, it's Class 3: watch out for a shallow rock ledge stretching across "river left". The channel is more open on the right-hand side — head for the waves where there is deeper water. But watch for rocks here too at low water. Moving on, look for the next drop in 25 or 30 minutes.

• Two Rocks, or Witness Drop, is next. At medium water, these rocks turn into the biggest hole on the run with large waves below them — standing waves up to 1¼ meters (4 feet) high for 180 meters (600 feet). It is a Class 3 rapid and is also difficult at lower water because of the boulders showing, one of the few places in the river where they do. It's also on the left-hand side. Open-canoeists might want to scout; a great number of canoes have piled up on this one. Pull out on "river left" when you see a bend to the left coming up. Past Two Rocks, expect the biggest, longest rapid of the river in another 15 or 20 minutes.

• Horseshoe Rapids, another Class 3, and the standing waves we found there were 1 meter (3 feet) high; there are a couple of sets of rapids. The first as you enter the horseshoe and go around a broad bend to the left, then another whole set of standing waves as you come out of the horseshoe and head for a straighter stretch again. Closed-boaters can "go for it" — head for the big stuff in the middle, and have a roller-coaster ride. Open-canoeists will want to scout; to avoid being swamped, keep just to the right-hand side of the big waves, but also keep to the left of the ledge and the back eddy on "river right". It's a fine line! As soon as open-canoeists are past this first set, they should land on the right-hand shore, walk across the peninsula and scout to see if they want to paddle or portage the next set of rapids in the second curve of the horseshoe. You run it along the right-hand shore. And rafters? They love this set — it's a rafter's special — just pure fun!

• Palliser Rapids is about 2½ hours past the horseshoe and it's more Class 3 standing waves, with some boulders at lower water. Then, another 15 or 20 minutes and you'll see the most beautiful sight on the run: Pedley Falls.

• Pedley Falls is what makes me think of Palliser Reach as a picture postcard. It's sheer scenery. But look at the water you're paddling into — it can be tricky, even at moderate levels, to pull out in time. Open-canoeists, especially, will want to check out the Class 2 to 3 rapids just upstream from the falls. At low water there is a ledge. You can pull out on either bank to look at it. Past this bridal-veil-like cascade, it's a couple hours to the take-out.

When we paddled the Kootenay, we saw remnants of an improvised river sauna on the beach on the left-hand shore at Horseshoe Rapids. It was not "fired up" — there were no hot rocks that day and we were warm and wanted to cool off. But I think anyone could stop and use it. Or you might want to take some plastic in the event you're inspired to build a new steam tent at another spot. We stopped for lunch later on a bouldery beach, savoured a rain shower with sun sparkling through it like a curtain of diamonds. On a really wet day those same lunch-spot boulders would be perfect for a riverside sauna.

Plan for the unplanned on this run: allow lots of time so you can grab onto whatever happens that is good for you — that's the mood to go with.

Access to take-out and put-in: Located off Settlers-Kootenay River Forest Road (often called Ravenshead Road by locals) on the east side of the Columbia-Windermere Valley which is the Rocky Mountain Trench. The Kootenay take-out is 20 minutes from Canal Flats. The put-in is 30 minutes from Radium Hot Springs and 3 hours from Calgary.

For the take-out: in Canal Flats, go past the post office, general store, and fire hall and turn right on McGrath Avenue, then left, and head north on Kootenay River Forest Road, a gravel logging road that runs along the west side of the river. There are new roads all along but keep going straight on the main one: from Canal Flats, go 32.5 kilometers (20.2 miles) to a fork in the road where one road veers to the left-hand side, but you go straight. Cross a cattle guard, and, shortly past it and before Kootenay-River-Lower-Crossing (26 Mile) Bridge, turn right into a small road to the river; it's an easy place for loading boats when you've finished your run. But park your shuttle vehicle somewhere else; keep this loading area, which has been built by the rafters, clear and accessible for all to use.

To go to the put-in, backtrack to the fork in the road, turn right and continue heading north on Kootenay River-Settlers (Ravenshead) Forest Road for 32.5 kilometers (20.2 miles) and turn right down a road with a signpost to "Nipika Riverbend Campground". Follow it down the hill, across the Kootenay-River-Upper-Crossing (Settlers) Bridge, and turn left into Nipika where you can put in.

From Calgary or Radium — if you're approaching on Banff-Windermere Highway 93, you'll probably want to go first to the put-in, then set up your shuttle. To do this, turn off the highway into Settlers Road which is a gravel logging road. It is signposted on the highway, but you'll find it more easily if you measure the distance:
• From Calgary, heading west on Highway 93, you'll go through Kootenay National Park. After passing Kootenay Crossing, watch for McLeod Meadows; when 8.2 kilometers (5.1 miles) past the McLeod Meadows Campground, turn left into Settlers Road. It is well signposted; if you're travelling during daylight hours you can easily see it but it's difficult to spot at night. From the Highway 93 turnoff, go south on Settlers Road for 12.1 kilometers (7.5 miles) to the "Nipika Riverbend Campground" signpost. Turn left and follow it down the hill, cross the Kootenay-River-Upper-Crossing (Settlers) Bridge, and then turn left into Nipika to the put-in.
• From Radium, head east on Highway 93 for 16.4 kilometers (10.2 miles) and turn right into Settlers Road. From Settlers Road and Highway 93, again, go south on Settlers for 12.1 kilometers (7.5 miles) and you'll see the Nipika signpost. Follow it to the put-in.

Pedley Falls

To reach the take-out from the put-in, return to Settlers Road, turn left and go south on Settlers-Kootenay River (Ravenshead) Forest Road. Go 32.5 kilometers (20.2 miles) to a fork in the road and turn left again. You'll see an easy take-out just downstream from Kootenay-River-Lower-Crossing (26 Mile) Bridge. It's on "river right".

The Settlers-Kootenay River (Ravenshead) Forest Road is open to the public. However, logging traffic might be on it too 24 hours of the day except on Saturdays, Sundays and holidays — so drive with your headlights on. To learn about possible fire-hazard closures, contact the Ministry of Forests, Invermere District, P.O. Box 189, Invermere, B.C. V0A 1K0, telephone (604)342-4200.

WHITE RIVER
Lower Section

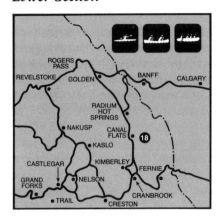

Who: Intermediate, advanced and expert kayakers; expert open-canoeists; and all rafters. At low levels, also guided novice kayakers and guided intermediate open-canoeists

Water to expect: Steady Class 3. At low levels, Class 2+; at very high levels, Class 3+. Small rock river with rock garden at the start; steady gradient through a remote canyon

Length of run: 34.3 kilometers (21.3 miles); at least 6 to 8 hours — it's a long one

Shuttle one way: depending on route

Why go: Mellow-yet-lively water, splendid game watching, the scenery never lets up, the wild strawberries are sweet — altogether it's a beautiful place to be. Allow plenty of time. Pick a nice day. Take lunch. Enjoy!

There are roller-coaster-like, super-smooth surfing waves at most corners, some whirly pools at high water. And it goes on for hour, after hour, after hour. The river is never boring, is always nice — at high and low water. We surprised a knobbly-kneed moose ankle deep at a river bend the first time we paddled it and saw one running between the trees beside the river the next trip. Everyone I've ever talked with who's been on this section of the river has seen a moose. You'll paddle past wind-carved hoodoos on high earth banks, like sand castles in the sky. Swallows fly in and out of caves in the cliffs. We met five elk while searching for a road to the river. In the morning while driving to the put-in, we saw a black bear, a whitetailed deer, hills splashed with Queen Anne's lace, orange tiger lilies and wild roses like a painting by Elizabeth Fisher. At dusk, while heading back to camp we saw a herd of elk — ten of them beside the road. *Alces* is the scientific name for the genus which includes elk and moose and Alces Lake near the put-in bears the name for good reason. Game abounds. But mostly the lure of this river is the water, all water! It shimmers clear and pale greeny-blue like a rivulet of aquamarines.

During June and July, non-paddlers might get onto a commercial rafting trip through this remote scenic canyon; you start with the upper White and go for two or three days, camping along the way. Arrange it in advance. Check with Glacier Raft Company, P.O. Box 2319E, Banff, Alberta T0L 0C0, telephone at Banff (403)762-4347; at Golden (604)344-6521. Or contact Kootenay River Runners, P.O. Box 81, Edgewater, B.C. V0A 1E0, telephone (604)347-9210.

Topographic maps: 1:50,000 Mount Peck 82J/3, Mount Abruzzi 82J/6 and Fairmont Hot Springs 82J/5.

Facilities: Camping for a fee at nearby provincial park campgrounds beside

you take, from 43.4 to 45.0 kilometers
(27.0 or 28.0 miles); 1 to 1½ hours.
Gravel logging roads

Season: May through September. Snow-
melt and rain-fed, and glacial-melt keep
the natural flow going. We paddled it in
late June and in early August; precise
riverflow unavailable; my guess is
riverflows ranging from 15 to 50 m³/s
(530 to 1770 cfs)

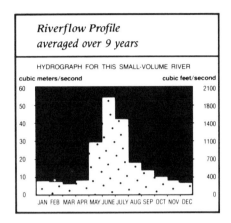

Riverflow Profile
averaged over 9 years

HYDROGRAPH FOR THIS SMALL-VOLUME RIVER

Alces Lake and Whiteswan Lake with picnic tables, pit toilets and fire rings
as well as a marine campsite across Whiteswan Lake that you could paddle to.

Lussier Hot Springs is nearby and perfect for after paddling, if you can still
move after a long day on the White; and there's camping for a fee at a small
provincial campsite very near it, if you can get in. My first time on the White, I
skipped dinner and went straight to the springs — don't leave the area without dipping in. It takes only 15 minutes from the put-in to Lussier; go back towards Highway 93/95 for 14.2 kilometers (8.8 miles). It's at the "16 km"
signpost, and you'll see a covered stairway on the Lussier River side of the
road. Park at the roadside and walk 100 paces down steep steps and a gravel
path to a wooden shack which houses one hot pool. Between the shack and

Roller wave at low water

Waves at corners

Tiger lilies

Bull elk

86

the Lussier River, there are three more pools beneath the stars, and the closer to the river you get, the cooler the water, but it's all steaming! Altogether there's room for two dozen or so people to luxuriate. They're magnificent primitive hot springs.

From the put-in, you could also reach primitive springs in a wild mountain setting at Ram Creek in 1 hour — these springs are warm not hot, but with their own special charm. Best on a warm, sunny day. They're situated in the cleft of a hillside. You sit in the pool looking out over a narrow, small valley with a big bright southern exposure in front of you and trees on the mountainside behind. When we were there, winds were wild and a tall tree crashed into the valley above and behind us. Despite the wild winds or whatever, sitting in these springs, you feel like you're King of the Mountain.

Another hot springs option is at Fairmont: if you've completed your shuttle the night before the run and you're leaving from the take-out, you could reach the commercially operated pools at Fairmont in 45 minutes.

Fishing at Alces Lake

Guidelines: Almost immediately after launching, you're into the most technically difficult rapid on the run. At low water, it's a rock garden and maneuvering is required. With very high water, it could be washed out. But with medium riverflow it's technical. So, watch for it. However, from then on the message is water, water, and more water. With high riverflow, fun waves 1 meter (3 feet) high and greater, are all down the river. Even with low riverflow, there are few rocks, and there's one big roller wave to play in.

Overall gradient averages 8 meters/kilometer (40 feet/mile). River width averages 30 meters (100 feet) and narrows to 12 meters (40 feet) in the canyon where a glistening waterfall spills over sparkly phyllite rock walls into the clear, pale greeny-blue river. At low water, the narrowest passage is 8 meters (26 feet). Again, it's in the canyon, where there's a series of three waves which are 1 meter (3 feet) high: spun silver plumes spray from the tops of them and the wonderful big roller wave is at the bottom of the set.

Riverflow is the biggest variable to consider on this run. During June and July, you can probably get an eyeball report on White riverflow — at the least you can get an idea of what the riverflow is like on the east side of the Trench: contact Glacier Raft Company, P.O. Box 2319E, Banff, Alberta T0L 0C0, telephone at Banff (403)762-4347 or at Golden (604)344-6521. Or try Kootenay River Runners, P.O. Box 81, Edgewater, B.C. V0A 1E0, telephone (604)347-9210. After riverflow, the greatest potential problem on this run is that you are far from any road; there is no place to climb out if you change your mind or if you get tired. It's a long run. And, if you go all the way to the Kootenay, there's an hour of flatwater paddling at the end. Set up your shuttle a day in advance so you can enjoy an unhurried day on the river.

Rocky Mountains behind

Access to take-outs and put-in: Located on the east side of the Columbia-Windermere Valley. The take-out is 45 minutes from Canal Flats.

Head north out of Canal Flats past the general store and post office, and just past the fire hall, turn right into McGrath and almost immediately left into Kootenay River Forest Road with sage brush beside it. New industrial roads appear all the time, but you continue on the west bank of the Kootenay for 34 kilometers (21 miles) to a junction; turn right and cross the Kootenay-River-Lower-Crossing (26 Mile) Bridge. Head up the hill. Go for 1.2 kilometers (0.7 mile) to a fork in the road, stay right and go 1.9 kilometers (1.2 miles) more to a dirt track on the right-hand side. If the roads are wet, this one might be impassable for some cars; check it out before you drive down; also there is very little turn-around space at the bottom. But it's 1.6 kilometers (1.0 mile) to the take-out and there is a good primitive campsite beside the river.

Alternate take-out: if the dirt track is washed out, you could return to the Kootenay River, cross it, and head downstream for 2.1 kilometers (1.3 miles) or to a point where you can see a river flowing in from the other side (it is the White) and leave a shuttle vehicle at the roadside. Bushwhack to the river making your own trail, and hang a colorful marker so you'll find your vehicle at the end of the day. Note that this is the easiest access to the water at this alternate take-out, but it is slightly upstream on the Kootenay from where the White River flows in. Therefore, at the end of the White River run, as soon as you paddle into the Kootenay, turn upstream and ferry across as quickly as possible. Then, line your boat upstream to the trail you made and scramble through the underbrush to your vehicle. The lining and portage were not difficult, but mosquitoes marauded us at this point. There are relatively few mosquitoes in most of this region, and they vary with the season but so does water. And they go together. So — good luck!

For the put-in: head uphill, turn right into White-Rock Forest Road, which is the main logging road. go 5.3 kilometers (3.3 miles) to a fork in it; keep right and go 24.7 kilometers (15.3 miles) to another fork in the road, where you stay right, again, and cross a bridge over Elk Creek. Continue for 11.3 kilometers (7.0 miles) to the put-in bridge over the White. Depending on the condition of the road, this direct route might take 1 to 1½ hours: whenever I've travelled White-Rock Forest Road it has been extremely rough and filled with potholes. An alternate approach to the put-in is possible and might be preferable. Before going, you might want to check on the condition of White-Rock Forest Road with the Ministry of Forests.

In the event that White-Rock Forest Road is impassable, or, if you simply choose to travel a greater distance on roads likely to be in better condition, but in about the same amount of time, you could return to Canal Flats, and go from there to the put-in. The circuitous route will take 1½ hours:

For this roundabout route to the put-in: from Canal Flats, head south on Highway 93/95; after crossing the bridge over the Kootenay, go 4.6 kilometers (2.9 miles) and turn left up the good gravel road signposted to "Whiteswan Lake Provincial Park". It's Whiteswan Forest Road. From the highway, it will take you 35 minutes to reach the put-in. When you've gone 17.9 kilometers (11.1 miles) you'll pass Lussier Hot Springs; continue, keeping on the main road past Alces and Whiteswan lakes, and go 14.2 kilometers (8.8 miles) more to the put-in bridge.

Travel is permitted 24 hours a day on Kootenay River, White-Rock and Whiteswan Forest Roads which are open to the public. However, logging traffic could be on them too, so drive with your headlights on. The best times to use them are weekends, holidays, and weekdays before 5 a.m. and after 5 p.m. To learn about road conditions and also about possible fire-hazard closures, contact the Ministry of Forests, Invermere District, P.O. Box 189, Invermere, B.C. V0A 1K0, telephone (604)342-4200.

WHITE RIVER
Upper Section

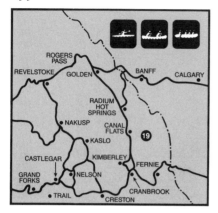

Who: Advanced and expert kayakers; advanced rafters with guides and expert rafters. At low water, also intermediate kayakers; expert open-canoeists and guided intermediates; advanced and intermediate rafters

Water to expect: Continuous Class 3, a Class 4 boulder rapid (easy to portage), some Class 2. Small volume; steady gradient most of the way; some technical

Length of run: 10.0 kilometers (6.2 miles); 2½ hours

Shuttle one way: 10.0 kilometers (6.2 miles); 15 minutes. Gravel logging road

Why go: Continuous action — you'll find good surfing waves, holes and rapids on the river, the most notorious being the S-Bend. Orange tiger lilies among the rocks on shore. Primitive hot springs to warm up in, 15 minutes from the take-out. And during June and July there are frequent commercially operated rafting trips but you must book for them; see the "Guidelines" section for a couple of rafting contacts.

Topographic map: 1:50,000 Mount Peck 82J/3.

Facilities: You could pitch tents on vacant Crown land at either of the put-ins where camping is free, which is especially convenient if you're going the back way to the Bull River next — crossing the mountains on logging roads. Or, you'll find a great variety of lakeside and riverside camping for a fee with picnic tables, pit toilets and fire rings at 100 sites scattered between Whiteswan Lake and Lussier Hot Springs — all in the highly developed Whiteswan Lake Provincial Park.

Lussier Hot Springs is close-by and a good hot soak in these casually developed primitive springs is an excellent treat after paddling — don't leave the region without going there. It's only 15 minutes from the take-out back towards Highway 93/95. Past Whiteswan and Alces lakes look for Coyote-Lussier Forest Road. Do not turn into it, but measure the distance. From this junction, continue along Whiteswan Road for 3.3 kilometers (2.0 miles) more to the hot springs. There is a canopy over the top few steps leading down the hill to the springs. Park by the roadside and walk 100 paces down the steep gravel path.

From the take-out, you could reach more primitive springs in a wild mountain setting beside Ram Creek in 55 minutes — they're warm not hot, but have their own special charm. And, after the upper White run, you might have time to reach them while it's still light: on your first visit to Ram Creek via the back roads, you need to look for the springs during daylight hours. The route was poorly signposted when we were there; in addition, the final road

Season: May through September. Best in late June. Snow-melt and rain-fed, and glacial-melt natural flow. We paddled it in late June during runoff; precise riverflow unavailable; my guess is 52 m³/s (1840 cfs)

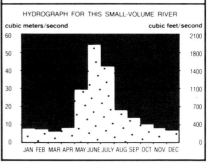

Riverflow Profile
averaged over 9 years

HYDROGRAPH FOR THIS SMALL-VOLUME RIVER

cubic meters/second | cubic feet/second

S-Bend in June

to Ram Creek over the mountain from the White was a restricted logging road. Be warned: during daylight hours, you might have to wait for the end of the working day to travel the last 5 kilometers (3 miles) over the mountain to the springs. But then, after you're blissed out from soaking, it's an easy drive in the dark down to Highway 93/95.

Or you could reach the giant commercially operated hot pools at Fairmont in 45 minutes by leaving the river on Whiteswan Forest Road and returning the way you came in. At Fairmont you can enjoy enormous hot pools and hot showers too.

Guidelines: The S-Bend calls for scouting. When you set up the shuttle, stop and view it from the bank above. And, on the river you can scout it from the rocks on the "river left" shore. New rockslides come down each year, changing the assortment of rubble that makes this rapid, but there are always lots of "paddle grabbers". When we kayaked it, this spot was a Class 4 stretch with a large hole across the top left-hand passage. On the right, there were a couple of projecting rocks the locals called the Shark's Teeth. Straight ahead, a rooster tail off one rock, another rock just barely showing — and the biggest hole was at the bottom of it all. For rafters, it's easier at very high and very low levels. It's steep in this section, but overall gradient averages only 11 meters/kilometer (60 feet/mile).

Throughout the run the river is 30 to 40 meters (100 to 130 feet) wide. It's not particularly narrow. Therefore I was surprised to be told of a tree that was low and very difficult to see. And it *was* there: a killer. So, watch for wood.

The river is often up. When the summer sun shines, glacial-melt combines with snow-melt and swells the White as well as making it murky with glacial flour. And it's cold. With high water, it's good to have an Eskimo roll.

If you want an idea of riverflow during June and July, you can probably get an eyeball report — at least you can get an idea of what riverflow is like on the east side of the Trench — from Glacier Raft Company, P.O. Box 2319E, Banff, Alberta T0L 0C0, telephone at Banff (403)762-4347 or at Golden (604)344-6521. Or try Kootenay River Runners, P.O. Box 81, Edgewater, B.C. V0A 1E0, telephone (604)347-9210.

Access to take-out and put-in: Located near Canal Flats off Highway 93/95 on the east side of the Columbia-Windermere Valley — or circle around by back roads from the Bull River Valley over the mountains to the White. To reach the take-out from these different directions:
• From Bull River Valley, head up Bull River Forest Road; at the top of the mountain pass it becomes White River (East Fork) Forest Road and follows the White River East Fork to its confluence with the White. From Bull River 40 Mile Campground to the White takes 1½ hours. When you cross the White River and turn left, you're at the put-in. From there, it's 9.8 kilometers (6.1 miles) downstream to the take-out.
• From Radium, Invermere and Canal Flats, head south on Highway 93/95 and turn off the highway onto a gravel logging road signposted to "White-swan Lake Provincial Park". It is 4.8 kilometers (3.0 miles) south of the Highway 93/95 bridge over the Kootenay at Canal Flats.

Warming up

• From Cranbrook, head north on Highway 93/95. Go for 64 kilometers (40 miles) and when you're 20 minutes past Skookumchuck turn off the highway following the signpost to "Whiteswan Lake Provincial Park".

• From Highway 93/95, it takes 35 minutes to reach the take-out: head up Whiteswan Forest Road. When you've gone 17.9 kilometers (11.1 miles) you'll pass Lussier Hot Springs; continue, keeping on the main road past Alces and Whiteswan lakes, for 14.2 kilometers (8.8 miles) more to the take-out bridge.

To reach the put-in, cross the bridge, turn right and head upstream on White River Forest Road. Go 5.0 kilometers (3.1 miles) to a lookout where you can view the S-Bend far below. After taking a look, continue 4.2 kilometers (2.6 miles) more and carry over a gravel bar and put in. Or, continue on the road for 0.6 kilometer (0.4 mile) and turn right to another put-in.

Travel is permitted 24 hours a day on Whiteswan and White River Forest Roads which are open to the public. However, logging traffic could be on them too, so drive with your headlights on. The best times to use them are weekends, holidays, and weekdays before 5 a.m. and after 5 p.m. To learn about possible fire-hazard closures, contact the Ministry of Forests, Invermere District, P.O. Box 189, Invermere, B.C. V0A 1K0, telephone (604)342-4200.

BULL RIVER
40 Mile to Sulphur Creek

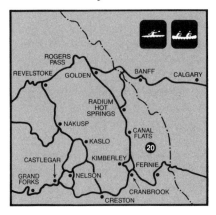

Who: Intermediate to expert kayakers and guided novices; expert open-canoeists and guided intermediates; no rafters

Water to expect: Class 2- to 2+, with a Class 5 to 6 drop (portagable). Medium volume, slowly flowing stream; mostly straightforward braided channels, but with surprise narrowing at bedrock

Length of run: 9.5 kilometers (5.9 miles); 2 to 3 hours

Shuttle one way: 9.7 kilometers (6.0 miles); 10 minutes. Gravel logging road with radio-controlled traffic

Why go: For a pleasant amble along a gravelly braided stretch; to see an elegant, natural rock gate and a perfectly-squared-off rock ledge forming a natural weir — all sitting in some of the most fabulous Rocky Mountain scenery in the world. This upper Bull run has a high mountain feeling and wild game is all around. While setting up shuttle, we saw two moose; you might also see black bears, blue herons, whitetailed deer, harlequin duck, grouse and porcupines.

Topographic maps: 1:50,000 Queen Creek 82G/14 and Fernie 82G/11.

Facilities: You'll find spacious camping at the 40 Mile put-in where picnic tables, a pit toilet and fire rings are provided free by the forest service. After paddling the Bull the first time, we celebrated at 40 Mile with an engagement party for two kayakers — it's a big area, good for a big party.

To reach the closest hot springs, cross over the mountains to White River (East Fork) Forest Road following signposts toward Whiteswan Lake and find your way to Lussier, some of the most wonderful primitive hot springs in the Kootenays. They're beside the Lussier River, 1½ hours from 40 Mile.

Guidelines: After putting in at 40 Mile, you'll drift along for more than an hour on the broad, braided stretch of the river with riffles. There are small standing waves that pile up at river bends that are fun. But watch for fallen trees and sweepers which are the greatest hazard. It's not pushy. However, if you don't pay attention the wood could be dangerous. The overall gradient averages 7 meters/kilometer (35 feet/mile), but in the last 5.5 kilometers (3.4 miles) of the run, the river drops at the rate of 11 meters/kilometer (60 feet/mile). In the braided section, width averages 45 meters (150 feet); later, near the end of the run, the canyon narrows to 8 meters (26 feet): this is the "Weir".

At the "Weir", the passage is narrow — the river also plunges ⅔ to 1 meter to 2 to 3 feet), depending on riverflow, to the base of the bedrock ledge. The "Weir" ledge forms an extremely dangerous hole across the width of the

Season: May through August. Snow-melt, rain-fed and glacial-melt. Natural flow, the dam on this one is below the runs. I've paddled it from early July through mid-August with riverflows ranging from 24 to 99 m³/s (850 to 3500 cfs)

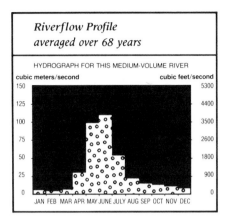

Riverflow Profile
averaged over 68 years

HYDROGRAPH FOR THIS MEDIUM-VOLUME RIVER

river. Scout the "Weir" on your way upstream, and flag it. On the river, once you're through the gorgeous rock gate, look for the next signs of approach:

When the canyon narrows and the walls on "river right" become smooth, straight rock and you see caves — look on "river left" for the flagged take-out you've decided on. Haul out on the right-hand bank, climb the rounded rocks, head downstream and you'll see the "Weir". It's a scramble of a portage — about 100 paces, and it is difficult to carry a heavy boat over the rocks, but if you paddle this run you'll probably want to. This natural weir *has* been run in a kayak, at higher levels, but is an extremely straight, steep ledge, and the hole at its base would be a killer keeper if you landed in it sideways.

Past the "Weir", put in to paddle the narrow straight rock gardens below, it's 5 minutes to the gravel bar take-out at Sulphur Creek.

Leaving killer "Weir" behind

Access to take-outs and put-ins: The Bull River is south of Canal Flats between Cranbrook and Fernie; also you can circle around the back way into the Bull River Valley by way of logging roads from Lussier Hot Springs and the White River. To reach the take-out from these different directions:

• From the White River, shortly past the put-in for the upper section, head south across the mountains on White River (East Fork) Forest Road. It will take 1½ hours to the take-out. You'll enter Bull River Forest Road at 40 Mile: this is the put-in. Head downstream to the bridge over Sulphur Creek. The take-out is at a gravel bar on the Bull just downstream from it.

• From Fernie it takes 1 to 2¼ hours to reach the take-out at Sulphur Creek. If you like back roads, one way to go is directly from Fernie to Sulphur Creek; it takes 1 hour on Hartley Lake Forest Road, a rough gravel logging road which is sometimes maintained. Before you try to drive it, check with the Ministry of Forests: Hartley Lake Forest Road might not be passable.

The surest route from Fernie to the Bull is on Highways 3 and 3/93 by way of Elko, Galloway and Jaffary; then on logging roads into the Bull. This takes 2¼ hours. Heading west on Highway 3/93, past Elko and Jaffray you descend a long hill to Lake Koocanusa. When you see the lake on your left-hand side and a bridge over it, do not cross the bridge. Look for signposts just before the bridge directing you to turn right to the "Kootenay Trout Hatchery", "Norbury Lake Provincial Park" and the "Bull River Guest Ranch". Follow these signposts. Pass the Bull River Pub on your left-hand side; cross the river, pass the trout hatchery, and climb a long hill to a major gravel road that cuts off of the secondary highway you're on. It is just before a major power-transmission line. Turn right up the gravel road with signposts to the "Bull River Guest Ranch" and to the "Power Plant". This is your turnoff to head upriver to the take-out.

• From Cranbrook, it takes 2 hours to reach the Sulphur Creek take-out. From Tamarack Shopping Centre, head east on Highway 3/95 toward Fort Steele, Wasa, Canal Flats, Invermere and Radium. Cross the Kootenay River and pass the Fort Steele Heritage Town on your left-hand side. Turn right in front of Fort Steele R.V. Park into the Wardner-Fort Steele Road; go on it for 22 kilometers (13½ miles) and then turn left up a gravel road following a large yellow signpost to "Bull River Guest Ranch" and a smaller signpost to the "Power Plant". This is your turnoff to head upriver to the take-out.

• From Radium, Invermere and Canal Flats, head south on Highway 93/95 to Fort Steele Heritage Town. At the junction, do not turn right toward Cranbrook; keep going straight, passing the Fort Steele R.V. Park on your left, and go 22 kilometers (13½ miles) on the Wardner-Fort Steele Road. On the way, you'll pass turnoffs to Horseshoe Lake and Norbury Provincial Park where you could camp. Go to the signposts for the "Bull River Guest Ranch" and the "Power Plant". This is your turnoff to head upriver to the take-out.

For the take-out: from the Wardner-Fort Steele Road turnoff, head upriver on Bull River Forest Road for 1¼ hours. It takes 15 minutes to reach the left-hand turnoff where you head up the road on which you might meet logging traffic. On the way, you'll cross a bridge over a narrow rock canyon of the Bull — a hint of what's to come. It's so narrow, you can see why the

Sparkling blue water, pristine peaks

river was dammed near here and you can see why some of the passages are like they are. Continue to a fork in the road and turn left. From this point, there might be a great deal of logging traffic. Head upstream past the Bull River Head Pond, soon cross a bridge over the Bull, then much later another one; continue to a third bridge, and the take-out is at a gravel bar downstream from this bridge over Sulphur Creek.

To reach the put-in: measure the distance from the bridge at Sulphur Creek, head upstream. Go for 0.6 kilometer (0.4 mile) and park at the roadside — you'll be just past the "50 km" signpost. Bushwhack 60 paces down a slope through the woods and look over the bank to the "Weir"; walk upstream and place a marker where you want to take out for the portage. Then continue driving upstream for 9.5 kilometers (5.9 miles) to a fork in the road near Quinn (Queen) Creek. Turn left down the dirt track into the 40 Mile Campground at the confluence of Quinn Creek and the Bull.

The creek was named after two brothers who were trappers and whose name was Quinn. Apparently the name of the creek was garbled when the first topographic maps were made and it's shown on them as Queen Creek, but it's referred to by locals as Quinn Creek, and the *Gazetteer of Canada, British Columbia* confirms that the name Queen has been rescinded and Quinn is the correct one.

Travel is open to the public on Bull River Forest Road; however, there is a great deal of logging traffic. The safest times to travel are on weekends, holidays, and weekdays before 5 a.m. and after 5 p.m. Logging traffic might be on the road, even then, so always drive with your headlights on and drive extremely cautiously.

During working hours, you could go in by following a radio-controlled vehicle; or if you have a VHF (very high frequency) radio, find out the frequency they're on, listen to it, and go. For information on radio frequency, where trucks are hauling, and fire-hazard closure, contact Galloway Lumber Company Ltd., General Delivery, Galloway, B.C. V0B 1P0, telephone (604)429-3496; or the Ministry of Forests, Cranbrook District, 1902 Theatre Road, Cranbrook, B.C. V1C 4H4, telephone (604)426-3391.

BULL RIVER
Mini-Canyon

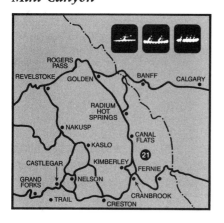

Who: Advanced and expert kayakers and intermediates with an Eskimo roll; no open-canoeists; advanced and expert rafters, at high levels. At low levels, intermediate to expert kayakers; and expert open-canoeists but no rafters

Water to expect: Class 3+ and 2, at high levels; at low levels, Class 3 and 2- with a Class 4 to 4+ drop (portagable). Medium volume. A continuous technical rapid, rock gardens and braided sections

Length of run: 9.5 kilometers (5.9 miles); 2 to 3 hours

Shuttle one way: 8.6 kilometers

Why go: Cruncher Drop is the snapper on this run. Good stuff! — or bad stuff! It depends on what happens to you. When I kayaked it the first time, this section provided a little too much Bull!

I was on an off-spell and swimming before the run had hardly begun, and had to pay off *two* rescuers with a bottle of wine each. When I kayaked it again, I found it to be summer paddling at its best, and on every visit I've found the camping and game-watching and flowers superb — not to mention Lussier Hot Springs which helped ease the bumps and bruises from my swims.

The contrasts of the Bull are extreme — there's a surprise on every run. The river comes in jerks and spurts. And it's bedrock that does it; bedrock creates Cruncher Drop at the start of the Mini-Canyon; bedrock makes the Slot in the Bull Canyon run; it makes the natural rock gates and the natural rock "Weir" in the 40 Mile to Sulphur Creek run. Bedrock makes the Bull.

Topographic map: 1:50,000 Fernie 82G/11.

Facilities: A campground is close-by beside Sulphur Creek. From the take-out, head upstream beside the Bull across the bridge over the creek. Almost immediately, turn right into a narrow dirt track and go for 2.0 kilometers (1.2 miles) to the grassy area beside the creek where you'll find picnic tables, pit toilets and fire rings provided free by the forest service. But this creekside site doesn't have the wonderful views that you find beside the Bull — and you might prefer the primitive tent space at the Sulphur Creek and the Bull River confluence even though there are no facilities there; or drive for 10 minutes upriver to the spacious campground at 40 Mile. At all sites, even when the water looks crystal clear, boil it before drinking it.

And the nearest hot springs from the take-out? Over the mountains — it's 2¼ hours to Lussier Hot Springs near the White River. If you're heading across the mountains to paddle the White, it's worth it. Or, going the other direction, from the junction of the Bull River Forest Road and the Wardner-

(5.3 miles); 10 minutes. Gravel logging road with radio-controlled traffic

Season: May through mid-August. Snow-melt and rain-fed, and glacial-melt keeps it going. Natural flow. We've paddled it from early July through mid-August with riverflows ranging from 24 to 99 m³/s (850 to 3500 cfs)

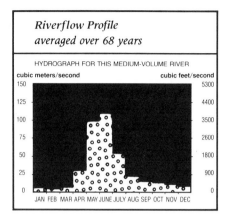

Riverflow Profile averaged over 68 years

HYDROGRAPH FOR THIS MEDIUM-VOLUME RIVER

cubic meters/second		cubic feet/second
150		5300
125		4400
100		3500
75		2600
50		1800
25		900
0		0

JAN FEB MAR APR MAY JUNE JULY AUG SEP OCT NOV DEC

Fort Steele Road, it takes an hour to reach the commercially operated hot springs at Fairmont; another 25 minutes to Radium.

Guidelines: At the Sulphur Creek put-in, you could easily be lulled into complacency by the mellow Class 2 riffles. But don't be. As you round the first corner to the left you're into it; continuous, bouncy Class 3 rapids feed into Cruncher Drop.

At high water, the Cruncher is a technical Class 3+ mine-bed of tricky, scattered holes requiring maneuvering. And you better be ready to maneuver and have your roll working. At low water, it's Class 4. At very low water, the sharp rocks choking the entry passage are exposed and it's plastic-boat country — possibly Class 4+. Short but intense. At all levels, scout Cruncher Drop

Brimming full

from the road before putting in. From the Cruncher on, the intensity eases and you can "come down". It's easy Class 3, then it's Class 2. The upper Mini-Canyon continues for 1.6 kilometers (1.0 mile); at the last drop in the upper section, a smooth flat slab of bedrock flows into a head wall. It would scrape a lot of bottoms at low water. After Bedrock Corner, the river banks expand into broad braided channels. And, at the end of the run, the river narrows and there's a gentle rock garden between low canyon walls. You can see it from the take-out.

Mini-Canyon run vital statistics: gradient averages 11 meters/kilometer (60 feet/mile); width ranges from 15 to 30 meters (50 to 100 feet); and it flows for a long season, but the entry to Cruncher Drop becomes dangerously bony in late summer. However, you could portage it.

Access to take-outs and put-ins: The Bull River is south of Canal Flats between Cranbrook and Fernie; also you can circle around the back way into the Bull River Valley by way of logging roads from Lussier Hot Springs and the White River. To reach the take-out from these different directions:
• From the White River, shortly past the put-in for the upper section, head south across the mountains on White River (East Fork) Forest Road. It will take 1¾ hours to reach the take-out. You'll enter Bull River Forest Road at 40 Mile; from there, head downstream following the Bull. You'll cross a bridge over Sulphur Creek — this is the put-in; continue downstream to another bridge across the Bull. This is the take-out.
• From Fernie it takes 1¼ to 2 hours to reach the take-out: it's located downstream from the Sulphur Creek and Bull River confluence.

If you like back roads, you might be able to go directly from Fernie to Sulphur Creek. When Hartley Lake Forest Road is open, it takes 1 hour to the Sulphur Creek put-in, then ¼ hour downstream to the take-out. Before you go, check with the Ministry of Forests in Cranbrook: Hartley Lake Forest Road might not be passable.

The surest route from Fernie to the Bull is on Highways 3 and 3/93 by way of Elko, Galloway and Jaffary; then on logging roads into the Bull. This takes 2¼ hours. Heading west on Highway 3/93, west of Elko and Jaffray you pass through some hilly country before descending a long hill to Lake Koocanusa. When you see the lake on your left-hand side and a bridge over it, do not cross the bridge. Look for signposts just before the bridge directing you to turn right to the "Kootenay Trout Hatchery", "Norbury Lake Provincial Park" and the "Bull River Guest Ranch". Follow these signposts. Pass the Bull River Pub on your left-hand side; cross the river, pass the trout hatchery and climb a long hill to a major gravel road leaving the secondary highway you're on. It is just before a major power-transmission line. Turn right up the gravel road with signposts to the "Bull River Guest Ranch" and to the "Power Plant". This is your turnoff to head upriver to the take-out.
• From Cranbrook, it takes 1¾ hours to reach the Mini-Canyon take-out. From Tamarack Shopping Centre, head east on Highway 3/95 toward Fort Steele, Invermere and Radium. Cross the Kootenay River and pass the Fort Steele Heritage Town on your left-hand side. Turn right in front of Fort Steele R.V. Park into the Wardner-Fort Steele Road; go on it for 22 kilometers

Campground at 40 Mile

(13½ miles) and then turn left up a gravel road following a large yellow signpost to "Bull River Guest Ranch" and a smaller signpost to the"Power Plant". This is your turnoff to head upriver to the take-out.

• From Radium, Invermere and Canal Flats, head south on Highway 93/95. When south of Skookumchuck, take the Wasa (not Kimberley) route toward Cranbrook and Fort Steele Heritage Town. At the Fort Steele junction, do not turn right toward Cranbrook; keep going straight, passing the Fort Steele R.V. Park on your left-hand side, and, again, go 22 kilometers (13½ miles) on the Wardner-Fort Steele Road to the signposts for the "Power Plant" and "Bull River Guest Ranch". This is your turnoff to head upriver to the take-out.

For the take-out: from the Wardner-Fort Steele Road turnoff, drive up Bull River Forest Road for 45 minutes. It takes 15 minutes to reach the fork in the road where you turn left and start following the river: on the way to this turnoff, you'll cross a bridge over a narrow rock canyon of the Bull; continue to the fork in the road and turn left. From this point, there might be a great deal of logging traffic. Head upstream past the Bull River Head Pond, soon cross a bridge over the Bull, then in 20 minutes another one. You'll see the take-out up a steep bank beside this bridge.

For the put-in: continue up Bull River Forest Road to the bridge over Sulphur Creek. From here, walk or drive downstream 0.6 kilometer (0.4 mile) to look at Cruncher Drop; then return to Sulphur Creek and put in.

Travel is open to the public on Bull River Forest Road *if* you are equipped for it with a VHF (very high frequency) radio or *if* you are willing to wait for a logging truck to follow in. The safest times to travel are on weekends, holidays, and weekdays before 5 a.m. and after 5 p.m. Logging traffic might be on the road, even then, so always drive with your headlights on and drive extremely cautiously.

During working hours, you could go in by following a radio-controlled vehicle; or if you have a VHF radio, find out the frequency the logging trucks are on, listen to it, and go. For information on radio frequency, where trucks are hauling, and fire-hazard closure, contact Galloway Lumber Company Ltd., General Delivery, Galloway, B.C. V0B 1P0, telephone (604)429-3496; or contact the Ministry of Forests, Cranbrook District, 1902 Theatre Road, Cranbrook, B.C. V1C 4H4, (604)426-3391.

BULL RIVER
Canyon

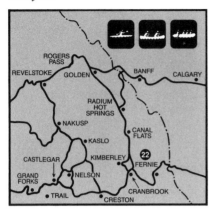

ROGERS PASS
REVELSTOKE GOLDEN BANFF CALGARY
RADIUM HOT SPRINGS
NAKUSP
CANAL FLATS
KASLO
CASTLEGAR KIMBERLEY **22**
FERNIE
GRAND FORKS NELSON
TRAIL CRANBROOK
CRESTON

Who: Advanced and expert kayakers; no open-canoeists; advanced and expert rafters who are guided, for canyon run.

Top warm-up section, also guided novice kayakers and intermediates; intermediate and expert open-canoeists; and all rafters

Water to expect: Canyon run, Class 4 to 4+, and Class 3. Drops and pools to the bridge, continuous technical rapids through canyon. Pushy at high levels, becoming dangerously bony when low.

Top warm-up section, Class 2; straightforward, swiftly flowing, steady gradient. Medium volume and cold

Length of run: 12.4 kilometers (7.7 miles) for full run; 4 hours.

Why go: Contrasty, short and snappy — it's one of the most dramatic runs in British Columbia. The river progresses from lively, sparkling blue water bubbling over a broad gravelly bottom with wild roses beside it, from Class 2 riffles and rock gardens to Class 3 boulder drops, to fun bouncy haystack waves that are 2 meters (6 feet) high beneath the bridge at high water, to the challenging and continuous churning rapids and holes in the Class 4 black-rock-walled canyon where you slip through the turbulent nozzle-like Slot into placid river then the reservoir. In the reservoir, each dip of your paddle makes myriad rings on the smooth surface as you head toward the take-out tree hanging out over the still water; and to complete the run, you climb sharp rocks up the steep bank to the road. The Bull has it all.

While paddling, you might see orange tiger lilies blooming close beside the river and glance upstream to see sweeping, Rocky Mountain scenery high above the clear blue water. The Bull is rough and tough but also beautiful. It's available for a long season because it is glacial-fed. Another thing about it — all boaters can enjoy the top warm-up run, it is excellent for groups with mixed abilities and different crafts. Non-paddlers might experience the Bull Canyon too from May through mid-August as there are occasional commercially operated rafting trips. Inquire in Fernie.

After paddling, you'll find some of the nicest informal camping in British Columbia beside the Bull, a great pub close-by, and wilderness hot springs that are 1½ to 2 hours away on your way to the next river.

Topographic map: 1:50,000 Fernie 82G/11.

Facilities: Excellent informal camping and a home-away-from-home kind of pub are near the canyon take-out.

Camping beside the Bull: you'll find space to pitch tents amongst wild strawberries, yellow peas, Indian paintbrush and wild roses at the put-in. And, camping is free in this open-range country where we were stopped on the road by hordes of cattle, and wakened by cows mooing around our tents

Canyon run, 5.1 kilometers (3.2 miles);
1 to 2 hours. (920 to 3670 cfs)
Top warm-up section, 7.2 kilometers
(4.5 miles); 2 to 3 hours

Shuttle one way: 12.6 kilometers
(7.8 miles) for full run; 35 minutes.
Canyon run, 5.7 kilometers (3.5 miles);
15 minutes.
Top warm-up run; 6.9 kilometers
(4.3 miles), 20 minutes
Gravel logging road with radio-
controlled traffic

Season: May through August; Snow-
melt, rainfall and glacial-melt keep the
natural riverflow going. I've paddled it
from early July through mid-August with
riverflows ranging from 26 to 104 m³/s

(920 to 3670 cfs)

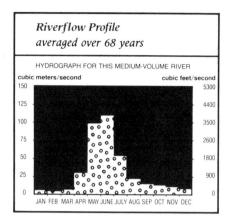

Riverflow Profile
averaged over 68 years

HYDROGRAPH FOR THIS MEDIUM-VOLUME RIVER

in the morning. A lovely riverside site. On your way in or out of the Bull River
area, you'll find free camping provided by the forest service at Horseshoe Lake
where there are picnic tables, pit toilets and fire rings; this recreation site sur-
rounds the lake and is wonderfully spacious for large groups. And, you'll find
camping for a fee with picnic tables, pit toilets and fire rings at Norbury Lake
Provincial Park. Both campgrounds are signposted off the Wardner-Fort Steele
Road and are 20 or 25 minutes from the canyon take-out. On your way out of
the Bull River Valley, turn right to find them.

Top warm-up section in late August

The Bull River Pub is 20 minutes from the canyon take-out. It's a great place to meet after a day on the river — the food and ambience are good enough to lure a great many locals. You'll find horseshoe tournaments on Sundays, historic artifacts, moose antlers, beautifully mounted bear and mountain goat, old photographs — you'll find the story of the Bull all over the walls of the pub. The river was named after a prospector named Bull who found small quantities of gold in the river. But the promise of water power and the wealth it would bring was what attracted settlers to Bull River in 1905, and the first hydro dam was built in 1910. To find the pub after paddling, turn left onto the Wardner-Fort Steele Road. It's just down the road.

Ram Creek Hot Springs is 1½ hours away — and it's the same to the commercially operated hot springs at Fairmont. The primitive springs at Lussier can be reached in 2 hours: go the back way up the Bull River Valley and over the mountains to White River (East Fork) Forest Road. If you're heading to the White River next, this hot springs stop makes sense.

Primitive campsite beside put-in

Guidelines: This Bull River run starts quietly and builds. Gradient of the top warm-up section averages 4 meters/kilometer (20 feet/mile); the canyon run gradient averages 7 meters/kilometer (35 feet/mile). It is evenly distributed and gradually increasing on both sections; the excitement in the canyon is created by the narrowing.

• Top warm-up section: at the put-in, the river is broad and gravel-bottomed: width averages 30 meters (100 feet) but watch for sweepers and fallen trees throughout the run. It's straightforward Class 2 for 7 kilometers (4 miles). Then subtly the pace changes; just past the take-out for the top warm-up section, boulders are scattered across the river signalling the start of serious paddling.

• Bull Canyon: Class 2 rock gardens spiked with Class 3 drops follow; there are some big holes and waves. And it builds.

When you go beneath the logging road bridge and then past the concrete piers of the washed-out bridge, be ready for continuous Class 3 rapids and/or holes, depending on water level, for the next 2 kilometers (1 mile). Canyon waves might be 1 to 2 meters (3 to 6 feet) high — when the water is piling up, this section is choice. While the river is getting slightly steeper, it is narrowing a great deal. The bedrock chokes in and the last rapid culminates in a passage that is a kayak-length wide at the nozzle-like Slot. You must get through it to exit the canyon and enter the final 1 kilometer (½ mile) stretch of slowly flowing river that goes into the head pond above Aberfeldie Dam which is referred to by paddlers as the reservoir. The Slot is guarded by a good roller wave. The length of the last rapid, the continuous nature of it and the difficulty of the last drop added together make this run a Class 4 — or more, depending on level. When it's very high or very low, it's Class 4+.

If you're paddling the canyon run for the first time on a given day, from the washed-out bridge on, you *must* be under complete control in your approach to the final narrow Slot. And this is true, whatever the riverflow.

However, if someone in your group has checked it out that day and you know the Slot passage is clear, you might take the less strong paddlers in your group, because you know if you muck up, probably the worst that will happen is that you'll wash out into the calm water of the reservoir. The day I swam in this section, I was towed to shore and climbed up the steep bank before the Slot; my running shoes were found circulating in an eddy in the quiet section of river past the Slot; my boat and paddle washed into the reservoir.

What are the usual moves through the canyon? Past the washed-out bridge, the river curves around to the left, and most boaters eddy out on the right-hand side just before the Slot for a breather and to check that it is not obstructed. Then, if the passage is clear, you can ferry across to "river left" and shoot through the nozzle into the slowly moving river and reservoir.

The Bull is not to be underestimated — I'm personally convinced. I had enjoyed a bombproof roll for a period of 1½ years immediately prior to my first time running the Bull. But, then, within two days I managed to demonstrate my swimming abilities in Class 2, 3 and 4 water. Therefore I wanted to go back to kayak, instead of swim it. The next year we returned to paddle the three runs described in this guidebook again; and, on the canyon run, just as we reached the washed-out bridge, sleet blew horizontally upriver into our faces, but we all negotiated the canyon successfully without a swim. The third time I was there, it hailed — the hailstones were the size of mothballs.

The Bull flows from the Rocky Mountains and is blessed and cursed with the gamut of weather and cold water and scenery that comes with high-mountains. Be prepared for it. And, take a rope to haul your boat up the Class 5 take-out!

Top warm-up section in early July

Access to take-outs and put-ins: The Bull Canyon is south of Canal Flats near Cranbrook. You can reach it from Highways 3 and 93 between Cranbrook and Fernie; or you can circle around the back way into the Bull River Valley by logging roads from Lussier Hot Springs and the White River. To reach the take-out from these different directions:

• From the White River, shortly past the put-in for the upper section, head east and south across the mountains on White River (East Fork) Forest Road. It will take 2 hours to reach the Bull River take-out. When you leave the White River, know that you'll soon come to the Bull and follow it down the valley with views all along. You'll cross a bridge over Sulphur Creek, then a bridge over the Bull. You'll see a braided section, pass the put-in, cross Van Creek and Dibble Creek, then another bridge over the Bull, and finally reach the Bull River Head Pond referred to by paddlers as the reservoir — it's the take-out for the full run.

• From Cranbrook, it takes an hour to reach the canyon take-out. From Tamarack Shopping Centre, head east on Highway 3/95 toward Fort Steele, Wasa, Invermere and Radium. Cross the Kootenay River and pass the Fort Steele Heritage Town on your left. Turn right in front of Fort Steele R.V. Park into the Wardner-Fort Steele Road; go on it for 22 kilometers (13½ miles) passing turnoffs to Horseshoe Lake and Norbury Lake Provincial Park and turn left up a gravel road following a large yellow signpost to "Bull River Guest Ranch" and a smaller signpost to the "Power Plant". Go upriver to the reservoir and to the midway access points for the canyon runs.

• From Radium, Invermere and Canal Flats, head south on Highway 93/95. When south of Skookumchuck, take the Wasa (not Kimberley) route toward Cranbrook and Fort Steele Heritage Town. At the Fort Steele junction, do not turn right toward Cranbrook; keep going straight, passing the Fort Steele R.V. Park on your left-hand side, and, again, go 22 kilometers (13½ miles) on the Wardner-Fort Steele Road. On the way, you'll pass turnoffs to Horseshoe Lake and Norbury Lake Provincial Park where you could camp. Go to the signposts for the "Bull River Guest Ranch" and the "Power Plant": this is your turnoff to head upriver for the canyon runs.

• From Fernie it takes 1½ hours to the take-out. Head west on Highway 3. Past Elko it becomes Highway 3/93; past Jaffray you descend a long hill to Lake Koocanusa. When you see the lake on your left-hand side and a bridge over it, do not cross the bridge. Look for signposts just before the bridge directing you to turn right to the "Kootenay Trout Hatchery", "Norbury Lake Provincial Park" and the "Bull River Guest Ranch". Follow these signposts. Pass the Bull River Pub on your left-hand side; cross the river, pass the trout hatchery, and climb a long hill to a major gravel road that cuts off of the secondary highway you're on. It is just before a major power-transmission line. Turn right up the gravel road with signposts to the "Bull River Guest Ranch" and to the "Power Plant". This is your turnoff to head upriver for the canyon runs.

For the canyon take-out, turn off the Wardner-Fort Steele Road into the gravel road with signposts, and drive for 15 minutes to reach the heavily travelled logging road. On the way, you'll cross a bridge over a narrow rock canyon of the Bull. When you reach a fork in the road, turn left and go 0.7 kilometer (0.4 mile) to the take-out tree leaning out over the reservoir. Just beyond the tree, there is a lay-by on the left-hand side of the road with room for two or three cars to park. The easiest route from the reservoir up the steep rocky slope is below the tree — but it's still a Class 5 take-out!

For the midway take-out and put-in: drive alongside the still reservoir then pass a short wooded section and you'll soon see the Bull. While driving, watch for the concrete piers of the washed-out bridge that are in the riverbed and take a quick look; this is where the continuous action begins in the canyon. A short way upstream you'll cross a bridge over the Bull; from here, drive 1.5 kilometers (0.9 mile) to a rough road leading to the water. Walk down it — don't drive. It's only 120 paces to the take-out eddy; downstream from the eddy, you'll see boulders scattered across the river that signal the entry to the serious canyon run.

For the top put-in, continue driving along the road winding high above the river — you can see views of the river for awhile, and then the road heads downhill and crosses Dibble and Van creeks. Continue driving past Van Creek for 0.9 kilometer (0.6 mile). Go to a dirt track and turn right into a large informal riverside campground and put in. From the midway put-in and take-out, altogether it's 6.9 kilometers (4.3 miles) upstream to this put in.

Travel is open to the public on Bull River Forest Road; however, there is a great deal of logging traffic. The safest times to travel are on weekends, holidays, and weekdays before 5 a.m. and after 5 p.m. Logging traffic might be on the road, even then, so always drive with your headlights on and drive extremely cautiously.

During working hours, you could go in by following a radio-controlled vehicle; or if you have a VHF (very high frequency) radio, find out the frequency they're on, listen to it, and go. For information on radio frequency, where trucks are hauling, and fire-hazard closure, contact Galloway Lumber Company Ltd., General Delivery, Galloway, B.C. V0B 1P0, telephone (604)429-3496; or contact the office of the Ministry of Forests, Cranbrook District, 1902 Theatre Road, Cranbrook, B.C. V1C 4H4, telephone (604)426-3391.

ELK RIVER
Canyon

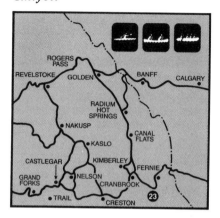

Who: Advanced and expert kayakers and guided intermediates with an Eskimo roll; no open-canoeists; advanced and expert rafters, at high levels. At low levels, intermediate, advanced and expert kayakers; expert open-canoeists; and all rafters

Water to expect: Depending on level, Class 3+ to 4 through remote canyons; Class 2+ to 3 at ledge drops, and Class 2. Large volume. Continuous technical rapids, squirrelly big water, ledge drops and pools

Length of run: 13.0 kilometers

Why go: The expansiveness of it all — big water, deep canyons, giant ledge drops, big birds. The precipitous put-in trail!

An excellent continuous rapid disappears around the corner at the start, worth climbing down the cliff just for it; then, if the water allows time to look as you go, you might see caves dug by prospectors in the walls of the Upper Canyon. But it can be big water. You could have your hands full just running the river. The Middle Canyon is filled with surprise twists and turns, squirrelly eddies, picturesque curvaceous rock walls carved by the current and there's no stopping when it's high water. Then you reach a series of ledge drops. As you paddle down the river, you see the broken off layered rock jutting from the water ahead — some like giant rectangular table tops tilted, with pointed edges sticking up. The irregular rocks create some good drops and some strange hydraulics, different with each riverflow, and each drop is followed by quieter water to recover in. The run ends in a mellow drift. When we were nearing the take-out, we saw six bald eagles, saw hawks wheeling and heard a rough-legged hawk shrieking like a cat.

Non-boaters can catch the thrills of the deep canyons on the Elk, too, as there are frequent commercially operated rafting trips from April through mid-August. Inquire in Fernie.

Topographic maps: 1:50,000 Elko 82G/6 and Lake Koocanusa 82G/3.

Facilities: Picnic tables, pit toilets and fire rings provided free by the forest service beside Fusee Lake. You reach it from Highway 93; the turnoff to it is 2.1 to 2.4 kilometers (1.3 to 1.5 miles) south of the put-in road, depending on which one you use. Turn west. Cross a cattle guard and wind down through the woods for 2.4 kilometers (1.5 miles) to the quiet, shallow little lake scattered with reeds. Watch for cow pies when you pitch your tent.

Hot springs? — whichever springs you choose, they're 2¼ hours from the put-in. But if you're heading north for your next river, any one is worth it. You could go north on Highway 93, then 93/95, to Fairmont where you'll find

(8.1 miles); 4 to 6 hours

Shuttle one way: 13.8 kilometers (8.6 miles); 15 minutes driving and 20 minutes climbing down the "cat" track. Paved highway for 10.3 kilometers (6.4 miles), the rest is gravel and dirt track

Season: April to September. Usually peaks end of May to early June. Snow-melt and rain-fed. Dam-controlled but responds like natural flow. We paddled it in mid-August with low riverflow of 44 m³/s (1550 cfs)

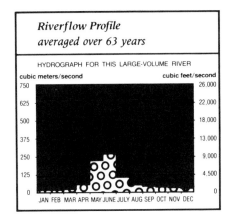

giant outdoor hot pools, changerooms and hot showers; or, past Skookum-chuck, turn off the highway to the primitive springs at Ram Creek or Lussier.

Guidelines: When you climb down the "cat" track to put in, you've made up your mind you're going, there's no turning back. Going down that steep

Upper Canyon in August

bank is hard enough, I can't imagine climbing out again — so check the river-flow, look at the water and decide if you want to be committed to it.

Riverflow continues from April throughout summer and you can expect the river to be extremely pushy in May and June, exciting in July, easier in August. Riverflow is dam-controlled for purposes of power and thus is not guaranteed to be predictable. We saw a signpost: "Elk River level may suddenly change without warning". However, a B.C. Hydro official assures me it responds like a natural river, and the hydrograph shows that it does with May and June being bonanza big water time.

River width averages 40 to 50 meters (130 to 160 feet). Gradient averages 9 meters/kilometer (45 feet/mile) in the Upper Canyon; and it drops at the rate of 5 meters/kilometer (25 feet/mile) in the Middle Canyon. The order of drops is as follows:

• Upper Canyon: you put in on an excellent Class 4 rapid that goes out of sight around the bend with rocks to maneuver around and waves that are up to 1 meter (3 feet) high at low water. At high water you'll be darting between holes, plunging through waves up to 1½ meters (5 feet) high.

• Middle Canyon: when you see the Wigwam River flowing in on "river left", expect the Middle Canyon soon. Once you're in it, the river twists and turns, the water is squirrelly, the eddies are squirrelly too. The passage narrows to 12 meters (40 feet) — it's narrow enough to become obstructed, so you need to be able to stop. At low water, you also must dodge all kinds of junk that's flown down the river with high water: we saw scraps of wrecked cars, which you don't want to tangle with, lodged between the boulders.

• Ledge drops: beyond the Middle Canyon, there are a dozen or so Class 2+ to 3 ledge drops that require maneuvering and which offer fun play spots — save time for it. Below each ledge, there is a slowly flowing pool to recover in.

• Braided section: as you approach the take-out at Lake Koocanusa the river eases off and becomes braided Class 1, ideal for bird watching.

Shortly past the take-out, the Elk flows into Lake Koocanusa which spans the international border; the lake was created in 1973 by damming the Kootenay River where it loops south and becomes the Kootenai at Libby, Montana. A new name was coined for the new lake: Koocanusa is an amalgamation of "Koo" for Kootenay, "can" for Canada, and "usa" for U.S.A.

Access to take-out and put-in: Off Highway 93, between Elko and Roosville which is the Canada/U.S.A. border town. The take-out is 15 minutes south of Elko, 45 minutes from Fernie and 1¼ hours from Cranbrook. To reach the take-out:

• From Elko or Fernie, go west of Elko on Highway 3 to the junction with Highway 93 and head south on it.

• From Cranbrook, head east on Highway 3 toward Elko, and before you reach it turn south onto Highway 93. After you've gone for 3.3 kilometers (2.1 miles) you'll pass one turnoff to the put-in. Then another. But continue south on Highway 93 to the bridge over the Elk where it flows into Lake Koocanusa. As soon as you cross the bridge, turn left into a gravel road that curls down to the water.

For the put-in, return toward Elko on Highway 93 for 10.3 or 10.6 kilo-

Climbing down to put in

meters (6.4 or 6.6 miles) to one of two gravel roads on the right-hand side: the first road is signposted "To Regional Garbage Disposal Site", the second road cuts off the highway opposite Caven Creek Forest Road. Turn right and go a short way to where these roads meet: then continue straight for 1.0 kilometer (0.6 mile) to the next fork in the road. You'll see a pipeline signpost on the right-hand side. (If you reach a gate into the sawmill, you have gone too far; a fence separates the pipeline right-of-way from the sawmill.) At the fork, the right-hand road veers off past the pipeline signpost: follow it and go straight for 1.4 kilometers (0.9 mile) passing a couple of gravel pits to where there is a metal building on the left-hand side and a wide swath cut where the pipeline goes down the hill on the right-hand side. Do not turn. Again, continue straight — go for 0.2 kilometer (0.1 mile) and park near a clump of trees surrounded by mauve and yellow Marguerites and rose hips. A short walk past this, you'll see the steep "cat" track and the irregular, rough steps that you go down the precipitous hill on to reach the put-in. It's extreme. From the canyon edge to the river is 275 meters (900 feet). But the steep pitch looks worse than it is; even before the stairsteps were there, we slid down in 20 minutes. Nevertheless, thanks be to the rafting operators who built them. Throw ropes are useful for lowering boats.

ST. MARY RIVER
To Marysville

Who: Intermediate, advanced and expert kayakers; expert open-canoeists; all rafters. At low levels, also guided novice kayakers and guided intermediate open-canoeists

Water to expect: Class 2 and 3-, with Class 3 to 3+ drops, at high levels. At low levels, Class 2 and 3-. Large volume. Small rock river, rock gardens and play spots

Length of run: 10.0 kilometers (6.2 miles) for the full run. To S-Corner: 8.7 kilometers (5.4 miles). Depending on play time, 3 to 4 hours

Why go: Mellow paddling spiked with fun play spots at Keer's Rock, at the drop open-canoeists have dubbed the World's Best Chute, and through an excellent rapid at the S-Corner — paddle past hoodoos and old homesteads, see cows, yellow and black flowers in the fields, hawks and bald eagles before cruising through town. When driving the shuttle, we saw two deer in the morning and two in the evening and a coyote. It's a well-blended mix of civilization and the wilds.

Topographic maps: 1:50,000 St. Mary Lake 82F/9 and Cranbrook 82G/12.

Facilities: At hot springs time you could go to Ram Creek or Lussier which are primitive mountain pools — or to Fairmont Hot Springs where you'll find huge commercially operated hot pools, changerooms and hot showers. It takes 1½ hours from the take-out to Fairmont, Ram Creek or Lussier.

There are no campgrounds near the St. Mary River; and the land rimming St. Mary Lake is privately owned. However, there are many casual campsites that are evident along the south shore of the lake, and using them will reduce the possibility of landowner conflicts. At the time of writing no one seems to object. Or you might pitch tents by the S-Corner.

Guidelines: You put in on quiet Class 2 water, the run begins as a quiet drift through the woods. But watch for sweepers and logjams on gravel bars at the corners where the river curls around; then, when you pass hoodoos and the river bends left towards the Keer's house, the action starts. The hazards too: watch for tangled wreckage of cars in the left-hand outside bend below the house and just before Keer's Rock — a menace at high water, because you wouldn't see the tangled mess. Past the junked cars, the fun.
• Keer's Rock: a huge house rock which provides squirrelly fun with high and low riverflow; it could become one whopping hole! Sometimes logs pile up on it, so, watch for a logjam. With nothing but water at Keer's Rock, it's Class 3 to 3+. Easy to miss, if you want to.
• World's Best Chute: a series of surfing waves that is around the next left-

Shuttle one way: 12.0 kilometers (7.5 miles) for the full run; paved roads for 9.4 kilometers (5.8 miles) of it, the rest is rough dirt tracks. For the sand pit take-out, 7.1 kilometers (4.4 miles); paved road for 4.6 kilometers (2.9 miles), the rest is rough dirt tracks. Takes 25 to 35 minutes

Season: May through September. High in May, peaks in June. Snow-melt and rain-fed, natural flow from lake which moderates it and extends its season. We paddled it in mid-August with riverflow of 23 m³/s (810 cfs)

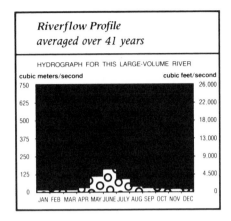

Riverflow Profile
averaged over 41 years

HYDROGRAPH FOR THIS LARGE-VOLUME RIVER

cubic meters/second		cubic feet/second
750		26,000
625		22,000
500		18,000
375		13,000
250		9,000
125		4,500
0		0

JAN FEB MAR APR MAY JUNE JULY AUG SEP OCT NOV DEC

hand corner; the river narrows and pushes the water up into classically scooped-out surfing waves with an excellent eddy on both sides. It's Class 2+ to 3. You could play for hours. But watch for junk here, too, as we saw an old car bumper caught on a rock.

• S-Corner: at low water, there's a continuous lively rock garden; at high water, a mine-bed of holes to negotiate. Expect action soon after you pass hoodoos high on "river right" and when going into the deep canyon section. Around a bend to the left and you're into it. And this excellent rapid continues around the next bend to the right and into a straight stretch. It goes for 150 meters (500 feet) and it's Class 3 to 3+.

Beyond the sand-pit take-outs, there are a couple more Class 2 rapids that I wouldn't want to miss. But watch for more junk in the river: past the pump-

Lunch stop

Approaching S-Corner

ing station beware of concrete blocks and steel reinforcing bars which were just below the surface when we paddled at low water. Don't tip. Then when you've gone beneath the pipeline bridge, there's very mellow water to the take-out.

River width ranges from 15 to 45 meters (50 to 150 feet). Gradient averages 5 meters/kilometer (25 feet/mile). Riverflow can be huge — maximum recorded flow was 501 m³/s (17,700 cfs) on June 17, 1974. Every spring, a great deal of rubbish washes down the river at runoff. Remember to look for logjams and rubble at every outside bend, especially the left-hand ones.

Access to take-outs and put-in: Located in Marysville off Highway 95A between Cranbrook and Kimberley on the west side of the Rocky Mountain Trench. It's 30 minutes from Cranbrook, 15 minutes from Kimberley to the take-out.

• From Cranbrook, heading north on Highway 95A, when going into Marysville you'll cross railway tracks on the outskirts of town, then almost immediately come to a signpost "Welcome to Marysville" and a reddish brown concrete block building — both on the right-hand side. Opposite the "Welcome" sign, there's a dirt road. Turn left and follow it for 1.9 kilometers (1.2 miles): many narrow dirt tracks branch off of this curving road, but keep to the main one and you'll reach the river. This is the take-out for the full run. The shore is unattractively stained a rusty red color with iron oxide effluent from a mine, but it's a good take-out and you'll find plenty of room to park.

• From Kimberley, heading south on Highway 95A, you'll come to St. Mary Lake Road; continue past it through Marysville for 2.1 kilometers (1.3 miles) to the "Welcome" sign and turn right down the dirt road to the river.

For the alternate sand-pit take-outs: from Highway 95A between Marysville and Kimberley, go west. Turn up St. Mary Lake Road and go for 2.7 kilometers (1.7 miles) and turn left into a rough dirt road which soon splits: the left-hand fork goes through the sand pit and the locals think it's fun to slide through it on the way to the river. We took the right-hand track. You'll probably find it's passable, but check before you drive down. It is steep, winding and narrow. Follow its curve to the right and then left for ½ kilometer (⅓ mile) to a second fork. Here the choice depends on the stretch of river you're running: the right-hand track goes to the take-out that is before the S-Corner, and if you continue straight you'll reach the take-out below it.

For the put-in: from the junction of Highway 95A and St. Mary Lake Road, proceed up St. Mary Lake Road for 2.7 kilometers (1.7 miles) and pass the sand-pit turnoff; continue 1.7 kilometers (1.1 mile) and pass a beautiful property overlooking the river. When we paddled, the Keers lived here. From the Keer's home, continue 2.9 kilometers (1.8 miles) up St. Mary Lake Road, then while St. Mary Lake Road curves to the right, you continue straight on a gravel road going toward a log house at the end of it. If you cross a bridge over a creek, you've gone too far. After going for 0.2 kilometer (0.1 mile) and before reaching the log house, turn left into a dirt track. Follow it, and when you reach a fork in it, follow the right-hand one to the river. This is a public road which is gazetted, but it is surrounded by privately owned property, so please respect it.

FINDLAY CREEK
Mini-Canyon to Skookumchuck Road

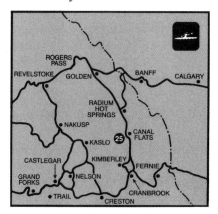

Who: Advanced and expert kayakers; no open-canoeists and no rafters

Water to expect: Class 3 and 4, two Class 5 drops (easy to portage) and braided Class 2. At very high and very low levels, unrunnable. Pushy small volume; technical

Length of run: 12.5 kilometers (7.8 miles); depending on scouting and play time, 5 to 7 hours for full run. Top canyons, 4.8 kilometers (3.0 miles); 3 to 4 hours. Camp 7 to Skookumchuck Road, 7.7 kilometers (4.8 miles); 2 hours

Shuttle one way: For full run, 13.7 kilometers (8.5 miles) and walk

Why go: To leap the "Mini-Waterfall", to leap the Frowning Hole — if that's not reason enough, add a red rock canyon, huge vistas from cliff tops when you scout, small play waves, broad braided gravel bars, the steep narrow rapids in Mini-Canyon, holes dug by gold seekers in the canyon walls, trees chewed by beavers, whirly chutes between low, narrow rock walls carved and polished smooth by the swirling water — all in wild-feeling country — and you have a day on Findlay Creek. Gooseberries grow along the banks reminding us that people have been exploring this region for a long time. There is a comfortable sense of history surrounding the creek, yet the country-side is still largely unsettled.

Topographic maps: 1:50,000 Findlay Creek 82K/1 and Canal Flats 82J/4.

Facilities: After paddling Findlay, you can choose from primitive or devel-oped hot springs. Only 20 minutes from the take-out you'll find hot showers, changerooms, and the largest commercially operated hot pools in British Columbia at Fairmont. They're open year-round. And you can reach the primitive springs at Lussier in 40 minutes, Ram Creek in 1 hour.

Low-key creekside camping near the take-out with no facilities; pitch your tent beneath the stars anywhere on Crown land. And there's camping for a fee overlooking Columbia Lake at Thunderhill Provincial Park with picnic tables, pit toilets and fire rings.

Guidelines: The Mini-Canyon, the Frowning Hole and the "Mini-Waterfall" are highlights on this challenging run: scout all of them from shore. At all levels, scout the Frowning Hole before putting in — it stretches across the creek. At high levels, also scout the Mini-Canyon as it becomes Class 5 and is so pushy that once you're on the water you're committed to run the Frowning Hole at the end of it. Be sure you want to.

Beyond the Mini-Canyon there's a braided section, then a higher, wider canyon with some small play waves; at corners you might have to climb from your boat to scout for fallen trees felled by beavers, hike to a high look-

300 paces at the take-out; 30 minutes
for driving, plus time for scouting.
Top canyons, 9.5 kilometers (5.9 miles);
10 minutes for driving. Camp 7 to
Skookumchuck Road, 7.8 kilometers
(4.8 miles) and walk 300 paces at the
take-out; 20 minutes. Gravel logging
roads

Season: Runoff, mid-May through July.
Best in late June. Snow-melt, rain-fed
and some glacial-melt; natural flow. We
kayaked it in late June during runoff;
precise riverflow unavailable; my guess is
40 m³/s (1410 cfs)

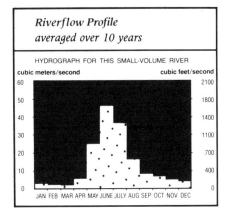

Riverflow Profile
averaged over 10 years

HYDROGRAPH FOR THIS SMALL-VOLUME RIVER

cubic meters/second · · · · · · cubic feet/second

out, pass hoodoos, paddle through a gorgeous red canyon to the campsite.

Past Camp 7, the creek narrows; look for the "Mini-Waterfall" which
comes soon. It is a *must scout* too. It becomes an extremely narrow Class 4+ to
5 drop at low water. You can walk to it from the road or scout from the

"Mini-Waterfall"

creek. The creek's not too pushy just before it, and you can climb out on the right-hand bank to take a look. When we ran Findlay Creek this was an irresistible (to me) clean swoosh of water that gushed over the 2- to 2½-meter (6- to 9-foot) drop, and when you shot out over it you landed in a squirrelly pool which flipped all four paddlers in our group who ran it. But there was time to recover before the water hit a head wall, and rounded a bend to the left into an extremely constricted, and — on that day — not too pushy canyon. I've been back since to look at the spot at low water and my waterfall (which was the first waterfall I had run at that time) turned out not to be a waterfall at all. It is now, and probably was then, an extremely constricted, low passage which the water piles up on it at high water, making it into a "Mini-Waterfall" — so that's why there's no keeper at the bottom of it. However locals tell me that it *was* a waterfall when I ran it, and that I ran it shortly after a landslide, but that rubble from that slide washed out of it again. Whichever, you must check it out for yourself before running it — be sure there are no logs beneath the surface. Beyond it, squirrelly whirly churning water between very narrow, very smooth rock walls. Check this out too at all levels of flow. There are stories of low-water times when people have had to climb out using ropes. Then look for your marker at the take-out. You do not want to miss it and go on to the waterfall that is below the bridge on Skookumchuck Forest Road.

Class 4+ to 5 judgment and skills are required to lead a trip on this small-volume but pushy creek. Class 4+ skills and control are required for each paddler on the trip, *even if you're portaging the Class 5 drops.*

From the put-in bridge at Findlay-Doctor Forest Road, the Findlay starts descending at the rate of 21 meters/kilometer (110 feet/mile), then eases off to 7 meters/kilometer (35 feet/mile). From Camp 7 to the take-out above Skookumchuck Forest Road, gradient averages 5 meters/kilometer (25 feet/mile), but there's excitement because of extreme narrowing. Width varies with riverflow: in the broader parts width averages from 18 to 24 meters (60 to 80 feet) narrowing between rock walls — some passages can become as narrow as 3 to 6 meters (10 to 20 feet). Watch for fallen trees and new rockslides; always be ready to pull out if you need to.

Access to take-outs and put-ins: Located off Highway 93/95 between Fairmont Hot Springs and Canal Flats in the Columbia-Windermere Valley on the west side of the Rocky Mountain Trench. From Fairmont to the take-out is 20 minutes; from Canal Flats, 15 minutes.

• From Fairmont, go south on Highway 93/95 for 22 kilometers (14 miles) to the Thunderhill Provincial Park turnoff which is on the west side of the valley.
• From Canal Flats, go north for 5 kilometers (3 miles) to the Thunderhill Park turnoff into Findlay Creek Forest Road.

For the take-out, head up Findlay Creek Forest Road past Thunderhill Park, cross a cattle guard and the road becomes gravel. From the cattle guard, go 5.0 kilometers (3.1 miles) and just past the "8 km" signpost, turn left into Skookumchuck Forest Road which goes to a bridge over the creek. Before the bridge, park on the right-hand side and walk to the right, heading upstream for ½ kilometer (¼ mile) down an overgrown dirt track — really just a trail, and place a marker at the take-out. You do not want to miss this point-of-no-return after which Findlay Creek disappears into a narrow gorge choked with fallen trees.

For the midway put-in or take-out: return to Findlay Creek Forest Road and head upstream; go 5.7 kilometers (3.5 miles) and, when you're between the "13 km" and "14 km" signposts, Findlay-Lavington Forest Road goes off to the left-hand side. From this junction, you can walk to the creek to look at the "Mini-Waterfall": face the creek with Findlay-Lavington Road at a one-o'clock angle, then walk at an 11-o'clock angle for 5 minutes down the grassy slope to see the "Mini-Waterfall". Then return to the junction and continue driving down Findlay-Lavington Road to the bridge at Camp 7 to put-in or to leave a shuttle vehicle if you're just running the top part.

For the Mini-Canyon put-in, return to Findlay Creek Road and head upstream for 1.6 kilometers (1.0 mile) to another fork in the road; Whitetail Lake Forest Road goes off on the right-hand side and it is signposted to "Blue Lake Forestry Centre" and "Findlay and Dutch Creek Multiple Use Resource Forest", but do not turn right. Continue straight. At the next fork in the road, go left and drive 6.1 kilometers (3.8 miles) along Findlay-Doctor Forest Road to the put-in bridge.

To see the Mini-Canyon, return for 0.5 kilometer (0.3 mile) on Findlay-Doctor Road along the way you just came down and park at the roadside. From here you can walk 50 paces to see the Mini-Canyon and decide whether to put in above it or below it. To put in below it, walk 125 paces downstream on a good fisherman's trail to a big eddy. This access below the Mini-Canyon is privately owned and at the time of writing the owners are happy to let kayakers cross it as long as they park well off the road. Trucks are hauling huge logs; many times long "sweepers" extend from the back of them. So avoid parking at a curve. And, if you see "No Trespassing" signs, please respect them and do not use this lower access.

———————————

Travel is permitted 24 hours a day on Findlay Creek, Findlay-Lavington and Findlay-Doctor Forest Roads which are open to the public. However, logging traffic could be on them too, so drive with your headlights on. To learn about where they're hauling, contact Crestbrook Forest Industries Ltd., P.O. Box 4600, Cranbrook, B.C. V1C 4J7, (604)426-6241. To learn about possible fire-hazard closures, contact the Ministry of Forests, Invermere District, P.O. Box 189, Invermere, B.C. V0A 1K0, telephone (604)342-4200.

TOBY CREEK
Through Slipping Rock Rapid

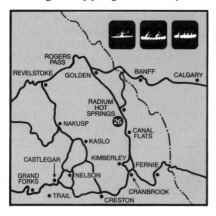

Who: Advanced and expert kayakers; no open-canoeists; advanced and expert rafters. At low levels, also solid intermediate kayakers and guided novices; expert open-canoeists; intermediate rafters and guided novices

Water to expect: Class 3 and 4, plus a Class 5 rapid (easy to portage). Small volume. Continuous, technical rock gardens and boulder drops. Freezing cold

Length of run: 5.1 kilometers (3.2 miles); 3 to 5 hours, depending on play time

Shuttle one way: 4.7 kilometers

Why go: Stairstep rapids are in a continuous cascade down the mountainside at Toby Creek. It's exciting paddling. And the holes at Toby are the best-known whitewater play spots in the Kootenays. Racers have spread the word.

The first Toby Creek Classic featured a slalom race which was followed by free-style rodeo boating. It was held on this stretch in 1980, sponsored by an active local club, the Toby Creekers. Next they ran a provincial-kayak-team selection race in the spring of 1981. And the Canadian national kayak races were on Toby from July 2 to 7, 1982. The slalom gates were hung just down-stream from Slipping Rock Rapid — a demanding course. Another Toby Creek Classic was held in 1983; it was part of the Alberta Foothills Cup, but the water was low so there was no hot-dog boating event. The best whitewater circus was at the Nationals. It's a great destination for squirt boaters.

Toby is good for the "Joe Blow" kayaker too, fun for you and me — it's so accessible, the shuttle is easy, and, if the run is too much for you, you can climb out at almost any point. It's not remote, as many of the East Kootenay runs are. This gives paddlers a chance to try something a bit more demanding than they're used to.

Non-paddlers can enjoy rafting Toby: there are commercially operated trips every day from June through August on the quieter section upstream from the run described here. They go to the bridge at Panorama. You can book through Off the Wall Adventures, Ltd., P.O. Box 7000, Invermere, B.C. V0A 1K0, telephone (604)342-6941.

And for everyone, it's a scenic place to be. The surrounding terrain is rugged: Mount Nelson is one of the highest and most beautifully shaped mountains around. It looks like a classic snow-capped volcanic peak, but is not. Mount Nelson rises to 3,300 meters (10,850 feet) and can be seen from Toby Creek. Glaciers are scattered throughout the Purcell Mountains above Toby Creek which flows straight out of Toby Glacier.

After paddling, a couple of kayakers from our boating group rode motor-bikes up Watch Peak to Paradise Mine — formerly Paradice, so named to

(2.9 miles); 10 minutes. Paved road

Season: Mid-May through August, usually peaking in late June. Natural flow with a great deal of glacial-melt and snow-melt, also rain-fed. We paddled it in late June with riverflow of 39 m³/s (1380 cfs)

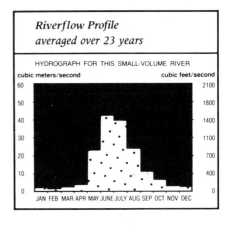

Riverflow Profile averaged over 23 years

HYDROGRAPH FOR THIS SMALL-VOLUME RIVER

cubic meters/second   cubic feet/second

JAN FEB MAR APR MAY JUNE JULY AUG SEP OCT NOV DEC

bring luck; and they brought snow back to camp for iced drinks! Wild roses bloom around camp and beside the creek and you'll find hot springs in every direction out of Toby on your way to the next river.

Canadian Nationals at Toby Creek

Topographic map: 1:50,000 Toby Creek 82K/8.

Facilities: Camping is free in a variety of primitive undeveloped spaces where you can pitch your tents on the way up the rough road to Paradise Mine. The dirt track to Paradise cuts off the paved road when you're 1.2 kilometers (0.8 mile) downstream from the put-in bridge at Panorama — the campsite we found on the road to Paradise was not only convenient, it *was* a nice place to be. There are many privately owned campgrounds beside the lake in the Windermere area, and there's also camping for a fee near Radium at Dry Gulch Provincial Park with picnic tables, pit toilets (some flush toilets), fire rings, and firewood. It has a spacious dry-belt-country feeling and is 10 minutes north after you turn onto Highway 93/95.

Fairmont Hot Springs and Radium Hot Springs are within 35 minutes of the take-out. For Fairmont, go to Highway 93/95 and head south for 10 minutes; for Radium, go to Highway 93/95 and head north for 15 minutes then turn right into Highway 93 and in 5 minutes you're at the springs. Both are commercially operated outdoor pools with changerooms and hot showers. The pools at Fairmont overlook the broad valley and they cover a vast area, like a football field — all steaming. They form one enormous pool. The hot and the cool pools at Radium feel smaller because they are separated, yet you can easily move from the hot to the cool to the hot pool and back again. While soaking in the steamy pool nestled in Sinclair Canyon, you'll probably see mountain sheep on the opposite hill.

Guidelines: Steady width, steady gradient on this run: the width averages 40 meters (130 feet); gradient averages 10 meters/kilometer (55 feet/mile) and it's all in stairsteps. Toby Creek is filled with glacial-melt, which means it flows for a longer season than many mountain streams — be prepared for paddling iced water. On a rainy midsummer day I wished for neoprene mitts.

Class 3 boulder gardens run from the put-in to the Class 5 Slipping Rock Rapid, which most boaters carry around; the portage might be flagged by local paddlers, but check it out when you set up shuttle. Most kayakers climb to the road, carry 300 meters (1000 feet) or so, put in as soon as possible below Slipping Rock and ferry across to "river right" to run the Class 4 rapid immediately past it; and there's more good water to the take-out. This section below Slipping Rock to the take-out is considered by many to be the best of Toby. The locals frequently make this 2.6 kilometer (1.6 mile) stretch their complete run as it is easy to get a good 2-hour paddle on it.

For an eyeball report on creekflow from mid-May through September, contact Off the Wall Adventures, Ltd., P.O. Box 7000, Invermere, B.C. V0A 1K0, telephone (604)342-6941. They're on Toby every day.

Access to take-out and put-in: Located off Highway 93/95 midway between Golden and Cranbrook in the Columbia-Windermere Valley at the Panorama Resort area near Invermere. Toby is on the west side of the Rocky Mountain Trench — only 15 minutes from the highway to the take-out.

Go to Invermere. From there, follow signs towards Panorama Resort: when you reach a right-hand turnoff to Wilmer, keep going straight on the main road and you'll pass Lillian Lake. From the lake, it is 7.8 kilometers

Below Slipping Rock

(4.8 miles) to the road-side take-out; there's a lay-by with room for a couple of cars to park just up the road.

Then continue upstream 2.5 kilometers (1.6 miles) to the put-in below Slipping Rock Rapid which most kayakers portage. Look at the rapid and see if you want to carry around it. If so, you'll probably want to take out at least 0.5 kilometer (0.3 mile) up the road where you'll see a huge house rock. Note the take-out you decide on — you might even want to flag it — then continue 2.0 kilometers (1.2 miles) to the put-in bridge at Panorama.

HORSETHIEF CREEK
14 Mile Bridge to Westside Road

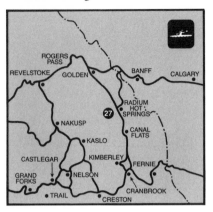

Who: Expert kayakers, and advanced kayakers with a guide; no open-canoeists and no rafters

Water to expect: Class 3 to 4+ with a difficult mandatory portage around an unrunnable Class 6 waterfall. Small volume. Steady gradient, except for the falls. Remote canyon with very limited access

Length of run: 19.2 kilometers (11.9 miles); 7 or 8 hours, minimum

Shuttle one way: 15.4 kilometers (9.6 miles); 20 minutes. Privately owned gravel logging roads

Why go: For the thrill of finding a waterfall — a wilderness falls that is not on any map. For the excitement of exploring. For all you see while you're scouting. For hoodoos. For swallows flying in and out of them. An otter. Wild roses, black-eyed Susans, tiny blue flowers, Queen Anne's lace, Indian paintbrush and daisies all over the hillsides. For the smell of sage brush. For the taste of wild strawberries. For lazy grey-green water. For crashing white spray. For rock gardens and playful waves. For lively whitewater rapids mile after mile after mile. For getting there. For reaching your shuttle, your camp. For making it.

Topographic maps: 1:50,000 Radium Hot Springs 82K/9. The Columbia River Basin MS series maps, sheets 47 and 48, are also extremely useful — if you can find them. This series is no longer in print. The falls are not shown even on these large scale 1:31,680 topos on which 3 centimeters equals 1 kilometer (1 inch equals ½ mile), but you *can see* a great deal of detail in the canyon.

Facilities: Camping is free at a spacious forest service site beside Lake Enid which is 10 minutes from Wilmer and has picnic tables, pit toilets and fire rings. Find it by heading out of Wilmer on Park Street which becomes Horsethief Road; when you've gone 5.8 kilometers (3.6 miles), look for an unmarked turnoff on the right-hand side. There's camping for a fee at Redstreak Campground in Radium and 5 minutes south of Radium at Dry Gulch.

Fairmont Hot Springs is 30 minutes from the take-out; to reach it, go via Wilmer and Invermere to Highway 93/95 and head south. You'll see a huge signpost on the highway. Radium Hot Springs is 35 minutes from the take-out; to reach it, go to the junction of Highway 93 and 95 in Radium and head east on Highway 93. From there, it's 5 minutes to the springs. Both are commmmercially operated outdoor pools with changerooms and hot showers. You'll find gigantic pools in the big open Columbia-Windermere Valley at Fairmont, and large but intimate feeling pools nestled in Sinclair Canyon east of Radium.

Guidelines: When you put in on the lazy grey-green water in the marshy,

Season: Late June to August. Best in June. Snow-melt, some glacial-melt and rain-fed; natural flow. We explored it in late June after the peak of runoff; precise riverflow unavailable; my guess is 30 m³/s (1060 cfs)

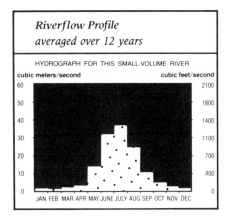

Riverflow Profile
averaged over 12 years

HYDROGRAPH FOR THIS SMALL-VOLUME RIVER

high valley at 14 Mile Bridge, there's no hint of the intensity to come. The width at the put-in is 35 meters (115 feet), but downstream it averages 20 to 24 meters (70 to 80 feet), and at one place the creek is as narrow as 8 meters (26 feet). Gradient averages 15 meters/kilometer (80 feet/mile); however, a lot of it is in one spot.

The waterfall comes 6.4 kilometers (4.0 miles) after putting in. It took us ½ hour to reach it. The creek plunges 10 meters (30 feet) onto messy jagged rocks at the bottom with trees scattered over them like the old-time game of Pick-Up-Sticks. Not something you want to go over. It comes without warning. You don't see spray. And you don't hear the falls. The mellow water

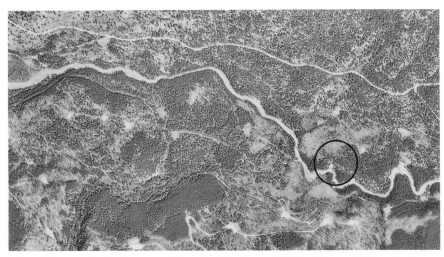

Waterfall not visible in air photo of Horsethief Creek: see 12 Mile Bridge on left-hand side, and downstream on the right-hand side the location of the waterfall is within the circle; there is not even a contour line on the topographic map to indicate this killer drop.

Past hoodoos, nearing end of run

Putting in

Lunch stop

Past waterfall, a fallen tree

simply slips over the lip of the falls smooth as taffy and crashes onto the ragged rocks and logs heaped at its base.

To spot the waterfall, eddy hop with extreme caution and watch for a tributary creek coming in on "river right". When Bruce Creek flows in from the right-hand side you have almost reached the waterfall on Horsethief Creek; when you are 100 meters (300 feet) past where Bruce Creek flows in, there's a big eddy on "river right", and the same distance again, the falls.

For the portage, eddy out on "river right". You have to climb 100 meters (300 feet) up the right-hand bank. It is steep, rocky and wooded. Once up the hill you'll find an overgrown logging road — really only a trail — curving around the edge of the hill and it is easier to walk. Past the falls, slide down the fairly steep open slope; a rope is useful to lower boats. You put in on lively continuous Class 3+ rapids. It's a narrow, small-volume creek and some of the rock gardens are bony. But basically it's good from here on: the water is Class 3 for most of the remaining trip with busy rock gardens — however, it's continuous enough and remote enough to make it a Class 4. There's one Class 4+ rapid, some gravel bars for lunch in the sun, and small play waves and holes in the canyon near the end of the run.

The waterfall is the one essential thing to look out for, but at least it's fixed. We also had to carry around a tree that had fallen across the creek. At another place, we chose to carry around a Class 4 rock garden as well: there was a clear passage on "river right", but if you messed up on that, the main flow would then wash you under a tree blocking the channel where you would be, so we were conservative — there's potential action all the way.

Take throw ropes, matches, duct tape, and food. It's a long day.

Our group explored the Horsethief on June 27, 1980, and it was probably a first descent. Mike Bohn, Ben Lemke, Betty Pratt-Johnson, John Pratt-Johnson, Klaus Streckmann and Dane Wray completed the run that day. Since then, many have kayaked it.

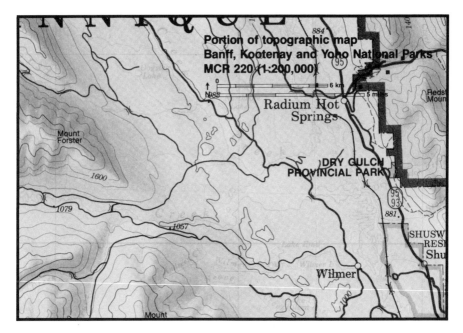

Access to take-out and put-in: Located off Highway 93/95 between Invermere and Radium in the Columbia-Windermere Valley. The Horsethief flows into the west side of the Rocky Mountain Trench. From Radium, it's 30 minutes to the take-out; from Invermere via Wilmer, 5 minutes to the take-out.

• From Radium at the four-way stop, head southwest on Forsters Landing Road. When you see the mill, bear left into Horsethief Forest Road. Continue on it to a well-signposted four-way junction at Westside Road, which is where you head upstream to put in, but first go to the take-out. Turn left into Westside: cross Forster Creek, then to the bridge over the Horsethief.

• From Invermere, head north out of town following signposts toward Panorama Resort and Wilmer. Shortly you'll cross a bridge; immediately turn right — it's 2.6 kilometers (1.6 miles) to Wilmer where the road becomes gravel. This is Westside Road. Continue on it. When heading downhill and you see hoodoos, you're nearly at the take-out bridge.

For the put-in, go north on Westside Road for 4.3 kilometers (2.7 miles) to Forster Creek. Cross Forster and go 2.1 kilometers (1.3 miles) north to the four-way junction where you turn left off of Westside Road into Horsethief Forest Road. There is a signpost pointing out that it's a privately owned road for the next 16 kilometers (10 miles) and directing you to Starbird and Commander glaciers and to Lake of the Hanging Glaciers. This is where the Horsethief springs from. Go 5.6 kilometers (3.5 miles) to a fork in the road. The right-hand fork is marked Forster Road; you stay left on Horsethief Forest Road and continue to the put-in bridge at 14 Mile.

On your way upstream to put in, when you're 2.6 kilometers (1.6 miles) past the Forster Road turnoff, you could cut off the main logging road and go to look at Horsethief Creek. This is your only chance to scout from the road. The rough track that sheers down the hill on the left-hand side. It goes to

Below waterfall, continuous rock garden rapids

12 Mile Bridge, *if* the bridge is still there. Bridges sometimes wash away, so, check it out. *Do not assume that it is there.* If 12 Mile Bridge is still intact, when you're paddling the creek and you reach it, it's a signal that you've got only 1.8 kilometers (1.1 miles) to go to reach the point where Bruce Creek enters above the falls.

Note: The Horsethief access described is on 16 kilometers (10 miles) of privately owned logging road, and a great deal of the northern creekbank is privately owned. At the time of writing, the public are welcome to use Horsethief Road as long as they don't stop. Travel with your headlights on and watch for logging trucks. Do not stop to camp or picnic. Do not litter. And do not light fires.

Drive with your headlights on. The best times to use this road are weekends, holidays, and weekdays before 5 a.m. and after 5 p.m. To learn where logging trucks are hauling and about possible fire-hazard closures, contact the Ministry of Forests, Invermere District, P.O. Box 189, Invermere, B.C. V0A 1K0, telephone (604)342-4200.

BOBBIE BURNS CREEK-SPILLIMACHEEN RIVER
Below Poet Creek

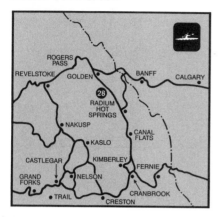

Who: Expert and guided advanced kayakers with a solid roll; no open-canoeists and no rafters

Water to expect: Class 3 to 4+, and a difficult mandatory portage around a Class 6 waterfall. Medium volume. Pushy drops and pools, remote from road; *a high risk run*

Length of run: 13.4 kilometers (8.3 miles); 5 to 6 hours

Shuttle one way: 12.2 kilometers (7.6 miles); 30 minutes. Gravel logging roads with radio-controlled traffic

Season: Late June to September. Best in

Why go: A waterfall. A touch of the wilds. Beautiful drops and pools . . . to meet the challenge!

Topographic map: 1:50,000 Bugaboo Creek 82K/15.

Facilities: You'll find camping for a fee in Radium at the huge Redstreak Campground in Kootenay National Park where there are more than 200 sites. Five minutes south of Radium, at the smaller Dry Gulch Provincial Park, you'll find more camping for a fee. At Dry Gulch, 25 sites are scattered beneath the Douglas fir trees. Both campgrounds have pit toilets and some flush toilets, picnic tables and fire rings, and there are hot showers at Redstreak. Or find your own place to pitch your tent near the run with no facilities, and no fee. That's what we usually do. It's one of the special delights of the Kootenays to me to have so much vacant Crown land to choose from and to be able, in many locations, to just stop where you are.

The closest hot springs to Bobbie Burns are the commercially operated hot pools at Radium where you might see bighorn sheep from the pool — they're on the hillside opposite it. There's also a cool pool for swimming. From the take-out, you could reach Radium in 1 hour. You could reach the giant-sized commercially operated pools at Fairmont in 1½ hours, and the primitive Lussier Hot Springs in 1¾ hours.

Guidelines: Steady, active stuff. The overall gradient is 13 meters/kilometer (70 feet/mile); however, early in the run the creek descends at the rate of 21 meters/kilometer (110 feet/mile). It's pushy all the way. Width averages 30 meters (100 feet). And there are lots of waves and water, fabulous drops and pools. Bobbie Burns Falls, which drops 8 or 10 meters (26 or 30 feet), is late in the run, therefore you must be ready for it throughout.

Most drops are challenging, many require scouting from shore, but cannot be seen from the road; allow time for scouting while paddling the river. The falls are almost impossible to see until you are almost over them: *all kayakers must paddle in control at all times. The situation demands that all boaters have the*

early July. Snow-melt, rain-fed and glacial-melt. Natural flow. We explored it in late June after its peak; precise riverflow unavailable; my guess is 61 m³/s (2150 cfs)

Good water, all the way

Bobbie Burns Falls

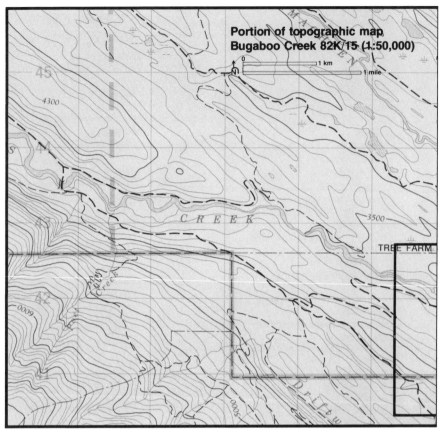

The Bobbie Burns Creek put-in is on this section of the topographic map: it is downstream from the bridge, which we could not reach when we were there because the road was washed out, and it is upstream from Poet Creek.

ability to stop. Demands control.

When exploring, our leader in that section pulled into the last eddy before the falls at the last possible moment — he ripped off his spray deck, jumped for shore, then grabbed our boats as each of us eddied out. Looking at photographs later that we had taken during the trip, we could see the approach to the falls. But while paddling we were so busy negotiating each drop and rapid we did not notice the classic, dropping tree line that warns of a waterfall — look for a descending tree line. Also, when you're approaching the falls, there is an island in the middle and the creek looks particularly placid and bland.

Beware of the pussycat sections! Maybe this waterfall is so difficult to see because it's such a clean waterfall, top and bottom. These are the only clues I know of to help you spot this falls. Look at the portion from a topographic map showing the section of creek where the falls are — the falls are missing from it, but it will help if you familiarize yourself with the creek in every way you can: look at the contours on the map and the path of the creek; and look

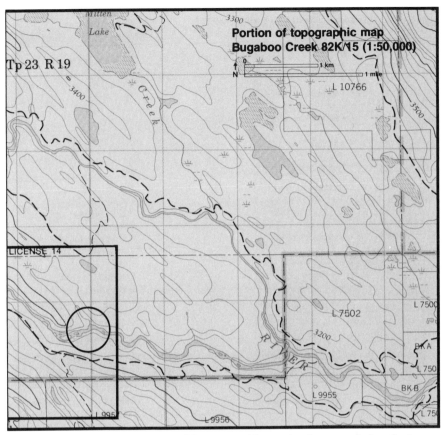

Bobbie Burns Falls is in this section of the topographic map but is not marked on the topo — not even by a contour line. The falls are located within the circle on this map. Also see air photo on page 134; the area covered by the air photo is indicated by the rectangle on this map.

at the air photo on page 134 in which you *can* see Bobbie Burns Falls.

Also, perhaps it helps just to know they are there. But ultimately you have to get out there and paddle the creek — *paddle very carefully, under control.* For the portage, eddy out on "river right" and climb around the right-hand side of this beautiful waterfall which plummets 8 or 10 meters (26 or 30 feet) into a large, calm pool — the ultimate drop and pool.

Go with a strong group. *Do not kayak* Bobbie Burns Creek until after it has peaked; paddle when the water is clear and dropping. Put your best boater well in the lead throughout. Paddle it like an exploration each time you go: this is a high risk run.

Our group explored this run on June 30, 1980, and it was probably a first descent. Mike Bohn, Elie Bowles, Betty Pratt-Johnson, John Pratt-Johnson, Klaus Streckmann and Dane Wray completed the run that day with Dane leading when we reached the waterfall. Many have kayaked the creek since.

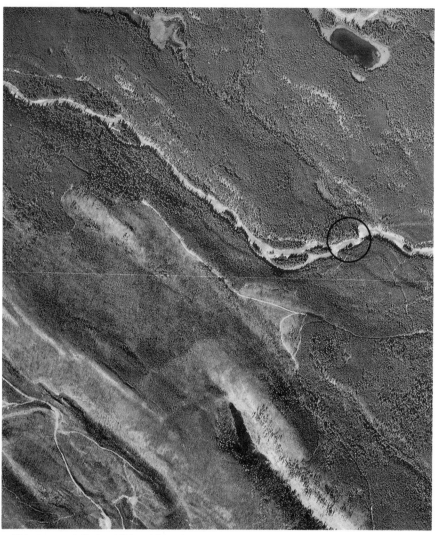

Bobbie Burns Falls is visible within the circle on this air photo taken in September when riverflow was very low. See reservoir in the top right-hand corner of the photo; see finger-like lake near the bottom of it: even without stereo viewing, you can detect changes in elevation. See the map on pages 132 and 133 where the area covered by this air photo is indicated by the rectangle. Compare them.

Travel is permitted 24 hours a day on these forest roads which are open to the public. However, logging traffic could be on them too, so drive with your headlights on and whenever possible follow a radio-controlled vehicle. To learn about where they're hauling, contact Crestbrook Forest Industries Ltd., General Delivery, Parson, B.C. V0A 1L0, (604)348-2211; or on the way to the creek, you could stop at the Crestbrook office in Parson. To learn about possible fire-hazard closures, contact the Ministry of Forests, Invermere District, P.O. Box 189, Invermere, B.C. V0A 1K0, telephone (604)342-4200.

Portion of topographic map
Banff, Kootenay and Yoho National Parks
MCR 220 (1:200,000)

Lead Mountain

Harrogate

Jubilee Mountain

Spillin

Access to take-out and put-in: Located off Highway 95 between Golden and Radium on the west side of the Columbia-Windermere Valley. From the community of Spillimacheen, drive for 10.9 kilometers (6.8 miles) on very rough logging roads to the take-out.

In Spillimacheen, turn off the highway onto Westside Road and head across the marshy Columbia River; go straight for 2.3 kilometers (1.4 miles) crossing two bridges; then turn left (still on Westside Road) for 0.8 kilometer (0.5 mile), and turn right up a rough fire access road. This is where you start heading upstream on the south side of the river: the forest roads keep changing all the time, but when we were there we went for 1.8 kilometers (1.1 miles) to a fork in the road; there we stayed left and went 1.0 kilometer (0.6 mile); at the next fork, we stayed left again, and went 1.1 kilometers (0.7 mile); then we followed the right-hand fork and drove 4.2 kilometers (2.6 miles) to the take-out, which is simply a point where the road comes close to the Spillimacheen River. Leave a shuttle.

For the put-in, head on upstream: go for 12.2 kilometers (7.6 miles); half-way up this road, we passed a log cabin; the road was in extremely poor condition when we were there — it might be impassable now — but hopefully you can still make it to the put-in where you climb down a bank to Bobbie Burns Creek.

High Noon at St. Leon

Inside steamy cave, looking out — at Ainsworth

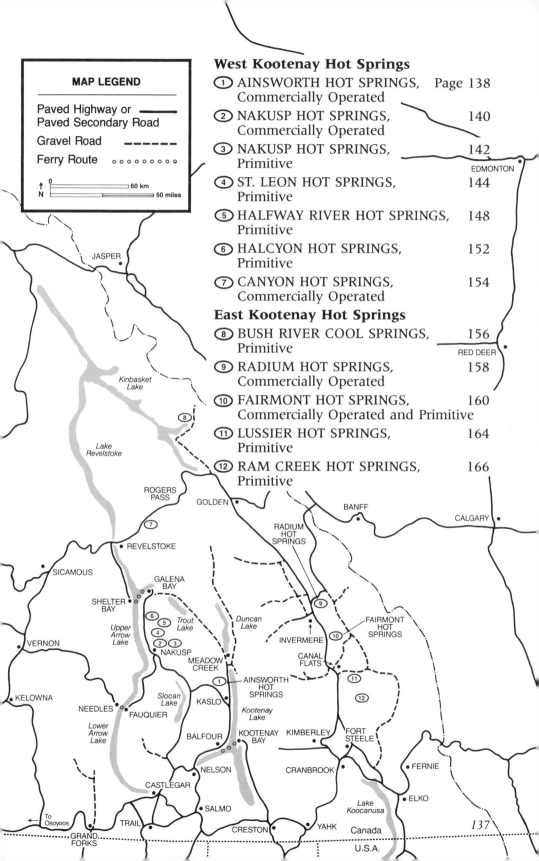

West Kootenay Hot Springs

(1) AINSWORTH HOT SPRINGS,   Page 138
Commercially Operated

(2) NAKUSP HOT SPRINGS,   140
Commercially Operated

(3) NAKUSP HOT SPRINGS,   142
Primitive

(4) ST. LEON HOT SPRINGS,   144
Primitive

(5) HALFWAY RIVER HOT SPRINGS,   148
Primitive

(6) HALCYON HOT SPRINGS,   152
Primitive

(7) CANYON HOT SPRINGS,   154
Commercially Operated

East Kootenay Hot Springs

(8) BUSH RIVER COOL SPRINGS,   156
Primitive

(9) RADIUM HOT SPRINGS,   158
Commercially Operated

(10) FAIRMONT HOT SPRINGS,   160
Commercially Operated and Primitive

(11) LUSSIER HOT SPRINGS,   164
Primitive

(12) RAM CREEK HOT SPRINGS,   166
Primitive

MAP LEGEND

Paved Highway or
Paved Secondary Road ————

Gravel Road ------

Ferry Route ∘∘∘∘∘∘∘∘∘

N ↑ 0   60 km   50 miles

EDMONTON

RED DEER

JASPER

Kinbasket Lake

Lake Revelstoke

ROGERS PASS

GOLDEN

BANFF

CALGARY

RADIUM HOT SPRINGS

(7)

REVELSTOKE

SICAMOUS

GALENA BAY

SHELTER BAY

(6) (5) Trout Lake

Duncan Lake

(9)

FAIRMONT HOT SPRINGS

Upper Arrow Lake

(4)

(2) (3)

NAKUSP

INVERMERE

(10)

VERNON

MEADOW CREEK

CANAL FLATS

AINSWORTH HOT SPRINGS

(1)

KELOWNA

Slocan Lake

KASLO

(11)

NEEDLES

FAUQUIER

Kootenay Lake

(12)

Lower Arrow Lake

BALFOUR

KOOTENAY BAY

KIMBERLEY

FORT STEELE

NELSON

CRANBROOK

FERNIE

CASTLEGAR

Lake Koocanusa

ELKO

To Osoyoos

TRAIL

SALMO

CRESTON

YAHK

Canada

GRAND FORKS

U.S.A.

137

AINSWORTH HOT SPRINGS
Commercially Operated

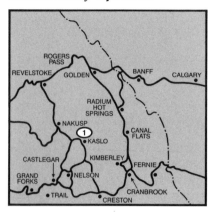

Who: soakers and swimmers — a great place for both sociable and private types as well as people wanting a cold plunge or a natural steam bath

Travel to springs: super-easy to reach. Paved highway to paved parking lot, then up a handicapped ramp to the resort and hot pools

Season: year-round

Why go: Hot springs in a cave — the pool follows two passages into a dimly lit cave in the rocky mountainside where peach and white colored stalactites drip hot rain. Inside the dark cavern the passages connect in a horseshoe shape, so you can go in one side and come out the other.

Deep in the cave there are secret places to hide. Hot water cascades over a colorful rock slope, above it there's a small cavern which is like a natural steam bath. You can crawl up the warm slope to it or just lie on the smooth rocks and luxuriate in the hot springs water streaming around you.

At the entrances to the cave you can meet other people in a small sociable hot pool. It has a ledge seat around the edge where up to 15 or 20 persons can sit in a circle and enjoy a snow storm or talk beneath summer stars. Next to it, there's a freezing cold plunge pool, with a waterfall pouring into it, which you can jump into for a stimulating splash — to my surprise it felt great after a deep-in-the-cave hot soak on a hot summer day! And on the other side of the sociable pool, there's a large curvaceous warm pool for swimming. It measures about 12 x 15 meters (40 x 50 feet). After swimming and soaking, and soaking and swimming you can go into the warm, well-appointed changerooms with electric outlets and hot showers to clean up. All facilities at this medium-sized operation are for use of persons passing through as well as for those eating at the restaurant overlooking Kootenay Lake or staying in the resort hotel — it's open year-round.

The temperature of the swimming pool ranges from 32° to 37° Celsius (90° to 99° Fahrenheit); the temperature of the cave hot pools ranges from 40° to 45° Celsius (104° to 113° Fahrenheit); there's no odor to the water.

The hot springs waters at Ainsworth have been enjoyed since at least 1882. The present cave started as tunnels dug by miners who were in the region looking for silver, lead and zinc. They followed the springs water into the mountain; the entrances to the tunnels were then dammed to contain the hot water at the high temperature it flowed from the ground at. The cavern has been improving ever since with the never-ending creation of beautiful

*Warm pool for swimming,
Kootenay Lake behind*

formations; the tufa builds up quickly with the constant flow of mineral water. Enough so that periodically the cavern is "cleaned out" by the management to keep it from filling up, and they might drill a bit farther in too — you never know what new nooks and crannies and ornaments you'll find on your next visit. It's an irresistible commercially operated hot springs.

For more information: contact Ainsworth Hot Springs Ltd., P.O. Box 1268, Ainsworth Hot Springs, B.C. V0G 1A0, telephone (604)229-4212.

Access to hot springs: Ainsworth is in the heart of the West Kootenays. The resort is nestled in the deep valley between the Selkirk and Purcell mountains and beside a deep lake. It's not on the road to anywhere, but I make it on the road to almost everywhere — I can produce a variety of imaginative excuses to go by way of these springs. You can approach by ferry or by leisurely roads from several directions, and by the time you reach the springs you've already started to relax. The pools and resort are right beside Highway 31 and overlook Kootenay Lake. If you approach from the south, notice the trail of neckties neatly tied 6 meters (20 feet) high on the telephone poles from Balfour to Coffee Creek — a zany manifestation of the delightful Kootenays whimsical spirit.
• From Creston, you could head north on Highway 3A and take the longest free ferry ride in the world. It crosses Kootenay Lake — goes between Kootenay Bay and Balfour. Then drive north for 10 minutes to Ainsworth Hot Springs.
• From Nelson, head northwest on Highway 3A to Balfour, then north on Highway 31 to Ainsworth Hot Springs. It takes 45 minutes.
• From Revelstoke, head south on Highway 23 to the free car ferry across Upper Arrow Lake. It sails from Shelter Bay to Galena Bay. Immediately off the ferry, turn left into Highway 31 which is unpaved for half the way to Ainsworth Hot Springs; this scenic big-mountain-route via Trout Lake and Lardeau to Ainsworth Hot Springs is also used for hauling logs, so drive with your headlights on. It could take as much as 3 hours to drive the 120 kilometers (75 miles) from Galena Bay to Ainsworth Hot Springs.

NAKUSP HOT SPRINGS
Commercially Operated

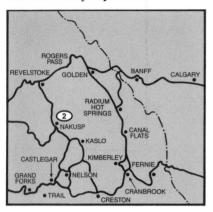

Who: soakers who want to enjoy a quiet, beautiful out-of-the way place; changerooms, campgrounds, a chalet

Travel to springs: you could drive to the door — from Highway 23, travel for 15 minutes up a paved road to the resort. Possibly logging traffic too

Season: open year-round except Christmas and two weeks in the fall

Why go: If you're wet and cold — or even if you're warm! — no nicer place to go after paddling than to Nakusp Hot Springs.

You'll find a commercially operated resort with tiled hot-swimming-pool-type outdoor springs as well as primitive natural hot pools in a couple of rock basins beside Kuskanax Creek. The commercially operated circular pool — affectionately referred to by some as the "Cannibal Pot" — is about 6 meters (20 feet) in diameter, and is split a third of the way across with a walkway. The smaller pool on one side of the walkway is hotter than the larger one. The temperature of these pools is 38° and 43° Celsius (100° and 109° Fahrenheit) and the water is odorless. At the resort, there are changerooms with electric outlets and hot showers; beside it, you'll find a resort-operated campground with flush toilets and hot showers as well as rental chalets. The pools are closed for maintenance for two weeks in the fall; and they're closed on Christmas day. Except for that, they're open year-round; and they're open in summer until 10 p.m. — late enough to reach the pools after paddling.

The civilized hot springs resort and the primitive pools are both superb. Take your choice — or go for it all!

For more information: Nakusp Hot Springs, P.O. Box 280, Nakusp, B.C. V0G 1R0, telephone (604)352-4033; or contact Nakusp Infocentre, P.O. Box 387, Nakusp, B.C. V0G 1R0, telephone (604)265-4234.

Access to commercially operated hot springs: the Nakusp Hot Springs are 15 minutes off Highway 23 near the village of Nakusp. The turnoff is north of the junction of Highways 23 and 6 and the side-road is paved highway. You can get to Nakusp in 3 hours from Vernon, and in 2 hours from Nelson, Castlegar and Revelstoke.

• From Revelstoke, head west on Trans-Canada Highway 1 and almost immediately turn south into Highway 23 toward the Shelter Bay-Galena Bay ferry. The moment you're off the Trans-Canada you begin to slow down to a pleasant Kootenays pace. Head south. Cross the Upper Arrow Lake on the

Early morning

free car ferry, then continue south again alongside the lake. From Galena Bay to the turnoff to Nakusp Hot Springs takes 35 minutes. You'll see signposts indicating the turnoff which is before you reach the village of Nakusp; head up this side-road for 15 minutes and you're there.

• From Vernon, head east on Highway 6 by way of Cherryville, cross the Monashee Mountains, ride the free car ferry across Lower Arrow Lake from Needles to Fauquier, and head north through Nakusp: follow Highway 6, then 23, to the hot springs turnoff.

• From Nelson, head west on Highway 3A to the junction with Highway 6; then go north on Highway 6 via Silverton and New Denver to Nakusp.

• From Castlegar, head northeast on Highway 3A to the junction with Highway 6. Then, again, follow the Slocan Valley north through Passmore, Silverton and New Denver to Nakusp.

• From Nakusp, go north on Highway 23, it's about 5 minutes from the village to the turnoff. Then, 15 minutes up the side-road to the commercially operated hot springs; see the description on pages 142 and 143 for directions to the primitive ones.

Travel is permitted 24 hours a day on the paved road from Highway 23 to the springs. However, on working days logging traffic could be on it too, so watch for logging trucks and drive with your headlights on.

NAKUSP HOT SPRINGS
Primitive

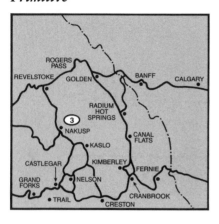

Who: soakers who are purists — the hot pool is 100% natural

Travel to springs: from Highway 23 it's a 15-minute drive on paved road — note that logging traffic might be on it too; plus a 15-minute walk for 2.0 kilometers (1.2 miles) along an easy path to the springs

Season: year-round

Why go: To soak, to play, to clean up. This one's incredible. There's no plastic, no tile. It's the only totally primitive hot pool I know of — the hot springs water collects in a natural basin of rock beside Kuskanax Creek. It's a completely natural pool, it's surrounded by tall green trees. Hot water spills over rough, rounded granite in a gentle waterfall you can sit in. There's room for three or four people in the pool and you can slide from one natural stone basin filled with hot springs water to another filled with freezing creek water; then back for a hot soak again. When you're tired of playing in the primitive pools, you've got the cleanly tiled commercially operated hot pools with smooth decks of native slate, attractive cedar buildings, heated changerooms, hot showers and hot coffee to go to.

Those who run the commercial operation are happy if visitors walk up the valley to enjoy the hot springs at their source as long as you don't divert them. Do not tamper with the flow. The primitive springs are within Nakusp Provincial Park so they're protected. Please keep them like they are.

For more information: Nakusp Hot Springs, P.O. Box 280, Nakusp, B.C. V0G 1R0, telephone (604)352-4033; or contact Nakusp Infocentre, P.O. Box 387, Nakusp, B.C. V0G 1R0, telephone (604)265-4234.

Access to primitive hot springs: The springs are located near Nakusp which you can reach in 3 hours from Vernon; in 2 hours from Nelson or Castlegar or Revelstoke. From Nakusp, it's a 5-minute drive north on Highway 23; a 15-minute drive up a paved side-road to the resort, plus a 15-minute walk.

• From Revelstoke, head west on Trans-Canada Highway 1 and almost immediately turn south into Highway 23 toward the free car ferry that sails from Shelter Bay-Galena Bay. Cross the Upper Arrow Lake on it and drive south again alongside the lake. From Galena Bay to the turnoff to Nakusp Hot Springs takes 35 minutes. You'll see signposts indicating the turnoff to the springs; if you reach the village of Nakusp, you've gone too far. Drive up the side-road for 15 minutes to the parking lot of the commercial operation.

Natural rock basin

• From Vernon, head east on Highway 6 by way of Cherryville across the Monashee Mountains then Lower Arrow Lake on the free Needles-Fauquier car ferry, then head north through Nakusp.

• From Nelson, head west on Highway 3A to the junction with Highway 6; then go north on Highway 6 via Silverton and New Denver to Nakusp.

• From Castlegar, head northeast on Highway 3A to the junction with Highway 6. Then, again, follow the Slocan Valley north through Passmore, Silverton and New Denver to Nakusp.

• From Nakusp, go north on Highway 23; it's a 5-minute drive from the village to the turnoff. Then, 15 minutes up the side-road to the parking lot beside the commercially operated pools and resort. Park there and walk upstream along a trail.

From the resort to the springs: walk 1.0 kilometer (0.6 mile) from the buildings that house the commercially operated pools to the primitive springs. Cross a footbridge and continue for another 1.0 kilometer (0.6 mile). Follow a rough trail along a steep bank beside the the pipeline to a clearing. In the clearing, you'll see a deep rectangular concrete tub. It measures 1 x 2 meters (3 x 6 feet) and it's filled with water too hot to climb into. Follow steaming trickles from the tub to the creekside and find just-the-right-temperature water in a natural rock basin.

Travel is permitted 24 hours a day on the paved road from Highway 23 to the springs. However, on working days logging traffic could be on it too, so watch for logging trucks and drive with your headlights on.

143

ST. LEON HOT SPRINGS
Primitive

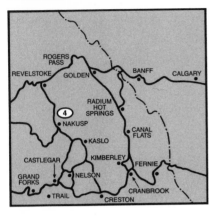

Who: soakers wanting a short or long walk to a quiet, tidy place in the wilds

Travel to springs: drive 10 minutes on a gravel logging road, then walk 15 minutes down a steep, difficult path to the springs; or hike from the paved highway to the springs — takes 2 hours on a rough but well graduated trail

Season: year-round

Why go: The hot springs pool at St. Leon is like a woodsy idyll from a story book — like a Hollywood movie set from the 40s or 50s. The springs are in the wilds, yet the steamy water is neatly contained in a kidney-shaped concrete pool. That's all that remains from a resort that was built because of the springs. The resort operated first in the early 1900s, and again from 1946 until the early 1950s when the hotel at St. Leon, which was beside Upper Arrow Lake and which was due to be expropriated for the Arrow reservoir, burnt to the ground. The springs water was never successfully piped to the hotel; the distance was too great and the guests had to go to the springs. In the early days they travelled by horse and buggy to reach them.

Today the pool at St. Leon is still lovely. The sides of it slope smoothly to its rounded center; when you slip down it there is hot, hot water up to your ears. The pool edge is encircled with flat rocks that are comfortable to sit on; there are a couple of rocks in it that you can sit on, too, and some spring-green algae. The pool sweeps in a gentle curve for a length of 6 meters (20 feet). Pine needles are scattered around it beneath a dense canopy of enormous evergreen trees. To catch the sun, plan to be in the pool by noon.

For more information: Nakusp Infocentre, P.O. Box 387, Nakusp, B.C. V0G 1R0, telephone (604)265-4234. Also see 1:50,000 topographic map St. Leon Creek 82K/5.

Access to hot springs: At the time of writing the public are permitted to visit St. Leon Springs; however, this property is privately owned. If you go there and find any signposts saying "No Trespassing", please respect them.

Located in the shady deep woods, St. Leon Hot Springs can be reached in 25 minutes to 2 hours from Highway 23. You can drive on a gravel logging road for 10 minutes, then head down a short steep hiking trail over slippery roots and deadfalls for 10 to 15 minutes — or start from Highway 23 and walk up a rough but well graduated trail in 2 hours. The logging road turnoff and the trail head are 20 minutes from Galena Bay, and 20 minutes from Nakusp.

Down steep bank

Climbing over deadfalls to pool

From Nakusp, head north toward the bridge over St. Leon Creek. When you have gone 15 minutes, start looking for a road-side rest area on the right-hand side. If you plan to drive to the springs, measure the distance from the rest area: go 2.6 kilometers (1.6 miles) more to St. Leon Forest Road and turn right. If hiking, continue past St. Leon Road and park at the roadside near the bridge over the creek.

From the Galena Bay-Shelter Bay free car ferry, head south. When you've driven for 20 minutes you'll cross a bridge over Halfway River, then another one over St. Leon Creek. Shortly past it you'll find the trail head, then St. Leon Road.

• If hiking all the way: you will find the trail head less than 0.4 kilometer (0.2 mile) south of the bridge over St. Leon Creek. Search along the east side of Highway 23 for this overgrown logging road that is now a trail. It is indicated by a faint gap between the trees. When you find it, the trail to the hot springs heads off obliquely to the left, and is fairly steep at the start. Then it flattens to a comfortable pitch. It takes 2 hours to walk up the cool wooded path. After about an hour, you'll cross a creek, then bear right and up the hill on a well-worn trail to the springs.

• If driving: you'll find St. Leon Road, which is a good gravel logging road, when you're 1.7 kilometers (1.1 miles) south of the bridge over St. Leon Creek and 2.6 kilometers (1.6 miles) north of a road-side rest area.

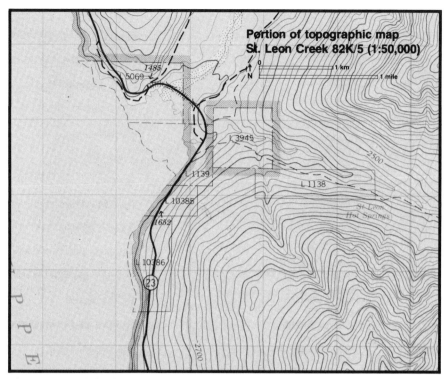

This map is included here to show the steepness of the incline from the Highway 23 "hot springs route" beside Upper Arrow Lake up to St. Leon Springs. The hiking trail to the springs is shown on this map as a logging road, but the road described in these access directions is not shown. It has been built since the region was mapped.

From Highway 23 to road-side parking for the springs, it is 3.5 kilometers (2.2 miles). Head up the steep hill and when you have gone for 1.3 kilometers (0.8 mile) there's a fork in the road. You stay left. Continue up the hill on the main road for 1.4 kilometers (0.9 mile) and another dirt track goes off on the left-hand side, but you continue straight for 0.8 kilometer (0.5 mile) more to a wide spot in the road where you can park and turn. You know you are there when the road starts to level off. After parking, walk a few paces back along the road and find a trail down the steep bank. Hike between the tall trees and angle to the right down the hill littered with deadfalls. It takes 10 or 15 minutes to reach the hot springs. Not easy — but it's worth it!

———————————————

Travel is permitted 24 hours a day on St. Leon Forest Road which is open to the public. However, logging traffic could be on it too, so drive with your headlights on. To learn about possible fire-hazard closures, contact the Ministry of Forests, Arrow District, 845 Columbia Avenue, Castlegar, B.C. V1N 1H3, telephone (604)365-2131; or contact the regional office of the Ministry of Forests, 518 Lake Street, Nelson, B.C. V1L 4C6, telephone (604)354-6200.

HALFWAY RIVER HOT SPRINGS
Primitive

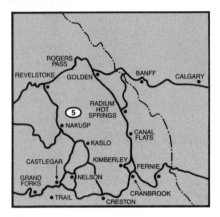

Who: soakers wanting very hot springs in a very private place. Camping too. In this Garden of Eden, you can cool off with a cold plunge in the river a few steps from the springs

Travel to springs: drive 35 minutes on gravel logging road from Highway 23; then walk for 5 to 10 minutes down a steep path to the river and springs

Season: year-round

Why go: At the base of the hill, you pass a tree with a signpost, but you want hot springs — you move on: pass two picnic tables, three tent sites, a pit toilet, firewood cut and stacked. You see the top small pool — it's 2 meters (6 feet) square; you lift its cover — yes, it's hot! You see a small cave, ferns beside it, a statue of the Virgin Mary in front of it. You dip a finger in the puddles at her feet. Yes, hot! You follow the steaming green algae trails that slowly circle the rocks and trickle toward the river — you follow them to the main pool where the hot springs are momentarily captured in a neat wooden tub that is 2½ meters (9 feet) square — you stop and climb in. Yes!

You soak for hours, but finally you *have* to leave. You have no food. No sleeping bag. No tent. But somehow you know this place will not go away. It's obviously so loved, so well tended. You'll come back too — to enjoy. To tend. To be. You like it quiet like you've found it. But also you wish to meet the other souls who tend this garden, who return to enjoy it. On the way out, you stop to read the signpost on the tree and you meet them — they never went away, they're here. And once you've been here, you'll never leave this place, it will never leave you. They, I, you, this place. We're all here together forever. I know because of the poem on the tree:

> *"There is no place*
> *Anything like this place*
> *Anywhere near this place*
> *So this must be the place."*

Temperature of the springs ranges from very hot to hot as the water trickles down to the river and there is a sulphur smell and taste to them. Also be aware that this Garden of Eden has its snake — there's lots of poison ivy.

For more information: Nakusp Infocentre, P.O. Box 387, Nakusp, B.C. V0G 1R0, telephone (604)265-4234.

Access to hot springs: Located beside Halfway River, which is halfway

Source of springs beneath cave

Ferns surround pool beside river — cool shade, hot water

Hottest pool beneath board, picnic table behind

along the east side of Upper Arrow Lake. You can get there in 3¼ hours from Vernon, in 2¼ hours from Nelson and Castlegar, 2 hours from Revelstoke, and 50 minutes from Nakusp. Look for huge osprey nests on the tops of telephone poles as you drive along this "hot springs route". When you reach the logging road turnoff, the springs are still 35 minutes off Highway 23; you'll find the turnoff when you're 20 minutes south of Galena Bay and 20 minutes north of Nakusp.

• From Nakusp, head north passing the turnoff to Nakusp Hot Springs, then St. Leon. When you're 0.6 kilometer (0.4 mile) past the bridge over St. Leon Creek, turn right up Halfway River Forest Road.

• From the Galena Bay-Shelter Bay free car ferry, head south; again, it's 20 minutes to your turnoff. When you've gone 12.5 kilometers (7.8 miles), you will pass Halcyon Hot Springs and you've still got 10.0 kilometers (6.2 miles) to go before reaching Halfway River, but you may not notice Halcyon. After crossing the bridge over Halfway River — which you can't miss — continue for 0.4 kilometer (0.3 mile) , turn left and head up the rough gravel logging road.

After leaving Highway 23, you'll have broad views of the wide gravelled river as you drive 6.1 kilometers (3.8 miles) to a fork in the road. Keep right and go 3.3 kilometers (2.1 miles) up a bumpy hill, along a flat stretch, then up another bumpy hill. You'll pass a "14" signpost on the left-hand side and then cross a creek.

Not much farther now — it's 1.5 kilometers (0.9 mile) more by road; go through a gravel pit. Past it, you'll see a fork in the road and a "Branch 48" signpost on the right-hand side; continue straight on the main road. You'll pass a rough dirt track that veers off down the hill on the left-hand side; again, continue straight. From "Branch 48", go straight for another 0.7 kilometer (0.4 mile), then go left down a dirt track to the logging landing, and park on the hard sandy part. This is the first clear-cut you see.

You'll find the trail to the river by walking 30 paces back up the turnoff road, almost to Halfway River Forest Road. Then look around. The steep path might be flagged: hike down it through tall trees. The trail curves to the right down the steep slope, then curls to the left past caves at the bottom of the hill. When you reach river level, head downstream and you'll find four casually developed hot pools between a cave on the left-hand side and the river. It's a world apart. But walking from the road down the hill to the springs, it takes only 5 or 10 minutes to reach this fern-clad Garden of Eden.

———————————————

Travel is permitted 24 hours a day on Halfway River Forest Road which is open to the public. However, logging traffic could be on it too, so drive with your headlights on. To learn about possible fire-hazard closures, contact the Ministry of Forests, Arrow District, 845 Columbia Avenue, Castlegar, B.C. V1N 1M3, telephone (604)365-2131; or contact the regional office of the Ministry of Forests, 518 Lake Street, Nelson, B.C. V1L 4C6, telephone (604)354-6200.

HALCYON HOT SPRINGS
Primitive

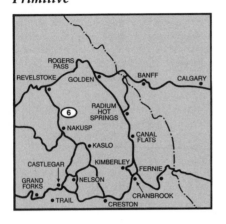

Who: lazy soakers looking for an easy-to-reach undeveloped campsite in the midst of steaming hot springs — on a hillside with a lake and snow-capped mountain view thrown in

Travel to springs: just off Highway 23. At the top of the rough road, no more than ten steps of walking to reach the hot springs. Drive 300 meters (1000 feet) up a steep road filled with potholes. Round a sharp curve. Pick a steamy patch, and drive the same distance again to where you can park, pitch your tent, "veg out"

Season: year-round

Why go: These primitive springs are magnificent — I remember camping beside Halcyon beneath a star-filled sky, another time making daisy chains while enjoying a hot soak on a sunny afternoon in July, another time leaping from the pool when a lightning storm threw orange forks into the black clouds over Upper Arrow Lake. It's a magical place in all its moods. There are several pools, all of them hot. We've hit the large pool at Halcyon when it's too hot to get in. It has been casually developed by someone who has built a couple of wooden tubs, one measuring 2½ x 5 meters (9 x 16 feet), the other 1¼ x 2½ meters (4 x 9 feet). They both have smooth log rounds for seats and are lined with plastic — depending on how friendly you are, there's room for 10 or 12 people to climb into the larger one, and 4 or 5 people to climb into the smaller one which is almost like a hot plunge pool. I think some cool water is mixed with the hot in the larger wooden tub to bring the temperature down a bit. The springs have some sulphur smell, but not enough to disturb me.

Nor others. These springs were developed at the turn of the century: first with a simple plunge pool — it's gone full-circle; within a couple of years, Halcyon grew to be an elegant resort. Guests came by sternwheeler — there were no roads — to soak in the hot baths and stay at the magnificent four-storey frame hotel beside Upper Arrow Lake. In 1955, just before the flooding of the lake would have drowned the large hotel, it burned. Today it feels to me like all West Kootenay roads lead to Halcyon. Many do. You can drive right to the springs, most of the way on paved highway. It's a rough dirt track for the last 300 meters (1000 feet) up the hill. Halcyon is so accessible and so well-known that it is visited by many people and you probably will not have it to yourselves. But if you don't want to hike for your hot springs stop, and you don't mind sharing your hot springs with others, Halcyon is superb.

The temperature of the springs as they bubble from the ground is 48° Celsius (118° Fahrenheit) — they're hot!

For more information: Nakusp Infocentre, P.O. Box 387, Nakusp, B.C.

From hot pool, looking across Upper Arrow Lake

V0G 1R0, telephone (604)265-4234. Also see the 1:50,000 topographic map Beaton 82K/12.

Access to hot springs: Situated overlooking Upper Arrow Lake and just above Highway 23, between Revelstoke and Nakusp; from Revelstoke, it takes 1½ hours to reach the springs; from Nakusp, 20 minutes.

From Revelstoke, head west on Highway 1, then almost immediately turn south on Highway 23 toward the free car ferry from Shelter Bay-Galena Bay. From Galena Bay, continue south for 12.5 kilometers (7.8 miles) to the turnoff to Halcyon. Look for a tall pole on the left-hand side.

From the right-angle bend in the center of Nakusp, go north for 36 kilometers (22 miles) or measure from the bridge at Halfway River and go north 9.9 kilometers (6.2 miles) to the Halcyon turnoff. It's on the right-hand side.

The steep dirt road filled with potholes that branches off Highway 23 to the springs is marked by a tall pole with the signpost "Private". You can drive up it for about 300 meters (1000 feet), make a sharp hairpin curve to the right-hand side and drive to within a few steps of the springs. At the time of writing the springs are frequented by the public and the owners do not seem to mind. However, this could change at any time. If you see a new "No Trespassing" sign, respect it.

CANYON HOT SPRINGS
Commercially Operated

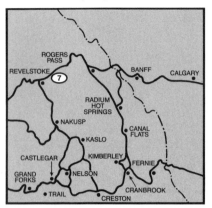

Who: soakers and swimmers — all will enjoy it

Travel to springs: so easy to reach, it's 10 on a scale of 1 to 10. Trans-Canada Highway 1 to the resort, then a short paved road to the parking lot which is a few steps from the pools

Season: mid-May through mid-September

Why go: The hot pool in Albert Canyon is so reachable — it's almost *on* Trans-Canada Highway 1, yet it feels hidden in deep mountains. We soaked in it after paddling the Kicking Horse, which also feels light years from anything, although much of that river too is within sight of the roaring Trans-Canada. An excellent wild river, an excellent medium-sized hot springs to follow it with. The river and springs are separated by 120 kilometers (75 miles) but linked by Canada's number 1. And the Canyon Springs are great!

There are two pools and they are only 3 meters (10 feet) apart: the water temperature of the hot pool is 41° Celsius (105° Fahrenheit) and it measures 10 x 10 meters (30 x 30 feet); the "cool" pool measures 12 x 20 meters (40 x 70 feet) and is 29° Celsius (85° Fahrenheit). The water in both pools is odorless. You'll find all the usual amenities of changerooms with electric outlets, hot showers and a small café as well as a spacious campground with 130 campsites scattered beneath the trees at this commercially operated hot pool where music is piped in. You can hear it under water.

You can arrange to go rafting on commercially operated ½-day and 1-day trips from Canyon Hot Springs — the pools and the resort are open from mid-May through mid-September.

For more information: Canyon Hot Springs, P.O. Box 2400, Revelstoke, B.C. V0E 2S0, telephone (604)837-2420.

Access to hot springs: Located beside Trans-Canada Highway 1 west of Rogers Pass; this resort is 1¼ hours from Golden, 1¼ hours from the Shelter Bay ferry; 30 minutes from Revelstoke. It's difficult to spot when driving at high speed: watch for it on the south side of the highway.

Beyond pools, snow-capped peaks of Monashees

Paddlers in steamy hot pool

BUSH RIVER COOL SPRINGS
Primitive

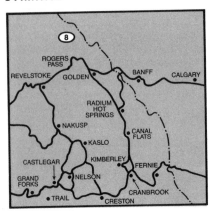

Who: adventure seekers with a canoe who'll settle for a cool soak — all near a low-key campsite

Travel to springs: 1½ hours off Trans-Canada Highway 1 on gravel logging roads; then a 5-minute paddle. Ferry across the Bush River to search for the cool springs

Season: year-round but best in summer

Why go: For wonderful scenery, for a good time looking, for a tepid paddle in a woodsy pool — if you're lucky!

We were lured to explore this wilderness spot by the rumor of primitive cool springs beside the Bush. However, there was so much rain the week before we were there that the cool springs were chilled and drowned and we didn't realize we'd found them. But these springs are part of the relatively remote forest service recreation site beside the Valenciennes and Bush rivers, and, the forest service recreation officer for this region has confirmed to me that the cool springs *are* there beside the trapper's cabin we found. They're across the Bush River, so take a boat and paddle. And have fun looking!

For more information: contact the Ministry of Forests, Golden District, at 600 Ninth Street North, P.O. Box 1380, Golden, B.C. V0A 1H0, telephone (604)344-7500.

Access to cool springs: The springs are located 1½ hours off Trans-Canada Highway 1; the turnoff to go there is at Donald between Golden and Rogers Pass. Donald is not easy to spot — it's a railway point that a great many locals relate to and refer to. It's a small settlement with a mill, a trailer park and a graveyard. There is little indication from the highway that you've reached it. So measure the time or distance. Heading east on Trans-Canada Highway 1, look for Big Bend Highway cutting off to the northwest when 1¼ hours east of Albert Canyon and 45 minutes east of Rogers Pass Summit. Heading west, look for Big Bend Highway when you're 23 kilometers (14 miles) west of Golden or 7.2 kilometers (4.5 miles) west of the Trans-Canada Highway 1 bridge over the Blaeberry. After you leave Trans-Canada Highway 1, refer back to the map on page 57 as well as to the directions that immediately follow on page 157 to help you find your way into the back country.

From Trans-Canada Highway 1, turn north into Big Bend Highway; it is a good gravel road. Travelling up the Big Bend, which becomes Bush River Forest Road after 4.2 kilometers (2.6 miles), you'll drive through countryside

Cool springs pool visible in air photo of Bush River: it is in circle opposite where Valenciennes River flows in; Surprise Canyon upstream

that's raw and scarred by logging for 30 kilometers (19 miles) and the region is honeycombed with confusing logging roads. Keep noticing where you are: you'll pass Blackwater, Comfort, Help and Aid lakes. From Help Lake onward, the countryside is pretty. To find the springs, travel up the east shore of Bush Arm of Kinbasket Lake to where the Valenciennes River flows into the Bush River. When you cross a small bridge over Goodfellow Creek, you're almost there. Go 6.6 kilometers (4.1 miles) more to the bridge over the Valenciennes and you'll see the Bush River on your left-hand side. The campground is on your right-hand side beside the Valenciennes with picnic tables, pit toilets, and fire rings, and there's a good trail you can walk along for 2 kilometers (1 mile) up the lovely Valenciennes Canyon. The springs are immediately across the Bush River on the opposite side of it from the campground.

With extremely low water you might be able to wade the stream. But it's better to ferry across the river in a canoe or kayak, even though it's difficult to pull a boat up the bank through the tangle of scrubby brush into the trees. Climbing through the bushes is scratchy and rough — we encountered mosquitoes too, but I always love poking around to see what's there. We found a rough trapper's cabin beside a small pond, and that pond is formed by the cool springs. They bubble through the rocks a little north of the cabin.

Travel is permitted 24 hours a day on Bush River and Chatter Creek Forest Roads which are open to the public. However, logging traffic could be on them too, so drive with your headlights on. To learn about possible fire-hazard closures, contact the Ministry of Forests, Golden District, 600 Ninth Street North, P.O. Box 1380, Golden, B.C. V0A 1H0, telephone, (604)344-7500.

RADIUM HOT SPRINGS
Commercially Operated

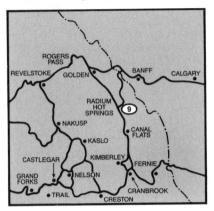

Who: soakers, game-watchers, serious swimmers — all will love it

Travel to springs: sooooooooo easy to reach — it's beside Highway 93.
Radium Aquacourt has a wheelchair to loan as well as handicapped access from parking lot to changerooms to pool and restaurants

Season: year-round

Why go: Rocky Mountain bighorn sheep are often on the red rock hillside opposite the springs nestled in Sinclair Canyon — game-watching from the hot pool is an everyday pastime at Radium.

While luxuriating in these delectably hot, smoothly tiled outdoor springs, you'll lie back, look through the steam, and almost always see wild bighorn sheep. You feel you could reach out and touch the prickly needles of an evergreen tree. The pools are odorless. The hot lounging pool is square at one corner and the rest of it curves around and follows the shape of the mountain; although there is room for 250 to 300 people to sit on the seats around the edges of the shallow hot pool, which is 50 meters (160 feet) long, the feeling is not of a crowd nor huge space — the feeling is of an intimate protected canyon, wild game, starry skies, and a totally warm friendly atmosphere.

There are two pools at Radium — a hot one and a cool one. The steaming mineral water that warms them comes from 2410 meters (1½ miles) below the ground. Up to 750 people can be accommodated in the two large pools which total 740 square meters (8,000 square feet) of surface water. But the mountains rising up close on all sides give them a comfortable, contained feeling. The cool pool is separate from the hot one and not visible from it. It is a rectangular shape with a length of 24 meters (80 feet), good for swimming lengths. The temperature of the cooler swimming pool is 29° Celsius (84° Fahrenheit); the hot lounging pool is 39° Celsius (103° Fahrenheit). You can lie back in it for hours looking up at the silhouette of the mountains against the starry sky.

Radium has civilized amenities yet a wild feeling. The commercially operated springs have been part of Kootenay National Park since 1922. And park management has done a beautiful job with them. At Radium, after a long soak in the hot pool you can swim in the cool pool, then take a warm shower, blow-dry your hair and stop in the café for a snack. You'll find a variety of accommodations nearby including hotels, motels, and camping for a fee at Redstreak and Dry Gulch. The pools are open year-round, in summer until

Sinclair Canyon

11:00 p.m., which gives you plenty of time to reach them after paddling.

For more information: Radium Hot Springs Aquacourt, P.O. Box 220, Radium Hot Springs, B.C. V0A 1M0, telephone (604)347-9485.

Access to hot springs: Located at the southern entry to Kootenay National Park beside Banff-Windermere Highway 93. From the junction of Highways 93 and 95 in the community of Radium Hot Springs, go 3.0 kilometers (1.9 miles) east on Highway 93. The aquacourt is 5 minutes east of the community of Radium; 20 minutes from Invermere; and 1½ hours from Golden.

FAIRMONT HOT SPRINGS
Commercially Operated and Primitive

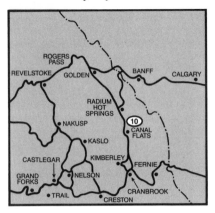

Who: who Fairmont *is not* for, is the more challenging question. Do you like things big? — little? — developed or rustic? Like crowds? — privacy? Want to swim lengths? — dive? — just have a hot soak? Looking for luxury? — or RV camping? You'll find it at Fairmont

Travel to springs: 1.8 kilometers (1.1 miles) on paved road off of Highway 93/95 right to the parking lot; located in the heart of the big broad Columbia-Windermere Valley

Season: year-round

Why go: "Land of the Smoking Waters" is what the Indians called the springs at Fairmont when they used branches to build tents over the hot pools they dug. And it's still a good name. Today the commercially operated open-air pools at Fairmont are gigantic — they've become the largest ones in British Columbia. They cover 930 square meters (10,000 square feet). To me, the hot pools area feels like a football field — all steaming!

At Fairmont, it's actually one giant pool divided into three smaller ones: a large 24-meter (80-foot) long rectangular pool with the water regulated at ideal temperature for active swimmers; there's a square pool for diving, and a triangular one for sociable soaking. The three pools together easily accommodate 900 people. This trio of hot pools sits on the east side of the broad Columbia-Windermere Valley and the snow-capped Rockies rise behind it. As you swim and dive and lounge in the steamy blue water, you look up to the "Mountain of Salt" behind the parking lot where there is still a primitive hot springs pool in the sunshine as well as three concrete tubs inside a stone bathhouse that was built in the early 1900s. This rustic open-air pool and the old stone bathhouse pools are called the Indian Baths, and soaking in them is free. Additional primitive hot pools pop up periodically on the hillside and then go away again, but the Indian Baths have continued bubbling up hot water ever since the stone bathhouse was built. And, above the Baths, you see the massive mountains where there's skiing in winter — it's a broad expansive scene. It's big. And it's got variety; that's what's different about Fairmont.

Twenty years ago at Fairmont the ambience of the commercially operated pool was rustic — log rail fencing was around the changeroom and up the stairsteps to it. After swimming, you could stop to squeeze the water from your swimsuit with the hand wringer attached to the log railing beside the pool. At that time, the pool in the commercial operation measured 6 x 15 meters (20 x 50 feet); it was situated on the valley side of the present giant pool. There were park benches beside it like you find today beside the primitive pool at the Indian Baths. The character of the resort is changing and developing and

Original bathhouse

moving with the times, but the warm welcoming atmosphere and the wonderful hot springs water, which is what it's all about, remain the same.

The temperature of the three pools ranges from 33° to 43° Celsius (92° to 110° Fahrenheit) but is consistent throughout each pool. The hot lounging pool is 43° Celsius (110° Fahrenheit); the swimming pool is cooler — it's temperature is maintained at 34° Celsius (94° Fahrenheit), while the diving pool is cooler again. It's kept at 33° Celsius (92° Fahrenheit); and all the water is odorless. The commercially operated pools are open daily year-round until 10 p.m. which gives you a chance to get there after paddling.

And, Fairmont *is* big, but the Fairmont of today has it all: those who like things intimate and simple can go to the Indian Baths which are available around the clock. Two or three people fit into the outdoor pool rimmed with wood. It has a cozy, friendly feeling. From it, you can see out across the big wide valley. A few steps below it, you'll find the old bathhouse where you can soak inside — it's still usable. There are three private rooms, each with a concrete tub which the hot springs water flows through, if you give it a little

Indian Baths

Triangular hot pool

Warm pool for swimming

encouragement, and this is the only hot springs setup I know of in the Kootenays where you're guaranteed to be able to soak in privacy if you want to. On the downhill side of the bathhouse the springs water runs out over a yellow-and-white petrified cascade — it's tufa deposited from the hot springs flow which is building the "Mountain of Salt".

The Fairmont of today is more than just hot pools, it's a many-faceted resort: there is a pleasantly low-lying (not high-rise) 139-room resort hotel with an intimate, round, brilliant blue hot pool for lodge guests. The lodge has a comfortable coffee shop available to day-guests too — I was welcomed into it while wearing my damp bathing suit; you will also find an elegant restaurant, two golf courses, tennis courts, and horseback riding as well as a trailer park with 265 units; fast food is available beside the changerooms. Other facilities day-guests will find are electric outlets and hot showers in the changerooms. The last time we were there the pools were temporarily closed because of a lightning storm, so they gave us *free* showers — and oh so nice to take a hot shower and get cleaned up after paddling.

For more information: Fairmont Hot Springs Resort, P.O. Box 10, Fairmont Hot Springs, B.C. V0B 1L0, (604)345-6311; in Calgary (403)264-0746 or 264-6061; toll-free throughout Canada and the U.S.A. 1-800-663-4979.

Access to hot springs: Situated near Highway 93/95 on the east side of the Columbia-Windermere Valley. Fairmont Hot Springs is 128 kilometers (80 miles) south of Radium Hot Springs and 112 kilometers (70 miles) north of Cranbrook, between Invermere and Canal Flats. As you approach, you'll see signposts and you'll see a huge signpost on the highway at the turnoff. The resort and the springs are 1.8 kilometers (1.1 miles) up the hill.

LUSSIER HOT SPRINGS
Primitive

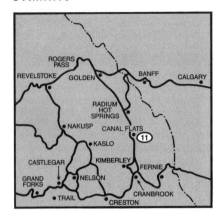

Who: Soakers who want to relax in natural pebbly hot pools beneath starry skies, who want to sink into a hot pool in the shelter of a wooden shack, plunge into the cold river — soakers wanting to meet new people. Great place for a party, they often happen here

Travel to springs: from Highway 93/95, it's 25 minutes on narrow gravel logging roads, then down stairsteps and a gravel path — 30 paces to the rustic shelter, springs and river

Season: year-round

Why go: These primitive springs in Whiteswan Lake Provincial Park are an incredible place to while away an hour beneath the stars, perfect for a rainy day.

Natural hot springs bubble up into a small, steamy wooden bathhouse beside the Lussier River: six people, at the most, fit into the springs in this rough shelter. Outside it, hot pools are scattered down the slope — they go in tiers to the riverbank. The pools change periodically as people rearrange the rocks that form them. The last time I was there, the first outdoor pool was small with a capacity for four or five people; steaming water cascaded from it, and trickled to the sandy-bottomed, rock-rimmed oval below, where there was room for 12 or 16 people to soak — this one was the right temperature for me to be happy in for hours. Below it was a small cool pool; and for people wanting a freezing plunge, the Lussier River.

The springs have a slight sulphurous odor and water temperature is hot but varies with runoff: so, when paddling is at its most exciting, the springs could be slightly cool. When we were there in mid-June the water was just passable; a week later it had warmed up and was perfect.

A great many visitors enjoy these springs, and the parks people who care for them ask that everyone help keep the area clean: take away all that you take in and all litter that you find, including cigarette butts, bottles, and broken glass after an accident. Leave it clean, ready for your next visit.

For more information: Contact the Ministry of Parks, P.O. Box 118, Wasa, B.C. V0B 2K0, telephone (604)422-3212. Also see the 1:125,000 topographic map Canal Flats 82J/SW; two portions of it, which also show Ram Creek Hot Springs, are reproduced on pages 168 and 169.

Access to hot springs: Located in the mountains on the east side of the Rocky Mountain Trench off Highway 93/95 between Canal Flats, Kimberley and Cranbrook. From the highway, it's 25 minutes on a gravel logging road to Lussier. To find it, look for the turnoff to Whiteswan Lake Provincial Park.
• From Radium, Invermere and Canal Flats, head south on Highway 93/95;

Inside hot springs shack, looking out

when you're 4.6 kilometers (2.9 miles) south of the bridge at Canal Flats, turn left into Whiteswan Forest Road.

• From Cranbrook and Kimberley, head north from the junction of 93/95 and 95A for 25 minutes to the Whiteswan turnoff on the right-hand side.

From the Highway 93/95 turnoff, drive 17.8 kilometers (11.1 miles) up Whiteswan Road — it's a twisting, narrow, gravel logging road. Lussier is at the "16 km" signpost. When you see the "Whiteswan Lake Provincial Park" signpost on the left-hand side, you're almost there. Look for a canopy on the right-hand side, which covers the first few stairsteps to the springs. From the road, only 30 paces down the steep stairsteps and then gravel path to Lussier.

Travel is permitted 24 hours a day on Whiteswan Forest Road which is open to the public. However, logging traffic could be on it too, so drive with your headlights on. And, if possible, follow a logging truck; its driver will inform other logging truck drivers of your presence and location on the road. To learn about possible fire-hazard closures, contact the office of the Ministry of Forests, Invermere District, P.O. Box 189, Invermere, B.C. V0A 1K0, telephone (604)342-4200.

RAM CREEK HOT SPRINGS
Primitive

Who: soakers who are happy with warm — not hot — springs, and who want it uncrowded

Travel to springs: from Highway 93/95 to Ram Creek takes 40 minutes of driving on gravel logging roads, then 40 paces of walking up a well-worn trail

Season: year-round; best on a sunny day

Why go: The best kept secret in the East Kootenays — the primitive springs at Ram Creek are a wonderful day-time place-to-go in summertime: not hot enough for a cold night; not hot enough for a winter warm-up. But perfect for a sunny day in August.

Wild flowers bloom around this deep pool where locals have placed rocks to collect the natural flow: pointed rocks dam up the large warm pool, flat rocks form stairsteps into it; and there are rounded rocks to sit on in the bottom of the pool. The water is odorless, and these delightful hot springs have been casually developed in a most natural and beautiful manner. The water is deep; you could sink in up to your chin and soak all day. The pool is about 5 x 8 meters (16 x 26 feet). It's situated a short way above the road in a small cleft in the hillside giving you an open feeling as you look out over the bright southern sky, and a feeling of tall trees rising behind, but well behind, not encroaching on you. When sitting in the springs, you feel you're King of the Mountain.

More and more people will be enjoying these springs. Again, be sure to take away all that you take in. Leave the area clean, ready for your next visit. There is supposed to be poison ivy nearby — we didn't see it, but if you wander from the springs, watch for it. I saw only the flowers.

For more information: contact the Ministry of Parks, P.O. Box 118, Wasa, B.C. V0B 2K0, telephone (604)422-3212. Ask for their Top of the World Provincial Park brochure with a map showing the way to the springs. Also see the 1:125,000 topographic map Canal Flats 82J/SW on pages 168 and 169.

Access to hot springs: Located in the mountains above the east side of the Rocky Mountain Trench between Cranbrook, Kimberley and Canal Flats. You can reach these springs by way of back roads from the White River and Lussier Hot Springs; if all industrial roads are open, it's 45 minutes from Lussier to Ram Creek. Or, you can go directly up a logging road; the turnoff to it from Highway 93/95 is north of Skookumchuck — that takes 40 minutes.

• From Cranbrook and Kimberley, heading north: watch for signposts to

Wild flowers at Ram Creek

"Premier Lake". When you're 2.5 kilometers (1.6 miles) north of the bridge over the Kootenay River at Skookumchuck, turn right off Highway 93/95 into Premier Lake Road.
• From Radium, Invermere and Canal Flats, heading south: you'll find the Premier Lake Road turnoff 27 kilometers (17 miles) south of Canal Flats.

Head up Premier Lake Road: after going 7.9 kilometers (4.9 miles) you will pass a right-hand turnoff to Premier Lake. Do not turn right. To this point, the road has been paved; but from here, continue straight on the gravel road with the "Sheep Creek Road North" signpost. After 1.6 kilometers (1.0 mile) there is another fork in the road; you follow the main road and turn right across the Lussier River (Sheep Creek). Continue on Sheep Creek Forest Road for 11.5 kilometers (7.1 miles) more to where the road curves right and up the hill; there is room to park on the left-hand side. You'll see hot springs water trickling toward the road over rocks green with algae. And you'll see a well-worn dirt path — it's 40 paces up the slope to the springs which are in an ecological reserve.
• From Lussier Hot Springs and the White River, you can head across the mountains on a network of logging and mining roads to Ram Creek. On your first visit to Ram Creek via the back roads, you need to go during daylight

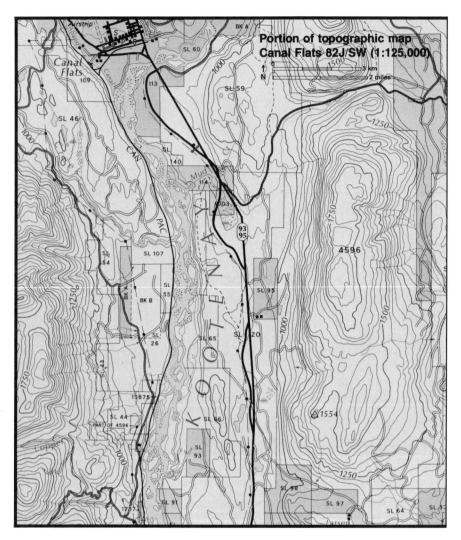

Portion of topographic map
Canal Flats 82J/SW (1:125,000)

hours. The route was poorly signposted when we were there. In addition, the last stretch to Ram Creek over the mountain from Lussier was a restricted logging road. Be warned: during daylight hours, you might have to wait for the end of the working day to travel the last 5 kilometers (3 miles).

If all industrial roads are open, it takes 45 minutes. From Lussier, go for 3.3 kilometers (2.1 miles) to Alces Lake and turn right into Coyote-Lussier Forest Road where you'll see the "Top of the World Park" signpost. After going 9.4 kilometers (5.8 miles) stay to the right-hand side of the big valley and cross the creek; do not bear left up Coyote Creek Forest Road. Continue more-or-less straight and go for 7.9 kilometers (4.9 miles). You'll find a maze of rough roads through this broad, high valley with a great deal of industrial traffic on them. When there are choices, it's probably safest to keep to the right. You'll reach a signpost (it was a very temporary one when we were there, and might now be gone) indicating that Top of the World Park is 15 kilometers (9 miles)

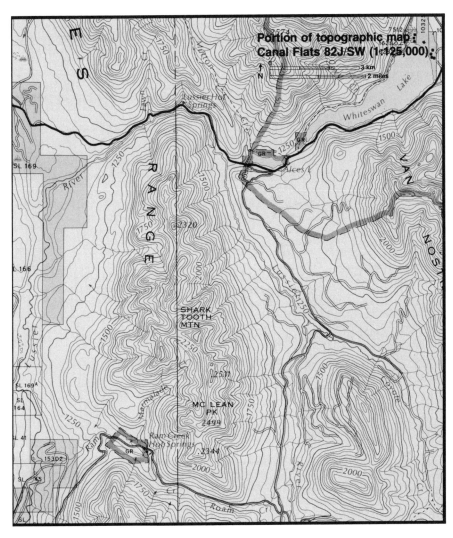

straight ahead. Do not go straight: turn right and go 5.8 kilometers (3.6 miles) over the mountains and down to Ram Creek Springs. When you head down the final steep hill to the springs, you'll see road-side parking in the switch-back curve at the bottom of it.

Travel is permitted 24 hours a day on Premier, Sheep Creek and Whiteswan Forest Roads, which are open to the public. However, logging traffic could be on them too, so drive with your headlights on. But note that travel might be restricted, with only in-dustrial traffic permitted on some of the roads in the region of Lussier and Top of the World Park until after 5 p.m. In addition, the Lussier Forest Road is extremely confus-ing with many poorly signposted roads veering off. It is not obvious which road to take; always be aware of how far you've gone and where you are or you might get lost.

To learn about possible fire-hazard closures, contact the office of the Ministry of Forests, Invermere District, P.O. Box 189, Invermere, B.C. V0A 1K0, telephone (604)342-4200.

WATER-GAUGING STATIONS
in the West and East Kootenays

River, Station Name, and Number (active or inactive)	Period of Record	Maximum Recorded Discharge and Date
Blaeberry River above Willowbank Creek 08NB012 (active)	17 years	153 m³/s (5,400 cfs) on May 29, 1986
Bobbie Burns Creek (no station)	None	No Records
Bull River near Wardner 08NG002 (active)	68 years	428 m³/s (15,100 cfs) on June 17, 1974
Bush River (no station)	None	No records
Columbia River at Birchbank 08NE049 (active)	50 years	10,700 m³/s (377,900 cfs) on June 9, 1961
Cross River (no station)	None	No records
Duncan River below B.B. Creek 08NH119 (active)	25 years	742 m³/s (26,200 cfs) on July 12, 1983
Elk River at Phillips Bridge 08NK005 (active)	63 years	949 m³/s (33,500 cfs) on May 24, 1948
Findlay Creek near Canal Flats 08NG001 (inactive)	10 years	121 m³/s (4,280 cfs) on June 10, 1948
Granby River at Grand Forks 08NN002 (active)	28 years	385 m³/s (13,600 cfs) on June 4, 1914
Horsethief Creek near Wilmer 08NA005 (inactive)	12 years	112 m³/s (3,960 cfs) on August 23, 1912
Kicking Horse River at Golden 08NA006 (active)	24 years	402 m³/s (14,200 cfs) on June 19, 1916
Kootenay River at Canal Flats 08NF002 (active)	36 years	876 m³/s (30,900 cfs) on May 29, 1986
Lardeau River at Marblehead 08NH007 (active)	45 years	422 m³/s (14,900 cfs) on June 11, 1972
Little Slocan River (no station)	None	No records
St. Mary River near Marysville 08NG046 (active)	42 years	501 m³/s (17,700 cfs) on June 17, 1974
Salmo River near Salmo 08NE074 (active)	39 years	462 m³/s (16,300 cfs) on June 2, 1968
Slocan River near Crescent Valley 08NJ013 (active)	63 years	719 m³/s (25,400 cfs) on June 7, 1961
Toby Creek near Athalmer 08NA012 (inactive)	21 years	143 m³/s (5,050 cfs) on July 12, 1983
Vermilion River near Radium Hot Springs 08NF004 (inactive)	11 years	191 m³/s (6,750 cfs) on June 5, 1956
White River near Canal Flats 08NF003 (inactive)	8 years	170 m³/s (6,000 cfs) on May 24, 1948
Wilson Creek near Rosebery 08NJ011 (inactive)	9 months	176 m³/s (6,220 cfs) on June 19, 1916

GLOSSARY OF SPECIAL TERMS USED BY RIVER RUNNERS

big water: large-volume, turbulent water characterized by boils and whirlpools as well as big waves and holes. Heavy water is similar but less violent.

boil: water welling up into a mound; occurs in big water.

bony: description of a river at low volume with many rocks showing, on which careful maneuvering is required to avoid hitting or scraping the rocks.

boulder garden: a boulder-strewn section of river.

braided river: a river split by sand or gravel bars into two or more channels that later converge and split again like a braid.

broaching: boat turning broadside to the river current and onto a rock or other obstacle; or boat turning broadside to the ocean surf.

busy water: water requiring a great deal of precision or maneuvering.

C-1: a decked (or closed) canoe propelled by one person in a kneeling position using a single-bladed paddle.

C-2: a decked (or closed) canoe propelled by two persons in a kneeling position, each using a single-bladed paddle.

canoe: see *open-canoe, closed-canoe, C-1* and *C-2*.

cascade: water coursing over a series of ledges or boulders; almost a waterfall.

channel: water flowing through a deeper part of the riverbed or a river route where a boat can go.

chicken route: a relatively easier way down the river.

chute: a channel in which fast water flows through a navigable gap in a drop.

clean river: a river that is normally free from sweepers and logjams.

closed-boat: a decked whitewater craft (kayak or C-1 or C-2).

closed-canoe: a decked boat paddled by one or two persons in a kneeling position, each using a single-bladed paddle.

continuous rapids: water flowing without stopping.

cushion: water piling up on the upstream side of a rock or other obstacle.

dam: a man-made barrier across a river that holds back the water. Often it is used to regulate the flow by allowing water to pass through it, or around it, but water does not flow over it.

discharge table: a record of volume of river-flow expressed in cubic meters per second (m³/s) and cubic feet per second (cfs), as it relates to the water height on the staff gauge or to the riverflow measurement made by the recording gauge on that river.

drop-and-pool river: a river in which still pools alternate with whitewater drops.

drop: a section of river, usually short, where the water descends relatively rapidly between two flatter stretches of water.

eddy: a resting place in a flowing stream where the water is still or the current flows upstream; an area of slack water downstream from a river bend, a rock, or other obstruction in the river where it is possible to stop.

eddy-hop: proceed downriver, across it, or upstream by moving from eddy to eddy and using each eddy to slow down or stop to scout, or to play.

eddy fence: a wall of water along the eddy line between the mainstream and the eddy; usually occurs in big water.

ender (endo): a maneuver — purposeful or accidental — in which the boat flips end over end, either forward or backward. It occurs on big, steep ocean surf, and in deep holes and on the upstream side of large standing waves on rivers.

Eskimo rescue: a technique whereby a paddler in an upright kayak assists a buddy in an overturned kayak to right it. The paddler in the overturned kayak beats the bottom of the boat to call for help, and the rescuer responds by placing his or her boat at right angles to the center of the overturned boat so that the upset paddler can grasp the bow and use it to become upright.

Eskimo roll: maneuver in which a closed-boater, remaining in an overturned kayak or decked canoe, uses a paddle and a hip-flick body motion to right the craft.

ferrying: a technique for crossing the current by angling the boat while paddling upstream.

flash rivers: rain-fed (sometimes snow-melt) rivers that rise and fall quickly.

frowning hole: a horseshoe-shaped drop that looks as if it is frowning (with a down-turned mouth) when viewed from upstream. This hole formation is more likely to be a dangerous keeper (see *keeper* listing) than is a smiling hole or a ledge drop.

gauge, water: see *recording gauge* and see *staff gauge*.

glacial-melt: description of a river that is sustained by the melting of glaciers. Normally these rivers reach large volume from mid-July to late September when the sun is hot.

gradient: the average amount that a river drops expressed in meters/kilometer (feet/mile).

haystacks: high, pointed standing waves.

head wall: a vertical rock wall or hard river-bank at a sharp bend in the river, often at a right angle. When the current is strong there will be a cushion of water on the wall, and often the wall is undercut.

heavy water: large-volume, turbulent water. Big water is similar but more violent.

hole: turbulent water in a river on the downstream side of a submerged rock or other obstacle — it is formed by the water flowing downriver with such great force over the rock that the surface water immediately downstream from the rock flows upstream to fill in the gap, then flows down to the riverbed before continuing downriver. Sometimes a hole is called a reversal. Also see *keeper, ledge, playing* and *play spot*.

hotdogging: playing in holes, eddies, and surfing waves to purposefully do pop-ups, enders, and other stunts on the water.

house rock: a very large rock or boulder, usually at least 3 meters (10 feet) high.

hydraulics: when used by whitewater boaters, this term refers to powerful waves, boils, whirlpools, and squirrelly, unpredictable surges of water found in large-volume rivers. Rollers, holes, reversals: "a thing that'll getcha."

K-1: a kayak for one person.

K-2: a kayak for two persons that is normally used on flat water.

kayak: a decked boat propelled by one or two persons from a sitting position, each using a double-bladed paddle.

keeper: a hole, or reversal, so powerful that it prevents a boat or a swimmer from leaving it. Holes formed below weirs or below bedrock ledges that are straight across become keepers with a lesser amount of water than does either a frowning hole or a smiling hole.

ledge: a horizontal rocky shelf, often at right angles to the current, over which the river drops abruptly; a hole formed on the downstream side of it is likely to become a keeper at higher water.

lining: pulling a boat upstream or downstream, guiding it with ropes attached to the bow or stern, or to both.

logjam: logs, branches, and debris piled up in the river with water straining through them and flowing beneath them; potentially one of the most dangerous hazards on rivers.

open-canoe (or open-Canadian canoe): a canoe without a deck (but sometimes with a spray deck of soft fabric and/or flotation) paddled by one or two persons in a kneeling position, each using a single-bladed paddle.

piling up: a description of water rising on the river.

pillow: water piling up on a rock and just barely covering it. If you are just learning to kayak, heed this vivid warning I had from those who taught me: "If you see something downstream that is smooth and round and looks like a pillow, it's filled with rocks!"

playing: maneuvering for fun, often repeatedly in the same patch of white water; going into standing waves or surfing waves, riding a hole, or doing pop-ups or enders on purpose.

play spot: a hole, a series of surfing waves, or any other water that offers the possibility for play.

pogies: covers that fit over your hands and paddle to protect your hands from the wind; usually made of nylon material with Velcro closures to secure them.

pop-up: a hot-dog maneuver performed purposefully — or accidentally — in which the bow, or stern, of a closed-boat drops vertically into the trough of a wave, or hole, and then forcefully pops up, sometimes clearing the water; a paddler with good balance can remain upright while doing this.

portage: the act of carrying boat and gear over land around a portion of river that the paddler does not want to run.

put-in: the launching point where you go onto the ocean surf or onto the river.

raft: an inflatable open boat that has a great deal of flotation and is rowed, paddled or motored down the river.

rain-fed: description of a river having rainfall as its primary source. Rivers fed by rain can rise at any time of the year, but those at lower altitudes usually are high in winter.

rapid (or rapids): a portion of river where the water flows over obstructions, causing waves and turbulent water.

reading water: looking at the water to guess what is beneath the surface, to decide where the power is and how to use that power, and to choose a route down the river.

recording gauge: an automatic device for measuring volume of riverflow that is enclosed and cannot be read by boaters.

riffles: small, ripply waves.

"river left": the left-hand side of the river as the paddler is facing downstream.

"river right": the right-hand side of the river as the paddler is facing downstream.

rock garden: a shallow portion of river that is scattered with many visible rocks.

roll: see *Eskimo roll*.

roller: a large wave that is breaking, or rolling, upstream toward you.

rooster tail: spray from a submerged rock.

runoff: surface water flowing off the land into creeks, rivers, and the sea. Sources are rainfall, melting snow, and melting glaciers.

scouting: looking ahead on the river, from your boat or by climbing onto shore and walking downstream, to study the water.

shuttle: transporting paddlers, boats, and gear between the put-in and the take-out.

smiling hole: a horseshoe-shaped drop which looks as if it were smiling (with upturned lips) when viewed from upstream. It is less likely to be a keeper than is a frowning hole, or especially a ledge that is straight across.

sneaking: the act of boating an easier route to by-pass a more difficult section of river.

snow-melt: description of a river which is sustained by melting snow; rivers with melting snow as a primary source are swollen in spring and in early summer during runoff.

squirrelly water: swirly, unpredictable hydraulics, usually occurring in medium-volume to large-volume rivers.

squirt boating: playing in eddy lines, holes and waves using "squirt" boats which are lower volume than slalom kayaks.

staff gauge: a vertical graduated rod or stick for measuring the depth of water in order to determine the volume of riverflow; it is read manually and can be read by boaters.

staircase: a series of ledge drops.

standing waves: waves that come in a series at the bottom of a drop where the river flattens and slows down.

stopper: a hole or a steep wave that momentarily stops a boat but does not keep it.

strainer: a sweeper or a fallen tree with branches hanging into the river and water flowing between them. Or, a gravel bar with small rocks scattered along its edge and water flowing between them: the latter type of strainer is usually deepest at either the upstream or the downstream end, and shallowest at its center.

surfing, ocean: riding the waves into shore.

surfing, river: coasting on a wave while facing upstream against the direction of the flowing current.

sweeper: a branch or tree extending from shore into the river and sticking out on the surface of the water or just beneath it; potentially one of the most dangerous hazards found on rivers.

table, discharge: see *discharge table*.

take-out: the point where you complete a run and leave the river.

technical water: this is water that requires precise maneuvering. Usually the term "technical" is used to describe smaller-volume, rocky streams; however, it also is used sometimes to describe heavy water requiring precision.

tight: description of a section of river in which precise maneuvering is required because the route or routes that can be taken are narrow and severely limited.

toggles: sticks attached to grab loops at the bow and stern of the boat; advisable to have them when ocean surfing. If you have to swim, they will save your hands from being twisted in the grab loops.

tributary: a smaller stream entering a larger one.

waterfall: flowing water in a river that drops freely, or very steeply.

water-gauging station: a place at the edge of the river where riverflow is measured by a staff gauge (which is read by someone) or measured by a recording gauge (which is automatic).

weir: a natural or man-made barrier across a river that might hold back water, but that normally allows water to flow over it; sometimes regulated. Weirs are usually so straight across that even when the drop is only a short distance a dangerous keeper is formed at the bottom of them.

whirlpool: a swirling vortex of water.

INDEX TO ACTIVITIES, CONDITIONS, FACILITIES, FEATURES, HOT SPRINGS AND WHITEWATER TRIPS

Aberfeldie Dam, 105

accommodations and resorts, 10, 22, 26, 41, 72, 74, 79, 82, 120, 122, 123, 128, 138, 139, 140, 142, 143, 154, 158, 160, 163; also see *camping,* and see *Tourism Infocard*
   photos, 78, 139, 141, 155, 159, 161, 162, 163

activities; see *clubs, courses, racing;* also see *beside the rivers*

Aid Lake, 56, 157

Ainsworth Hot Springs, 7, 12, 14, 21, 22, 26, 32, 34, 41, 45, 46, 48, 138-139
   maps, 5, 137
   photos, 136, 139

air photos, 11, 133; also see *Air Photos Infocard*

Air Photos Infocard, in back pocket of book

Albert Canyon, 154, 156

Alberta
   maps, 19, 80

Alberta Foothills Cup Race, 120; also see *Clubs for Canoeists and Kayakers Infocard*

"Alberta" Time; see *Mountain ("Alberta") Time*

Alces Lake, 84, 85, 89, 90, 93, 168

American Whitewater Affiliation; see International Scale of River Difficulty on *Regional-River-Conditions Infocard*

Argenta, 44, 45, 46, 48, 50

Arrow Dam; see *Hugh Keenleyside (Arrow) Dam*

Arrow Lake; see *Lower Arrow Lake* and see *Upper Arrow Lake*

Arrow reservoir, 144; also see *Lower Arrow Lake* and see *Upper Arrow Lake*

Balfour, 139
   maps, 5, 19, 80, 137

Banff, 55, 64, 70
   maps, 5, 19, 80, 137

bathhouses, primitive, 160, 161, 163, 164
   photos, 8, 161

BCRCA; see *Recreational Canoeing Association of British Columbia*

beaches, cobble, 42

beaches, sandy, 8, 16, 21, 30, 33, 42, 68, 70
   photo, 32

Beatrice Creek, 51

Beaver Creek Provincial Park, 21

Beaverfoot (Cozier) Bridge, 62, 64, 66, 67

Bedrock Corner, 100

berries, 7, 52, 84, 102, 116, 124; also see *bird watching, fish (and fishing), flowers and plants,* and *game*

Bert's Drop, 10, 22, 24, 25
   photo, 23

beside the rivers; see *hot springs (primitive and commercially operated), showers,* and *steam baths;* see *caves, canals, ecological reserve, ghost towns and historic sites, locks, mines, parks,* and *pubs;* also see *berries, bird watching, flowers and plants, fish (and fishing),* and *game; golf courses, hiking, horseback riding,* and *tennis courts*

Big Bend Highway, 56

big water, 16, 17, 21, 48, 62, 76, 79, 108, 110; also see Glossary, 171

Birchbank, 21

bird watching, 7, 18, 48, 52, 84, 108, 110, 112, 124, 151; also see *berries, flowers and plants, fish (and fishing),* and *game*

Black Bart, 62, 65

Black Bluffs, 22

Blackwater Lake, 56, 157

Blaeberry Campground, 60

Blaeberry River, 8, 56, 58-61, 156, 170
   maps, 19, 80
   photos, 59, 61

Blaeberry River, To Columbia River, 58-61
   map, 5
   photos, 59, 61

Boats-and-Skills Infocard, in back pocket of book

boats; see *Boats-and-Skills Infocard*

Bobbie Burns Creek, 8, 130-135, 170
   maps, 19, 80, 132-133, 135
   photos, 131, 134

Bobbie Burns Creek-Spillimacheen River, Below Poet Creek, 130-135
   maps, 5, 19, 80, 132-133, 135
   photos, 131, 134

Bobbie Burns Falls, 130, 133
   map, 133
   photos, 131, 134

Bonners Ferry
   maps, 19, 80

Boulder Garden, 50, 51

boulders, 7, 14, 22, 24, 48, 49, 50, 51, 62, 65, 70, 81, 90, 102, 105, 107, 110, 120, 122; also see *boulder garden* in Glossary, 171, and see *house rock* in Glossary, 172
   photo, 65

Boundary Dam
   maps, 19, 80

Boundary Waters Treaty (1909), 20

Box Canyon Dam
   maps, 19, 80

braided sections, 12, 34, 40, 41, 42, 55, 58, 60, 72, 73, 74, 94, 98, 100, 110, 116: also see Glossary, 171, and see *Topographic Maps Infocard*
   photo, 54

Bridge Rapids, 81
   photo, 78

bridges, named, 42, 43, 62, 64, 66, 67, 82, 88, 124, 125, 128, 129
   photos, 78, 125

Brilliant, 79

Brilliant Dam
   maps, 19, 80

British Columbia
maps, 5, 19, 80, 137

British Columbia provincial kayak-team-selection races, 120; also see *racing, kayak*

brook trout, 14; also see *brown trout, char, Gerrard rainbow trout, kokanee salmon, rainbow trout, sockeye salmon,* and *sturgeon;* and see *Tourism Infocard*

brown trout, 16; also see *brook trout, char, Gerrard rainbow trout, kokanee salmon, rainbow trout, sockeye salmon,* and *sturgeon;* and see *Tourism Infocard*

Bruce Creek, 127, 129

Bull Canyon, 106

Bull River, 8, 90, 94-97, 98-101, 102-107, 170
maps, 19, 80
photos, 6, 95, 97, 99, 103, 104, 106

Bull River, 40 Mile to Sulphur Creek, 94-97
map, 5
photos, 95, 97, 101

Bull River, Canyon, 102-107
map, 5
photos, 6, 103, 104, 106

Bull River Guest Ranch, 96, 100, 101, 106, 107

Bull River, Mini-Canyon, 98-101
map, 5
photo, 99

Bull River Head Pond, 97, 101, 106

Bull River Pub, 100, 102, 104

Bull River Valley, 103, 104, 106

Burrell Creek, 13, 14, 15

Bush Arm (Kinbasket Lake), 56, 157

Bush Mountain, 56

Bush River, 8, 52-57, 156, 157, 170
maps, 19, 80
photos, 54, 157

Bush River Cool Springs, 52, 56, 156-157
map, 5, 137
photo, 157

Bush River, To Kinbasket Lake, 52-57
maps, 5, 57
photos, 53, 54, 157

C-1: see Glossary, 171; and see *Boats-and-Skills Infocard*
photos, 43, 53, back cover

C-2; see Glossary, 171; and see *Boats-and-Skills Infocard*

Cable Car Rapids, 64

Cairnes Glacier, 60

Calgary, 64, 66, 70, 74, 82
maps, 5, 137

Camp 7, 116, 117, 118, 119

camping, 12, 14, 18, 22, 26, 31, 32, 34, 36, 38, 39, 40, 41, 44, 45, 48, 52, 56, 58, 60, 61, 64, 70, 72, 74, 79, 82, 85, 89, 90, 94, 96, 97, 98, 102, 103, 104, 107, 108, 112, 116, 117, 120, 122, 124, 130, 140, 148, 152, 154, 157, 158; also see *accommodations and resorts,* and see *Tourism Infocard*
photos, 36, 45, 53, 101, 104, 150

Canadian Heritage Rivers System (CHRS) program; 63

Canadian national kayak races, 120; also see *racing, kayak*
photo, 121

Canal Flats, 18, 74, 81, 82, 88, 89, 92, 96, 100, 101, 106, 118, 163, 164, 166, 167
maps, 5, 19, 80, 137

canals, 17, 18, 79
maps, 19, 80

"Cannibal Pot", 140
photo, 141

canoeing courses; see *How-to-Learn Infocard* and *Where-to-Learn to Canoe/Kayak Infocard;* also see *Boats-and-Skills Infocard* and *Clubs for Canoeists and Kayakers Infocard*

canoeing/rafting combination trips; see *Rafting Infocard*

canoes; see *open-canoes, C-1,* and *C-2;* also see Glossary, 171

Canyon Hot Springs, 55, 60, 64, 154-155
maps, 5, 137
photos, 155

canyons, 7, 8, 14, 15, 22, 23, 24, 26, 28, 52, 53, 55, 56, 58, 60, 62, 66, 70, 72, 74, 76, 84, 87, 94, 95, 96, 98, 100, 101, 102, 103, 104, 105, 106, 107, 108, 109, 110, 111, 113, 117, 118, 119, 122, 124, 127, 154, 156, 157; also see *Air Photos Infocard* and see *Topographic Maps Infocard*
photos, 61, 103, 106, 109, 111, 157, back cover

Cascade Creek, 42, 43

Castlegar, 12, 18, 20, 21, 25, 33, 36, 79, 140, 141, 142, 143, 151
maps, 5, 19, 80, 137

caves, 7, 14, 21, 46, 48, 95, 108, 138, 139, 148
photo, 136

char, Dolly Varden, 39, 40, 44; also see *brook trout, brown trout, Gerrard rainbow trout, kokanee salmon, rainbow trout, sockeye salmon,* and *sturgeon;* and see *Tourism Infocard*

charts, nautical; see *Tourism Infocard*

Cherryville, 141

Class 1 water, 52, 110; also see International Scale of River Difficulty on *Regional-River-Conditions Infocard*

Class 2 water, 12, 16, 22, 26, 30, 34, 40, 42, 44, 52, 58, 62, 64, 68, 72, 76, 79, 81, 90, 94, 98, 99, 100, 102, 105, 108, 110, 112, 113, 115; also see International Scale of River Difficulty on *Regional-River-Conditions Infocard*

Class 3 water, 12, 14, 15, 16, 22, 26, 28, 30, 34, 38, 40, 44, 48, 50, 52, 62, 64, 66, 68, 70, 72, 76, 79, 81, 84, 90, 98, 99, 100, 102, 105, 108, 110, 112, 113, 120, 122, 124, 127, 130; also see International Scale of River Difficulty on *Regional-River-Conditions Infocard*

Class 4 water, 14, 15, 22, 38, 48, 50, 62, 64, 65, 90, 92, 98, 99, 102, 105, 108, 110, 116, 117, 118, 122, 124, 127, 130; also see International Scale of River Difficulty on *Regional-River-Conditions Infocard*

Class 5 water, 22, 24, 25, 48, 50, 62, 94, 116, 118, 120, 122; also see International Scale of

River Difficulty on the *Regional-River-Conditions Infocard*

Class 6 water, 36, 94, 124, 130; also see International Scale of River Difficulty on *Regional-River-Conditions Infocard*

closed-boater runs: see *river runs for kayakers*

closed-boats; see *C-1, C-2,* and *kayaks;* also see Glossary, 171

closed-canoes; see *C-1* and *C-2;* also see the Glossary, 171

clothing; see *Regional-River-Conditions Infocard*

clubs: see *Clubs for Canoeists and Kayakers Infocard* and see *How-to-Learn Infocard*

Clubs for Canoeists and Kayakers Infocard, in back pocket of book

Cockscomb Mountain, 56

Coffee Creek, 139

Columbia Ice Fields, 55

Columbia-Kootenay River System, 11
maps, 19, 80

Columbia Lake, 17, 18, 116
maps, 19, 80

Columbia River, 8, 11, 16-21, 56, 58, 60, 63, 76, 135, 170
maps, 19, 80
photo, 17

Columbia River, Rock Island Play Spot, 8, 16-21
maps, 5
photo, 17

Columbia River Treaty (1964), 20

Columbia-Windermere Valley, 74, 82, 88, 92, 122, 124, 128, 135, 160, 163

combination trips: rafts with kayaks/canoes; see *Rafting Infocard*

Comfort Lake, 56, 157

Commander Glacier, 128

commercially operated rafting trips; see *rafting trips, commercially operated*

competitions; see *racing, kayak* and *racing, raft*

conditions of rivers: see *When-to-Go Infocard;* see *Regional-River-Conditions Infocard* with International Scale of River Difficulty; also see *flash rivers, natural riverflow, dam-controlled riverflow, hydrographs,* see *riverflows,* and see *features of rivers*

C-1; see at *start of "C" listings*

continuously flowing, 14, 15, 22, 30, 34, 38, 40, 44, 48, 52, 62, 90, 98, 99, 102, 105, 108 113, 120, 127; also see *continuous rapids* in Glossary, 171

cool springs, primitive, 52, 55, 56, 156-157
maps, 5, 137
photo, 157

Cooper Creek, 44, 46, 50

Corra Linn Dam, 79

courses, (kayaking and open-canoeing): see *How-to-Learn Infocard* and *Where-to-Learn to Canoe/Kayak Infocard;* also see *Boats-and-Skills Infocard* and *Clubs for Canoeists and Kayakers Infocard*

courses, rafting: see *How-to-Learn Infocard* and *Rafting Infocard;* also see *Boats-and-Skills Infocard* — all in back pocket of the book

Cozier Bridge; see *Beaverfoot (Cozier) Bridge*

Cranbrook, 93, 96, 100, 101, 106, 110, 115, 122, 163, 164, 165, 166
maps, 5, 19, 80, 137

creeks, 7, 8, 12, 13, 14, 15, 17, 26, 28, 31, 32, 34, 35, 36, 38-39, 40-43, 44, 45, 46, 48, 50, 51, 52, 56, 61, 87, 89, 94-97, 98, 99, 100, 101, 106, 107, 116-119, 120-123, 124-129, 130-135, 139, 140, 142, 146, 151, 157, 164, 170; also see *rivers*
maps, 5, 19, 80, 128, 132-133, 128, 135
photos, 6, 117, 121, 123, 125, 126, 127, 129, 131, 134

Crescent Valley, 30, 33, 36, 39

Creston, 17, 25, 139
maps, 5, 19, 80, 137

Cross River, 7, 72-75, 170
maps, 19, 80
photos, 73, 75

Cross River, Above Natural Bridge, 72-75
map, 5
photos, 73, 75

Crown land, 22, 26, 32, 34, 44, 48, 60, 64, 72, 90, 116, 130; and see the *Topographic Maps Infocard*
photos, 36, 45

Cruncher Drop, 98, 99, 100, 101

Crystalline Mountain, 51

C-2; see at *start of "C" listings*

current riverflow information; see the *When-to-Go Infocard*

dam-controlled riverflow, 17, 109, 110

dams, 17, 18, 20, 21, 24, 42, 45, 49, 79; also see Glossary, 171
maps, 19, 80

Davis Creek Campground, 41, 45, 48

decked canoe; see *Boats-and-Skills Infocard*

Deluge Mountain, 48, 51

Devil's Elbow, 8, 40, 42, 43

Dibble Creek, 106, 107

difficulty, degree of: see *Class 1 water, Class 2 water, Class 3 water, Class 4 water, Class 5 water, Class 6 water;* also see *river runs for kayakers, river runs for open-canoeists, river runs for rafters* and see International Scale of River Difficulty on *Regional-River Conditions Infocard*

discharge table: see *hydrographs,* see *discharges, maximum recorded,* see *When-to-Go Infocard,* and see Glossary, 171

discharges, maximum recorded, 21, 66, 115, 170; also see *When-to-Go Infocard, flash rivers, dam-controlled riverflow, natural riverflow, hydrographs, riverflows,* and see *lakes, effects of*

Dolly Varden; see *char*

Dolly Varden Picnic Site, 70

Donald, 56, 156

drops and pools, 15, 22, 102, 108, 110, 118, 130, 133; also see Glossary, 171

drops with names, 8, 10, 22, 24, 25, 30, 32, 40, 42, 43, 50, 51, 52, 53, 55, 56, 62, 64, 65, 66, 67, 76, 81, 90, 92, 93, 94, 95, 96, 97, 98, 99, 100, 101, 102, 105, 112, 113, 114, 116, 117, 118, 119, 120, 122, 123
photos, 6, 23, 63, 65, 78, 91, 95, 114, 117, 123, 157

Dry Gulch Provincial Park, 122, 124, 130, 158

Duncan Dam, 42, 44, 49

Duncan Lake, 41, 44, 45, 46, 48, 50
maps, 5, 137

Duncan River, 7, 34, 44-47, 48-51, 170
maps, 19, 80
photos, 45, 47, 49

Duncan River, Hume Creek to Westfall River (Upper Section), 48-51
maps, 5, 51
photo, 49

Duncan River, Westfall River to Giegerich Creek (Lower Section), 44-47
map, 5
photos, 45, 47

East Creek, 46

East Kootenays, 7, 8, 9, 16, 18, 52-135, 156-169
maps, 19, 57, 71, 80, 128, 132-133, 135, 168-169
photos, front cover, 6, 8, 11, 53, 54, 59, 61, 63, 65, 69, 73, 75, 77, 78, 83, 85, 86, 87, 88, 91, 93, 95, 97, 99, 101, 103, 104, 106, 109, 111, 113, 114, 117, 121, 123, 125, 126, 127, 129, 131, 134, 157, 159, 161, 162, 163, 165, 167

ecological reserve, 167
maps, 168-169
photo, 167

Edmonton
maps, 5, 137

Ego Mountain, 56

Eight Mile Flats, 12, 13

Elk Creek, 89

Elk River, 7, 8, 108-111, 170
maps, 19, 80
photos, 109, 111, back cover

Elk River, Canyon, 7, 108-111
map, 5
photos, 109, 111, back cover

Elko, 96, 100, 110
maps, 5, 137

5 Mile (Yoho) Bridge, 66, 67

14 Mile Bridge (Horsethief Creek), 124, 125, 128

40 Mile Campground, 92, 94, 97
photo, 101

Facchina's Rapid, 30, 32

Fairmont Hot Springs, 18, 60, 87, 92, 99, 104, 108, 112, 116, 118, 122, 124, 130, 160-163
maps, 5, 19, 80, 137
photos, 161, 162, 163

falls; see *waterfalls*

Fauquier, 141, 143
maps, 5, 19, 80, 137

features of rivers: see *big water, boulders, braided sections, bridges, canyons, conditions of rivers, continuously flowing, dams, drops and pools, drops with names, flash rivers, gravel-bottomed rivers, ledges, lock, play spots, rock gardens, steady gradient, technical water, waterfalls,* and *weirs;* also see *Air Photos Infocard, Regional-River-Conditions Infocard, Topographic Map Infocard* and *When-to-Go Infocard*

Fernie, 96, 100, 102, 106, 108, 110
maps, 5, 19, 80, 137

ferries, 32, 43, 139, 140, 141, 142, 143, 146, 151, 153, 154; also see *Tourism Infocard*

Field, 66, 67

Findlay Creek, 7, 8, 16, 116-119, 170
maps, 19, 80
photos, 6, 117

Findlay Creek, Mini-Canyon to Skookumchuck Road, 116-119
map, 5
photos, 6, 117

first descents, 24, 46, 50, 127, 133

fish (and fishing): also see *brook trout, brown trout, char, Gerrard rainbow trout, kokanee salmon, rainbow trout, sockeye salmon,* and *sturgeon;* and see *Tourism Infocard*
photo, 87

fish hatchery, 96, 100, 107

5 Mile (Yoho) Bridge; see at *start of "F" listings*

flash rivers, 23, 27, 35, 63; also see *Glossary,* 171, and see *When-to-Go Infocard*

flatwater marathon racing, kayak; see *Clubs for Canoeists and Kayakers Infocard*

flowers and plants, 7, 12, 34, 37, 52, 84, 86, 88, 90, 98, 102, 111, 112, 120, 124, 166; also see *berries, bird watching, fish (and fishing),* and *game*
photos, 35, 86, 167

Forster Creek, 128

Fort Steele Heritage Town, 96, 100, 101, 106
maps, 5, 137

40 Mile Campground; see at *start of "F" listings*

14 Mile Bridge (Horsethief Creek); see at *start of "F" listings*

Franklin D. Roosevelt Lake
maps, 19, 80

free-style boating, 120

Frowning Hole, 116; also see *Glossary,* 171
photo, 6

Fruitvale, 21

Fusee Lake, 108

future outlook for riverflow; see *When-to-Go Infocard*

Gable Creek, 13, 14, 15

Galena Bay, 32, 43, 48, 139, 140, 141, 142, 144, 146, 151, 153
maps, 5, 19, 80, 137

Galloway, 96, 100

game, 7, 8, 12, 26, 34, 40, 44, 52, 68, 70, 72, 76, 84, 94, 98, 104, 112, 122, 124, 130, 158; also see *berries, bird watching, flowers and plants,* and *fish (and fishing)*
photo, 86

gates, slalom, 26, 28, 120; also see *Clubs for Canoeists and Kayakers Infocard*

gauge, recording; see *Glossary,* 172

gauge, staff, 14; also see *Glossary,* 173

Gerrard (ghost town), 40, 41, 43, 45, 48

Gerrard rainbow trout, 7, 8, 40; also see *brook trout, brown trout, char, kokanee salmon, rainbow trout, sockeye salmon,* and *sturgeon;* and see *Tourism Infocard*

ghost towns and historic sites, 9, 10, 17, 18, 20, 40, 41, 56, 63, 67, 68, 72, 73, 97, 104, 116, 138, 144, 152, 158, 160, 161

giant-volume hydrograph (riverflow monthly average), 17; also see *riverflows* and see *When-to-Go Infocard*

Giegerich Creek, 44

glacial-melt creeks and rivers; see under *river sources*

Glacier Creek, 45, 48

Glenogle (Rafters' Take-out), 62, 64, 66, 67

glossary, 171-173

Gold Hill Bridge, 42, 43

Golden, 17, 18, 56, 59, 60, 62, 63, 64, 66, 122, 135, 154, 156, 159
maps, 5, 19, 80, 137

golf courses, 18, 163

Goodfellow Creek, 56, 157

gradients: see *continuously flowing, drops and pools, ledges, steady gradient;* also see *Regional-River-Conditions Infocard*
averaging up to 5 meters/kilometer (25 feet/mile), 42, 55, 60, 70, 79, 104, 110, 115, 118
averaging from 6 to 10 meters/kilometer (30 to 55 feet/mile), 27, 32, 35, 44, 50, 73, 87, 94, 110, 118, 122
averaging from 11 to 15 meters/kilometer (60 to 80 feet/mile), 12, 22, 35, 38, 64, 92, 94, 100, 125, 130
averaging from 16 to 20 meters/kilometer (85 to 105 feet/mile) and greater, 14, 55, 118, 130

Granby Burrell Campground, 15

Granby River, 7, 12-13, 14-15, 18, 170
maps, 19, 80

Granby River, Canyon, 14-15
map, 5

Granby River, Howe Creek through Eight Mile Flats, 12-13
map, 5

Grand Forks, 12, 13, 14, 15
maps, 5, 19, 80, 137

gravel-bottomed rivers, 12, 26, 27, 39, 40, 41, 42, 44, 60, 68, 70, 72, 74, 84, 93, 95, 97, 102, 104, 112, 127
photos, 35, 43, 73

Grizzly Creek, 31

Gwendoline, 17

Grohman, 18

Halcyon Hot Springs, 20, 30, 32, 34, 151, 152-153
maps, 5, 19, 80, 137
photo, 153

Halfway River, 146, 151, 153

Halfway River Hot Springs, 32, 34, 148-151
maps, 5, 137
photos, 149, 150

Hatchery, Kootenay Trout, 96, 100, 107

Head Wall, 50, 51

head walls, 48, 50, 51, 100, 118; also see Glossary, 172

Hector Gorge, 68, 70
photo, 69

Hector Gorge Lookout, 70

Hector Gorge Picnic Site, 70

Help Lake, 56, 157

hiking, 24, 25, 39, 41, 52, 58, 72, 74, 143, 144, 146, 147, 157
photo, 54

historic sites; see *ghost towns and historic sites*

historical riverflow information; see *When-to-Go Infocard*

Hopi Hole, 62, 64, 66, 67

horseback riding, 58, 163

Horseshoe Lake, 96, 103, 106

Horseshoe Rapids, 76, 81

Horsethief Creek, 7, 8, 124-129, 170
maps, 19, 80, 128
photos, 125, 126, 127, 129

Horsethief Creek, 14 Mile Bridge to Westside Road, 124-129
maps, 5, 128
photos, 125, 126, 127, 129

Hot Line, Paddle; see *How-to-Learn Infocard*

hot springs, commercially operated, 8, 9, 10, 11, 12, 14, 18, 20, 21, 22, 26, 32, 34, 38, 41, 45, 46, 48, 53, 55, 60, 64, 70, 72, 73, 79, 87, 92, 99, 104, 108, 112, 116, 122, 124, 130, 138-139, 140-141, 151, 153, 154-155, 158-159, 160-163; also see *hot springs, primitive*
maps, 19, 80, 137
photos, 136, 139, 141, 155, 159, 162, 163

hot springs, primitive, 8, 9, 10, 11, 18, 20, 30, 32, 34, 38, 60, 85, 87, 89, 90, 93, 94, 96, 98, 100, 102, 104, 106, 109, 112, 116, 130, 140, 142-143, 144-147, 148-151, 152-153, 160-163, 164-165, 166-169; also see *cool springs, primitive*
maps, 19, 80, 137, 147, 168-169
photos, 8, 136, 143, 145, 146, 149, 150, 153, 161, 162, 165, 167

hot-dog boating, 120; also see Glossary, 172

house rocks, 65, 112, 123; also see the Glossary, 172

how to learn; see *How-to-Learn Infocard, Rafting Infocard* and *Where-to-Learn to Canoe/Kayak Infocard*

how to use this guidebook, 10-11

Howe Creek, 12

Howe Creek Campground, 12

Howser, 41, 43

How-to-Learn Infocard, in back pocket of book

Hugh Keenleyside (Arrow) Dam, 17, 18, 20, 21
maps, 19, 80

Hume Creek, 51

Hunter Creek access (Rafters' Lunch Stop), 62, 63, 64, 65, 66, 67

Hunter Creek Bridge, 67

hydrographs; 10; also see *giant-volume hydrograph, large-volume hydrographs, medium-volume hydrographs,* and *small-volume hydrographs;* and see *When-to-Go Infocard*

Idaho, 77
  maps, 19, 80

Indian Baths, 160, 161
  photos, 161, 162

Indian reserves; see *Topographic Map Infocard*

infocards, whitewater; see in back pocket of book

instruction (kayaking and open canoeing): see *How-to-Learn Infocard* and *Where-to-Learn to Canoe/Kayak Infocard;* also see *Boats-and-Skills Infocard* and *Clubs for Canoeists and Kayakers Infocard*

instruction, rafting: see *How-to-Learn Infocard* and *Rafting Infocard;* also see *Boats-and-Skills Infocard*

instruction, safety; see *Rafting Infocard* and *Where-to-Learn to Canoe/Kayak Infocard*

International Canoe Federation; see the International Scale of River Difficulty on *Regional-River-Conditions Infocard*

International Scale of River Difficulty; see *Regional-River-Conditions Infocard*

Invermere, 92, 96, 100, 101, 106, 122, 124, 128, 159, 163, 164, 167
  maps, 5, 137

Jaffary, 96, 100

Jasper
  maps, 5, 137

John Fenger Memorial Trail, 41

Johnsons Landing, 44, 46, 50

K-1: see *kayaks;* also see Glossary, 172; and see *Boats-and-Skills Infocard*

K-2: see *kayaks;* also see Glossary, 172; and see *Boats-and-Skills Infocard*

Kaslo, 39, 43, 44, 45, 46, 48, 50
  maps, 5, 137

kayakers, trips for; see *river runs for kayakers,* and see Combination Trips: Rafts with Kayaks/Canoes on *Rafting Infocard*

kayaking courses; see *How-to-Learn Infocard* and *Where-to-Learn to Canoe/Kayak Infocard;* also see *Boats-and-Skills Infocard* and *Clubs for Canoeists and Kayakers Infocard*

kayaking/rafting combination trips; see *Rafting Infocard*

kayaks: see *Boats-and-Skills Infocard;* also see Glossary, 172
  photos, 6, 11, 17, 23, 27, 28, 32, 35, 45, 47, 49, 53, 59, 61, 65, 69, 73, 83, 86, 88, 91, 97, 99, 106, 111, 117, 121, 123, 126, 131

Keenleyside Dam; see *Hugh Keenleyside (Arrow) Dam*

Keer's Rock, 8, 112

Kelowna
  maps, 5, 137

Kettle Falls
  maps, 19, 80

Kettle River
  maps, 19, 80

Kicking Horse River, 7, 62-67, 154, 170
  maps, 19, 80
  photos, 63, 65

Kicking Horse River, Beaverfoot Bridge to Glenogle, 7, 62-67
  map, 5
  photos, 63, 65

Kimberley, 115, 164, 165, 166
  maps, 5, 137

Kinbasket Lake, 18, 21, 52, 55, 56, 157
  maps, 5, 19, 80, 137
  photo, 53

Koch Creek, 31, 32, 34, 36

kokanee salmon, 40; also see *brook trout, brown trout, char, Gerrard rainbow trout, rainbow trout, sockeye salmon,* and *sturgeon;* and see *Tourism Infocard*

K-1; see at *start of "K" listings*

Koocanusa Lake; see *Lake Koocanusa*

Kootenai River (U.S.A.), 77, 110
  maps, 19, 80

Kootenay Bay, 139
  maps, 5, 19, 80, 137

Kootenay Canal, 18, 77
  maps, 19, 80

Kootenay Canal Dam, 79

Kootenay Crossing, 70, 74, 82

Kootenay Lake, 40, 41, 42, 45, 77, 138, 139
  maps, 5, 19, 80, 137
  photo, 139

Kootenay Lake Provincial Park, 41, 45, 48

Kootenay National Park, 68, 69, 70, 73, 74, 82, 130, 158, 159
  map, 71
  photos, 69, 159

Kootenay River, 7, 8, 11, 16, 17, 18, 30, 33, 68, 70, 72, 74, 76-83, 88, 89, 96, 100, 106, 110, 167, 170
  maps, 19, 80
  photos, front cover, 77, 78, 83

Kootenay River, Palliser Reach, 76-83
  map, 5
  photos, front cover, 77, 78, 83

Kootenay River System
  map, 80

Kootenay Trout Hatchery, 96, 100, 107

Kootenay-River-Lower-Crossing (26 Mile) Bridge, 82, 83, 88

Kootenay-River-Upper-Crossing (Settlers) Bridge, 82
  photo, 78

K-2; see at *start of "K" listings*

Kuskanax Creek, 38, 140, 142

Ladylove Mountain, 56

Lake Enid, 124

Lake Koocanusa, 77, 96, 100, 107, 110
  maps, 5, 19, 80, 137

Lake Louise
  maps, 5, 19, 80, 137

Lake of the Hanging Glaciers, 128

Lake Revelstoke, 18, 21
  maps, 5, 19, 80, 137

lakes, 7, 17, 18, 19, 20, 21, 24, 38, 39, 40, 41, 42, 43, 44, 45, 46, 48, 50, 52, 55, 56, 68, 84, 85, 89, 90, 93, 94, 96, 100, 103, 106, 107, 108, 110, 112, 113, 116, 122, 124, 128, 138, 139, 141, 142, 143, 144, 147, 151, 152, 153, 157, 167, 168
  maps, 5, 19, 80, 137
  photos, 53, 139, 153
lakes, effect of; see *When-to-Go Infocard*
Land of the Smoking Waters, 160
land-status information; see *Topographic Maps Infocard*
Lardeau (community), 42, 43, 45, 46, 48, 50, 139
Lardeau River, 7, 34, 40-43, 170
  maps, 19, 80
  photo, 43
Lardeau River, Rapid Creek through Devil's Elbow, 40-43
  map, 5
  photo, 43
large-volume hydrographs (riverflow monthly averages), 31, 41, 45, 49, 77, 109, 113; also see *riverflows*, and see *When-to-Go Infocard*
Ledge (Surprise) Rapids, 81
ledges, 81, 94, 95, 108, 110; also see *ledge* in Glossary, 172, and *staircase* in Glossary, 173
  photo, 95
Libby
  maps, 19, 80
Libby Dam
  maps, 19, 80
Lillian Lake, 122
Little Slocan River, 7, 34-37, 170
  maps, 19, 80
  photos, 35
Little Slocan-Slocan Rivers, To Passmore, 34-37
  maps, 5, 37
  photos, 35, 36
locator maps, 10
locks, navigational, 10, 18, 20, 21
Lost Ledge Campground, 45, 48
Lower Arrow Lake, 18, 20, 141, 143; also see *Upper Arrow Lake*
  maps, 5, 19, 80, 137
Lower Bonnington Dam, 79
lower Duncan River; see *Duncan River, Westfall River to Giegerich Creek*
lower Salmo River; see *Salmo River, To Seven Mile Reservoir*
Lussier Hot Springs, 7, 60, 85, 89, 90, 93, 94, 96, 98, 100, 104, 106, 109, 112, 116, 130, 164-165 166, 167, 168
  maps, 5, 137
  photos, 8, 165
Lussier River (Sheep Creek), 85, 87, 94, 164
McGillivray's Portage, 18
McLeod Meadows, 70, 74, 82
maps, scales of; see *Topographic Maps Infocard*
marathon racing, kayak (flatwater); see *Clubs for Canoeists and Kayakers Infocard*
Marble Canyon, 68

Marblehead, 42
marine campsite, 85
marshes, 18
Marysville, 112, 115
maximum recorded discharges; see *discharges, maximum recorded*
Meadow Creek (community), 41, 42, 43, 44, 46, 48
  maps, 5, 137
medium-volume hydrographs (riverflow monthly averages), 13, 15, 23, 27, 39, 63, 69, 95, 99, 103; also see *riverflows*, and see *When-to-Go Infocard*
Mica Creek (community), 18, 56
Mica Dam, 18
  maps, 19, 80
Middle Canyon (Elk River), 108, 110
mines, 7, 120, 138
Mini-Canyon (Bull River), 98-101
  photo, 99
Mini-Canyon (Findlay Creek), 116, 119
"Mini-Waterfall", 116, 117, 118, 119
  photo, 117
Monashee Mountains, 141, 143
  maps, 19, 80
  photo, 155
Montana, 76
  maps, 19, 80
Mount Hatteras, 51
Mount Nelson, 120
Mountain ("Alberta") Time, 11, 55, 60, 64; also see *Pacific Time*
"Mountain of Salt", 160, 163
  photo, 161
Mummery Glacier, 60
Nakusp (village), 20, 32, 33, 39, 43, 140, 141, 142, 143, 144, 146, 151, 153
  maps, 5, 19, 80, 137
Nakusp Hot Springs, 20, 32, 34, 38, 140-143, 151, 153
  maps, 5, 137
  photos, 141, 143
Nakusp Provincial Park, 142
  photo, 143
national kayak races, 120
  photo, 121
National Topographic System; see *Topographic Maps Infocard*
Natural Bridge, 72, 74
  photo, 75
natural riverflow, 10, 13, 15, 23, 27, 31, 35, 39, 41, 44, 49, 53, 59, 63, 69, 73, 77, 85, 91, 95, 99, 103, 113, 117, 121, 125, 131
Needles, 141, 143
  maps, 5, 19, 80, 137
Nelson, 12, 14, 21, 28, 32, 33, 36, 77, 79, 139, 140, 141, 142, 143, 151
  maps, 5, 19, 80, 137
Nelway, 25
New Denver, 34, 36, 39, 43, 141, 143
Nipika Riverbend Campground, 72, 74, 79, 82
  photo, 78

Norbury Lake Provincial Park, 96, 100, 104, 106, 107

North Star, 17

Olympic-style flatwater sprint racing; see *Clubs for Canoeists and Kayakers Infocard*

open-Canadian canoes; see Glossary, 172

open-canoeing instruction: see *How-to-Learn Infocard* and *Where-to-Learn to Canoe/Kayak Infocard;* also see *Boats-and-Skills Infocard* and *Clubs for Canoeists and Kayakers Infocard*

open-canoeists, trips for; see *river runs for open-canoeists,* and see Combination Trips: Rafts with Kayaks/Canoes on *Rafting Infocard*

open-canoes: see Glossary, 172; also see *Boats-and-Skills Infocard*
  photos, front cover, 6, 31, 77, 85, 87, 95, 103, 109, 114

Outdoor Recreation Council of British Columbia; see *How-to-Learn Infocard*

Pacific Time, 11, 55, 60, 64; also see *Mountain ("Alberta") Time*

Paddle Hot Line; see *How-to-Learn Infocard*

Palliser, 64, 66, 67

Palliser Rapids, 81

Palliser Reach (Kootenay River), 76-83
  photos, front cover, 77, 78, 83

Panorama Resort, 120, 122, 123, 128

Paradice Mine, 120

Paradise (Paradice) Mine, 120, 122

Park Bridge, 62, 66, 67

parks, 21, 38, 39, 40, 41, 45, 48, 63, 64, 67, 68, 73, 74, 82, 84, 90, 96, 100, 103, 106, 116, 122, 124, 130, 142, 158, 159, 164, 165; and see *Tourism Infocard*
  photos, 8, 69, 143, 159, 165

Passmore, 32, 34, 36, 141, 143

Pedley Falls, 81
  photos, front cover, 83

Pend-d'Oreille (Seven Mile) Reservoir, 24

Pend-d'Oreille River (Canada), 24

Pend Oreille River (U.S.A.)
  maps, 19, 80

Pete's Pond (Seven Mile Reservoir), 24

photos, air; see *air photos,* and see *Air Photos Infocard*

picnic sites, 30, 70

play spots (and surfing), 8, 16, 18, 26, 27, 30, 32, 34, 35, 39, 42, 48, 58, 60, 62, 65, 68, 70, 72, 73, 84, 87, 90, 110, 112, 113, 120, 124, 127; also see Glossary, 172
  photos, 17, 27, 35, 69, 73

Poet Creek, 130

pogies; see Glossary, 172, and see *Regional-River-Conditions Infocard*

pool-and-drop rivers; see *drops and pools*

Poplar Creek, 42, 43

Porcupine Creek, 26, 28

Portage Rapid, 62, 65
  photo, 65

Porto Rico, 26

Premier Lake, 167

provincial-kayak-team selection race, 120

pub, 26, 28, 96, 100, 102, 104, 107

Purcell Mountains, 50, 120, 139
  maps, 19, 80

Queen Creek; see *Quinn (Queen) Creek,* 97

Quinn (Queen) Creek, 97

racing, kayak, 120; also see *Clubs for Canoeists and Kayakers Infocard*
  photo, 121

racing, raft, 26

Radium Hot Springs (community), 55, 60, 69, 70, 74, 82, 92, 96, 99, 100, 101, 106, 122, 124, 128, 135, 159, 163, 164, 167
  maps, 5, 137

Radium Hot Springs (hot pools), 64, 70, 72, 73, 79, 122, 130, 158-159
  maps, 5, 137
  photo, 159

rafters, trips for; see *river runs for rafters (paddle and rowing),* and see Combination Trips: Rafts with Kayaks/Canoes on *Rafting Infocard*

Rafters' Lunch Stop (Hunter Creek access, Kicking Horse River), 65, 66, 67

Rafters' Take-out (Glenogle, Kicking Horse River), 66, 67

rafting courses: see *How-to-Learn Infocard* and *Rafting Infocard;* also see *Boats-and-Skills Infocard* — all in back pocket of the book

Rafting Infocard (Combination Trips: Rafts with Kayaks/Canoes, and Where-to-Learn Rafting), in back pocket of book

rafting instruction: see *How-to-Learn Infocard* and *Rafting Infocard;* also see *Boats-and-Skills Infocard* — all in back pocket of the book

rafting trips, commercially operated, 58, 62, 64, 66, 68, 72, 76, 79, 84, 90, 102, 108, 120, 122, 154; also see *How-to-Learn Infocard* and see *Rafting Infocard*

rafts (paddle and rowing): see *raft* in the Glossary, 172; also see *Boats-and-Skills Infocard*
  photos, 63, 78, 93

rainbow trout, 14, 16, 26, 34, 39; also see *brook trout, brown trout, char, Gerrard rainbow trout, kokanee salmon, sockeye salmon,* and *sturgeon;* and see *Tourism Infocard*

rain-fed creeks and rivers; see under *river sources*

Ram Creek Hot Springs, 60, 87, 90, 104, 109, 112, 116, 166-169
  maps, 5, 137, 168-169
  photo, 167

Rapid Creek, 40, 42, 43

reading water; see Glossary, 172

Recreational Canoeing Association of British Columbia (RCA); see *How-to-Learn Infocard*

Red Deer
  maps, 5, 137

Redburn Creek, 61

Redstreak Campground, 70, 124, 130, 158

Regional-River-Conditions Infocard, in back pocket of book

reservoirs, 22, 24, 25, 102, 105, 106, 144
maps, 19, 80
photo, 134

Revelstoke, 18, 43, 44, 46, 48, 50, 56, 139, 140, 142, 151, 153, 154
maps, 5, 19, 80, 137

Revelstoke Dam, 18
maps, 19, 80

river conditions: see *When-to-Go Infocard;* see *Regional-River-Conditions Infocard* with International Scale of River Difficulty; also see *dam-controlled riverflow, flash rivers, hydrographs, natural riverflow, riverflows,* and see *river features*

river features: see *big water, boulders, braided sections, bridges, canyons, continuously flowing, dams, drops and pools, drops with names, flash rivers, gravel-bottomed rivers, ledges, locks, play spots, river conditions, rock gardens, steady gradient, technical water, waterfalls,* and *weirs;* also see the *Air Photos Infocard, Regional-River-Conditions Infocard, Topographic Map Infocard,* and *When-to-Go Infocard*

River Outfitters Association of British Columbia (ROABC); see *How-to-Learn Infocard*

Riverbend Campground; see *Nipika Riverbend Campground*

river reading: see *reading water* in the Glossary, 173

river runs for kayakers,
advanced, guided, 12-13, 14-15, 16-21, 22-25, 26-29, 30-33, 34-37, 38-39, 40-43, 44-47, 48-51, 52-57, 58-61, 62-67, 68-71, 72-75, 76-83, 84-89, 90-93, 94-97, 98-101, 102-107, 108-111, 112-115, 116-119, 120-123, 124-129, 130-135

advanced, unguided, 12-13, 14-15, 16-21, 22-25, 26-29, 30-33, 34-37, 38-39, 40-43, 44-47, 48-51, 52-57, 58-61, 62-67, 68-71, 72-75, 76-83, 84-89, 90-93, 94-97, 98-101, 102-107, 108-111, 112-115, 116-119, 120-123

expert, guided, 12-13, 14-15, 16-21, 22-25, 26-29, 30-33, 34-37, 38-39, 40-43, 44-47, 48-51, 52-57, 58-61, 62-67, 68-71, 72-75, 76-83, 84-89, 90-93, 94-97, 98-101, 102-107, 108-111, 112-115, 116-119, 120-123, 124-129, 130-135

expert, unguided, 12-13, 14-15, 16-21, 22-25, 26-29, 30-33, 34-37, 38-39, 40-43, 44-47, 48-51, 52-57, 58-61, 62-67, 68-71, 72-75, 76-83, 84-89, 90-93, 94-97, 98-101, 102-107, 108-111, 112-115, 116-119, 120-123, 124-129, 130-135

intermediate, guided, 12-13, 14-15, 16-21, 22-25, 26-29, 30-33, 34-37, 38-39, 40-43, 44-47, 52-57, 58-61, 62-67, 68-71, 72-75, 76-83, 84-89, 90-93, 94-97, 98-101, 102-107, 108-111, 112-115, 120-123

intermediate, unguided, 12-13, 16-21, 26-29, 30-33, 34-37, 38-39, 40-43, 44-47, 52-57, 58-61, 62-67, 68-71, 72-75, 76-83, 84-89, 90-93, 94-97, 98-101, 102-107, 108-111, 112-115, 120-123

novice, guided, 12-13, 16-21, 26-29, 30-33, 34-37, 40-43, 44-47, 52-57, 58-61, 62-67, 68-71, 72-75, 76-83, 84-89, 94-97, 102-107, 112-115, 120-123

novice, unguided, 12-13, 40-43, 44-47, 52-57, 72-75

river runs for non-paddlers, 58-61, 62-67, 68-71, 76-83, 84-89, 90-93, 102-107, 108-111

river runs for open-canoeists,
expert, guided, 12-13, 14-15, 16-21, 26-29, 30-33, 34-37, 38-39, 40-43, 44-47, 52-57, 58-61, 62-67, 68-71, 72-75, 76-83, 84-89, 90-93, 94-97, 98-101, 102-107, 108-111, 112-115, 120-123

expert, unguided, 12-13, 14-15, 16-21, 26-29, 30-33, 34-37, 38-39, 40-43, 44-47, 52-57, 58-61, 62-67, 68-71, 72-75, 76-83, 84-89, 90-93, 94-97, 98-101, 102-107, 108-111, 112-115, 120-123

intermediate, guided, 12-13, 26-29, 34-37, 38-39, 40-43, 52-57, 58-61, 68-71, 72-75, 76-83, 84-89, 90-93, 94-97, 102-107, 112-115

intermediate, unguided, 12-13, 34-37, 40-43, 52-57, 58-61, 72-75, 102-107

novice, guided, 52-57, 72-75

novice, unguided, 52-57

river runs for rafters (paddle and rowing),
advanced, guided, 12-13, 26-29, 30-33, 34-37, 38-39, 40-43, 44-47, 52-57, 58-61, 62-67, 72-75, 76-83, 84-89, 90-93, 98-101, 102-107, 108-111, 112-115, 120-123

advanced, unguided, 12-13, 30-33, 34-37, 38-39, 40-43, 44-47, 52-57, 58-61, 62-67, 72-75, 76-83, 84-89, 90-93, 98-101, 102-107, 108-111, 112-115, 120-123

expert, guided, 12-13, 14-15, 22-25, 26-29, 30-33, 34-37, 38-39, 40-43, 44-47, 52-57, 58-61, 62-67, 72-75, 76-83, 84-89, 90-93, 98-101, 102-107, 108-111, 112-115, 120-123

expert, unguided, 12-13, 30-33, 34-37, 38-39, 40-43, 44-47, 52-57, 58-61, 62-67, 72-75, 76-83, 84-89, 90-93, 98-101, 102-107, 108-111, 112-115, 120-123

intermediate, guided, 12-13, 26-29, 30-33, 34-37, 38-39, 40-43, 44-47, 52-57, 58-61, 62-67, 72-75, 76-83, 84-89, 90-93, 102-107, 108-111, 112-115, 120-123

intermediate, unguided, 12-13, 30-33, 34-37, 38-39, 40-43, 44-47, 52-57, 58-61, 62-67, 72-75, 76-83, 84-89, 90-93, 102-107, 108-111, 112-115, 120-123

novice, guided, 12-13, 26-29, 30-33, 34-37, 40-43, 44-47, 52-57, 58-61, 62-67, 72-75, 76-83, 84-89, 102-107, 108-111, 112-115, 120-123

novice, unguided, 12-13, 30-33, 34-37, 40-43, 44-47, 52-57, 58-61, 62-67, 72-75, 76-83, 84-89, 102-107, 108-111, 112-115

river sources,
glacial-melt, 7, 8, 41, 44, 49, 53, 55, 56, 58, 59, 60, 63, 66, 68, 69, 77, 79, 83, 91, 92, 95, 99, 102, 103, 117, 120, 121, 122, 125, 131; also see *Regional-River-Conditions Infocard,* see *When-to-Go Infocard,* and see

glacial-melt in Glossary, 172, and runoff in Glossary, 173

rain-fed, 13, 15, 23, 27, 31, 35, 39, 41, 44, 49, 53, 56, 59, 63, 66, 69, 73, 77, 85, 91, 95, 99, 103, 109, 113, 117, 121, 125, 131; also see *Regional-River-Conditions Infocard,* see *When-to-Go Infocard,* and see *rain-fed* and *runoff* in Glossary, 172

snow-melt, 13, 15, 23, 27, 31, 35, 39, 41, 44, 49, 53, 59, 63, 69, 73, 77, 85, 91, 92, 95, 99, 103, 109, 113, 117, 121, 125, 131; also see *Regional-River-Conditions Infocard,* see *When-to-Go Infocard,* and see *runoff* and see *snow-melt* in Glossary, 173

riverflow information (historical data, current data, and future outlook); see *When-to-Go Infocard*

riverflow profiles; see *hydrographs,* and see *When-to-Go Infocard*

riverflows,
  giant-volume, ranging from 751 m³/s to 8850 m³/s (26,500 to 312,500 cfs), 17, 21, 170
  large-volume, ranging from 151 to 750 m³/s (5350 to 26,450 cfs), 30, 31, 40, 44, 49, 66, 77, 108, 112, 115, 170
  medium-volume, ranging from 61 m³/s to 150 m³/s (2200 to 5300 cfs), 12, 13, 23, 30, 41, 45, 52, 53, 59, 63, 94, 95, 98, 99, 102, 103, 130, 131, 170
  small-volume, ranging up to 60 m³/s (2100 cfs), 15, 24, 26, 27, 34, 35, 38, 39, 59, 68, 69, 72, 73, 85, 90, 91, 95, 99, 103, 109, 113, 116, 117, 118, 120, 121, 124, 125, 127

rivers, 7, 8, 12-15, 16-21, 22-29, 30-33, 34-37, 40-43, 44-51, 52-57, 58-61, 62-67, 68-71, 72-75, 76-83, 84-93, 94-107, 108-111, 112-115, 130-135, 146, 151, 153, 154, 156, 157, 164, 166, 167, 170; also see *creeks*
  maps, 19, 29, 33, 37, 51, 57, 71, 80
  photos, front cover, 6, 17, 23, 27, 28, 31, 32, 35, 43, 45, 47, 49, 53, 54, 59, 61, 63, 65, 69, 73, 75, 77, 78, 83, 85, 86, 87, 88, 90, 93, 95, 97, 99, 103, 104, 106, 109, 111, 114, 157, back cover

rock gardens, 22, 34, 38, 70, 84, 87, 95, 98, 100, 102, 105, 110, 112, 113, 120, 124, 127; also see Glossary 173
  photos, 6, 28, 103, 106, 129

Rock Island, 16-21
  photo, 17

Rocky Mountain Trench, 16, 18, 55, 60, 74, 76, 82, 115, 118, 122, 128, 164, 166
  maps, 19, 80

Rocky Mountains, 8, 10, 52, 62, 68, 76, 94, 102, 105, 160
  maps, 19, 80
  photos, 53, 88, 97, 104

rodeo boating, 120

Rogers Pass, 56, 64, 154, 156
  maps, 5, 137

Rogers Pass Summit, 56, 60, 156

Roller Coaster Rapid, 62, 66

Roosevelt Lake; see *Franklin D. Roosevelt Lake*

Roosville, 110

Rosebery, 38, 39, 43

Rosebery Provincial Park, 38

Rossland, 21

7 Mile Dam; see *Seven Mile Dam*

7 Mile Reservoir; see *Seven Mile Reservoir*

St. Leon Creek, 146, 151

St. Leon Hot Springs, 20, 32, 34, 144-147
  maps, 5, 19, 80, 137, 147
  photos, 136, 145, 146

St. Mary Lake, 112

St. Mary River, 8, 112-115, 170
  maps, 19, 80
  photo, 114

St. Mary River, To Marysville, 112-115
  map, 5
  photos, 113, 114

safety instruction; see *Rafting Infocard* and *Where-to-Learn to Canoe/Kayak Infocard*

Salmo (village), 21, 22, 24, 25, 28
  maps, 5, 137

Salmo River, 7, 18, 22-25, 26-29, 170
  maps, 19, 29, 80
  photos, 23, 27, 28

Salmo River, Porto Rico through Ymir (Upper Section), 7, 26-29
  maps, 5, 29
  photos, 27, 28

Salmo River, To Seven Mile Reservoir (Lower Section), 7, 22-25
  map, 5
  photos, 23, 25

salmon; see *kokanee salmon*

saunas, 9, 26, 81

S-Bend (White River), 90, 92, 93
  photo, 91

S-Corner (St. Mary River), 112, 113, 115
  photo, 114

seasons, 7, 8; also see *Air Photos Infocard, Regional-River-Conditions Infocard* and *When-to-Go Infocard*

selection site, kayak-racing-team, 120; also see *Clubs for Canoeists and Kayakers Infocard*

Selkirk Mountains, 50, 139
  maps, 19, 80

Settlers (Kootenay-River-Upper-Crossing) Bridge, 82
  photo, 78

Seven Mile Dam, 24
  maps, 19, 80

Seven Mile Reservoir, 24
  maps, 19, 80

Shark's Teeth Rocks (White River), 92

Shark's Tooth Rock (Kicking Horse River), 65

Sheep Creek (Lussier River), 85, 87, 94, 164

Shelter Bay, 32, 43, 139, 140, 142, 146, 151, 153, 154
  maps, 5, 19, 80, 137

Shenango Canyon, 7, 22

Shotgun Drop, 62, 64, 65
  photos, 63, 65

showers, 10, 22, 26, 32, 41, 60, 64, 70, 72, 73, 92, 109, 112, 116, 122, 124, 130, 138, 140, 142, 154, 158, 163

Sicamous
maps, 5, 137

Silverton, 36, 141, 143

Sinclair Canyon, 122, 124, 158
photo, 159

skill levels; see *Boats-and-Skills Infocard,* and see International Scale of River Difficulty on *Regional-River-Conditions Infocard*

Skookumchuck (community in East Kootenays), 93, 101, 106, 109, 166, 167

slalom gates, 26, 28, 120

slalom racing, kayak, 120; also see *Clubs for Canoeists and Kayakers Infocard*
photo, 121

Slipping Rock Rapid, 120, 122, 123
photo, 123

Slocan Lake, 38, 39
maps, 5, 137

Slocan Park (community), 36

Slocan Pool, 79

Slocan River, 7, 30-33, 34-37, 39, 170
maps, 19, 33, 80
photos, 31, 32

Slocan River, Crescent Valley to Kootenay River, 30-33
maps, 5, 33
photos, 31, 32

Slocan Valley, 141, 143

Slot, 98, 102, 105

small-volume hydrographs (riverflow monthly averages), 59, 85, 91, 117, 121, 125; also see *riverflows,* and see *When-to-Go Infocard*

snow-melt creeks and rivers; see under *river sources*

Snowman Peak, 48

snowpack data; see *When-to-Go Infocard*

sockeye salmon, 40; also see *brook trout, brown trout, char, Gerrard rainbow trout, kokanee salmon, rainbow trout,* and *sturgeon;* and see *Tourism Infocard*

sources; see under *river sources*

South Slocan Dam, 79

Spillimacheen (community), 135

Spillimacheen River; see *Bobbie Burns Creek-Spillimacheen River, Below Poet Creek*

squirt boating, 120; also see *Glossary,* 173

St. Leon; see on page 181 alphabetized under *Saint*

St. Mary; see on page 181 alphabetized under *Saint*

Starbird Glacier, 128

steady gradient, 27, 32, 38, 44, 68, 76, 84, 90, 102, 104, 122, 124

steam bath, 46, 138

sturgeon, 16; also see *brook trout, brown trout, char, Gerrard rainbow trout, kokanee salmon, rainbow trout,* and *sockeye salmon;* and see *Tourism Infocard*

Sulphur Creek, 94, 95, 96, 97, 98, 99, 100, 101, 106

Surprise Canyon, 8, 52, 53, 55, 56

Surprise (Ledge) Rapids, 81

12 Mile Bridge (Horsethief Creek), 125, 128, 129

26 Mile (Kootenay-River-Lower-Crossing) Bridge, 82, 88

technical water, 14, 15, 22, 30, 34, 48, 87, 90, 98, 99, 102, 108, 116, 120; and see the Glossary, 173

tennis courts, 163

Tetragon Peak, 51

Thompson Falls, 58

Thunderhill Provincial Park, 116, 118

tide and current tables; see *Tourism Infocard*

Toby Creek, 7, 8, 120-123, 170
maps, 19, 80
photos, 121, 123

Toby Creek Classic (kayak race), 120

Toby Creek, Through Slipping Rock Rapid, 120-123
map, 5
photos, 121, 123

Toby Glacier, 120

toggles; see Glossary, 173

Top of the World Park, 168

topographic maps, 11, 29, 33, 37, 51, 57, 71, 128, 132-133, 134, 147, 168-169; also see *Topographic Maps Infocard*

Topographic Maps Infocard, in back pocket of book

tourist information; see *Tourism Infocard*

Tourism Infocard, in back pocket of book

Trail, 8, 16, 18, 21
maps, 5, 19, 80, 137

trips for kayakers; see *river runs for kayakers*

trips for open-canoeists; see *river runs for open-canoeists*

trips for rafters; see *river runs for rafters*

trout; see *brook, brown, char, Gerrard rainbow,* and *rainbow*

Trout Lake, 40, 41, 43, 44, 45, 50, 139
maps, 5, 137

12 Mile Bridge (Horsethief Creek); see at *start of "T" listings*

26 Mile Bridge (Kootenay River); see at *start of "T" listings*

Two Rocks (Witness) Drop, 81

Upper Arrow Lake, 18, 20, 21, 139, 140, 142, 144, 147, 151, 152, 153; also see *Lower Arrow Lake*
maps, 5, 19, 80, 137
photo, 153

Upper Bonnington Dam, 79

Upper Canyon (Elk River), 108, 110
photo, 109

upper Duncan River; see *Duncan River, Hume Creek to Westfall River*

upper Salmo River; see *Salmo River, Porto Rico to Ymir*

Valenciennes Canyon, 157
Valenciennes River, 52, 55, 56, 156, 157
  photos, 53, 157
Vallican, 36
Van Creek, 106, 107
Vermilion Crossing, 70
Vermilion River, 7, 8, 68-71, 79, 170
  maps, 19, 71, 80
  photo, 69
Vermilion River, Hector Gorge to Kootenay River, 68-71, 79
  maps, 5, 71
  photo, 69
Vernon, 140, 141, 142, 143, 151
  maps, 5, 137
vertical drop, effect of; see Regional-River-
Conditions Infocard
volume; see Regional-River-Conditions Infocard and see When-to-Go Infocard
Waneta Dam, 24
  maps, 19, 80
Waneta Reservoir, 24
Wasa, 96, 101, 106
Washington
  maps, 19, 80
Watch Peak, 120
water to expect; see river runs for kayakers,
river runs for open-canoeists, river runs for rafters;
also see When-to-Go Infocard, and Regional-
River-Conditions Infocard
waterfalls, 8, 34, 36, 58, 72, 74, 76, 77, 87,
118, 120, 121, 126, 127, 130, 132, 133, 138,
142; see Air Photos Infocard, see Topographic
Maps Infocard, and see Glossary, 173
  maps, 128, 133
  photos, front cover, 83, 117, 125, 131, 134
water-gauging stations, active, 42, 46, 170;
also see Glossary, 173
water-gauging stations, inactive, 170; also
see Glossary, 173
weirs; see "Weir" Drop (Bull River) and see
Glossary, 173
"Weir" Drop (Bull River), 94, 95, 97, 98
  photo, 95
West Kootenays, 7, 8, 11, 12-51, 77, 138-155
  maps, 19, 29, 33, 37, 51, 80, 147
  photos, 17, 23, 25, 27, 28, 31, 32, 35, 36,
43, 45, 47, 49, 136, 139, 141, 143, 145, 146,
149, 150, 153, 155
Westfall River, 44, 46, 48, 50
When-to-Go Infocard, in back pocket of
book

where to learn canoeing and kayaking;
see Where to Learn to Canoe/Kayak Infocard
where to learn rafting; see on Rafting Infocard in back pocket of book
Where-to-Learn to Canoe/Kayak Infocard, in back pocket of book
White Man Pass, 72
White River, 7, 8, 84-89, 90-93, 96, 98, 100,
104, 106, 166, 167, 170
  maps, 19, 80
  photos, 85, 86, 87, 88, 91, 93
White River, Lower Section, 8, 84-89
  map, 5
  photos, 85, 86, 87, 88
White River, Upper Section, 7, 90-93
  map, 5
  photos, 91, 93
Whiteswan Lake, 85, 89, 90, 93, 94
Whiteswan Lake Provincial Park, 89, 90,
92, 93, 164, 165
  photos, 8, 165
Whitewater Canoeing Association of
British Columbia; see How-to-Learn Infocard
Whitewater Infocards for British Columbia, 10; see in back pocket of book
whitewater information sources; see infocards in pocket on the inside of the back cover
whitewater racing, kayak, 120; also see
Clubs for Canoeists and Kayakers Infocard
whitewater rodeo, 120
width, effect of; see Regional-River-Conditions
Infocard
Wigwam River, 110
wildlife; see berries, bird watching, fish (and
fishing), flowers and plants, and game
wildwater racing, kayak; see Clubs for
Canoeists and Kayakers Infocard
Wilmer, 122, 124, 128
Wilson Creek, 7, 38-39, 170
  maps, 19, 80
Wilson Creek, To Rosebery, 7, 38-39
  map, 5
Windermere Lake, 18
Winlaw, 36
Witness (Two Rocks) Drop, 81
World's Best Chute, 112
Yahk
  maps, 5, 137
Ymir, 26, 27, 28
Yoho (5 Mile) Bridge, 66, 67
Yoho National Park, 63, 64, 67